Elementary
SOCIAL STUDIES

4th Edition

Elementary
SOCIAL STUDIES

A Practical Approach

Ian Wright

Nelson Canada

I(T)P An International Thomson Publishing Company

Toronto • Albany • Bonn • Boston • Cincinnati • Detroit • London • Madrid • Melbourne • Mexico City
New York • Pacific Grove • Paris • San Francisco • Singapore • Tokyo • Washington

I(T)P™
International Thomson Publishing
The trademark ITP is used under licence

© Nelson Canada,
A Division of Thomson Canada Limited, 1995

Published in 1995 by
Nelson Canada,
A Division of Thomson Canada Limited
1120 Birchmount Road
Scarborough, Ontario M1K 5G4

Cover: Mick Wiggins

Canadian Cataloguing in Publication Data

Wright, Ian, 1941–
    Elementary social studies : a practical approach to teaching and learning

4th ed.
Includes bibliographical references and index.
ISBN 0-17-604200-8

1. Social sciences – Study and teaching (Elementary).
I. Title.

LB1584.5.C2W75 1994   372.83'044   C94–931203–7

Acquisitions Editor	Charlotte Forbes
Production Editor	Bob Kohlmeier
Developmental Editor	Heather Martin
Art Director	Liz Nyman
Design	Julia Hall

Printed and bound in Canada
1 2 3 4 (BG) 98 97 96 95

CONTENTS

This book is not a text in the usual sense of the word. Textbooks usually require you to absorb information first and then carry out certain activities, such as answering questions based on the text's content. Maybe this is how you learned Social Studies in school. The assumption in most methods texts is that if you read about the theory and practice of Social Studies teaching, you will become an effective teacher. This book is based on the assumption that if you are actually *involved* in Social Studies activities, you are more likely to be able to understand and implement these activities in your classroom. In other words, you are encouraged to "learn by doing" and to reflect critically on what you are doing.

The emphasis, then, is on the procedures and standards of critical thinking in the Social Studies. The philosophy behind *Elementary Social Studies* is that students of all ages should be actively engaged in finding, applying, interpreting, analyzing, synthesizing, and evaluating information in order to make rational decisions. I hope this book challenges you to think critically about what you teach and how you teach it, in addition to providing you with many practical ideas.

ORGANIZATION

This book is divided into four parts. Part 1 examines the nature and purposes of Social Studies education and some of the factors involved in curriculum development.

Part 2 is concerned with conceptual and empirical claims. Concepts are dealt with first because students must have some understanding of the concepts that inform a sentence, or a question, before they can fully understand it. The discussion on concept teaching/learning is followed by an examination of the teaching/learning of empirical claims. The term "fact" is not used here because the use of this term assumes the truth of any claim made about what was, is, or will be the case. Rather, I encourage you and your students to evaluate empirical claims. If a claim is deemed to be true or believable, then the term "fact" is appropriate. Thus, this section provides activities that emphasize inquiry procedures and the evaluation of information. We next examine how to obtain information from a variety of sources (graphs, maps, and so on), how to use that information, and, finally, how to present it in different formats.

Part 2 concludes in chapter 16 with a discussion of generalizations, in which information is synthesized, and a unit plan format, in which concept, generalization development, and inquiry are tied together. Once you have completed this section, you will be able to create a structured unit plan that focuses on the active learning of information.

Part 3 deals with matters of value through the medium of decision-making. It outlines approaches to values education and explores the value questions that arise in citizenship, multicultural, global, human rights, peace, and law-related education.

Part 4 provides a detailed framework for unit planning that goes beyond the learning of information. It includes a discussion, with examples, of unit rationales, the scope and sequence of a unit, and actual unit episodes, some of which involve value questions. Receiving further emphasis in this section is the writing of objectives and ideas for motivating student interest in a topic.

A selected bibliography, organized by topic, appears at the end of the book.

Critical thinking and integration with other subject areas are emphasized throughout. In order to arrive at conclusions about social phenomena, students will have to bring information to bear from many subject areas, both in the sciences and in the arts. Further, students are encouraged to locate data found in a variety of sources and to present their conclusions in a variety of forms—written, pictorial, and oral. *Elementary Social Studies* demonstrates that many of the "whole language" objectives in the language arts curriculum can be realized through Social Studies.

This fourth edition also contains separate sections on the teaching of history and geography. Despite the recent focus in elementary schools on integration, students still need to have some familiarity with the basic disciplines of the Social Studies. All Canadian Social Studies curriculums include distinct history and geography topics. The other social sciences, such as economics, political science, sociology, and anthropology, are not accorded separate treatment here, for they do not receive separate treatment in the elementary school curriculum. This does not mean that this book ignores these disciplines. You will find that some of the strategies outlined here focus on knowledge taught in particular disciplines. There is a simulation game that emphasizes economic concepts; there are activities that focus on teaching knowledge drawn from political science; and much of what is learned about families and communities, in Canada and elsewhere, relies on sociological and anthropological concepts and procedures of inquiry.

A NOTE TO INSTRUCTORS

Each section contains activities that are designed to help teachers (pre-service and in-service) work through particular ideas and "learn by doing." Thus, this book is best used in a classroom situation where teachers can work together and engage in discussion. You may decide to lecture on a particular topic and then use the text to reinforce the lecture, or you may prefer to use the activities in the book as a springboard for a lecture or discussion. Lectures can be supplemented by having students read books and articles suggested in the bibliography.

The activities in this book have been used with both pre-service and in-service teachers over the last fifteen years. They have been—and will no doubt continue to be—redesigned and modified. Teachers have appreciated this approach because it serves the philosophy of "active" learning.

I wish you success in using this book.

ACKNOWLEDGMENTS

I am indebted to my Social Studies instructors at the Universities of Calgary and Alberta; to my colleagues at the the University of British Columbia, and to the university itself for granting me a sabbatical in which to write this fourth edition; to my students, who have endured my classes and the use of this book; to the people who provided illustrative materials; to Lily Kuhn, who took my scribblings and turned them into a finished product; to the following reviewers, who helped in the development of this revision: Elspeth Deir (Queen's University), Blye W. Frank (Mount Saint Vincent University), Susan Gibson (University of Calgary), Rick A. Hesch (University of Lethbridge), and John Schaller (University of Regina); to the staff at Nelson Canada, particularly Charlotte Forbes, for her enthusiasm, and Bob Kohlmeier and Heather Martin, for being everything developmental editors should be; to Cy Strom, for his skill as a copy editor; to Nancy, for the chair; to Penney Clark, who read every word in the book and whose insightful advice has been incorporated; and last but not least, to Carol, for her much-needed criticism, her exceptional editing ability, and her love.

Ian Wright
Vancouver, British Columbia
August 1993

PART 1

The Nature & Purposes of Social Studies

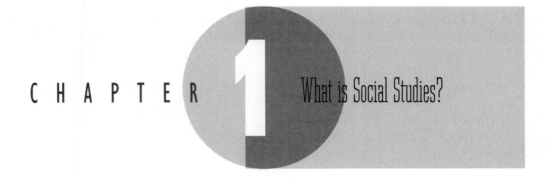

C H A P T E R 1 What is Social Studies?

Imagine you have a class of elementary school students (you can choose which age level) and are free to plan and implement your own one-year Social Studies program. What will you do? How you answer this question depends mainly upon what you think "Social Studies" means, what you think the goals of Social Studies are or should be, and what you think students are capable of learning.

These three conditions are related. If you decide that it is a worthwhile goal to teach about the Quebec conscription crisis during World War I to your Grade 1 students, then your decision is questionable because Grade 1 students would have a very hard time making much sense of the topic. (This does not mean, of course, that the topic is not worth teaching at another grade level.) On the other hand, a decision to teach your Grade 6 students to play the recorder because they are capable of learning to play it also needs further thought. Although teaching the recorder is a worthwhile endeavour, it does not fall under the Social Studies label.

Let us first look at how you define Social Studies.

ACTIVITY 1-A

1. What words, phrases or images come to mind when you think of SOCIAL STUDIES? Write down one word or phrase, or draw an image, in each of the segments of the reaction wheel.
2. Exchange your reaction wheel with a peer.
3. Try to clarify what your peer means by his or her reactions.
4. If necessary, rewrite/redraw your reactions so that they are clear and understandable.
5. In a large group (five or more people), collect all reactions. Try to classify these into *content reactions, skill reactions*, and *expressions of attitude*. Looking just at the *content* classification, can you agree on what Social Studies is?

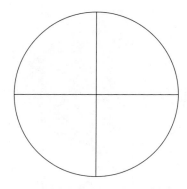

Content reactions	Skill reactions	Expressions of attitude
What one "knows"	What one "does"	How one "feels" What evaluations one makes

You may find that your group was able to agree on what the content of Social Studies is, at least in general terms. You have all studied some history and geography in Social Studies and may remember making models of Egyptian pyramids or colouring maps of Canada. There is not likely to be much disagreement that these are Social Studies activities. However, not all activities fall so clearly under this label.

ACTIVITY I-B

Read the following. Which of these would you consider to be Social Studies? Indicate your answers on the chart, and then refer to the ANSWERS section.

1. The students have conducted a survey on people's attitudes toward litter on downtown streets. The students are now learning a simple statistical procedure in order to discover whether males and females differ significantly in their attitudes.

2. The students are creating a mural in order to display what they learned from a field trip to a farm.

3. The students are acting out the arrival of some of the first settlers in New France.

4. The students are listening to a nurse tell them how to apply a tourniquet.

5. Having read a story about the life of two children in Japan, the students are answering comprehension questions in their notebooks.

6. The students are discussing how to welcome a new immigrant from India to their class.

7. The students are reading a fairy tale from China.

8. The students are learning songs sung by children in Israel.

9. The students are making scale drawings of their classroom.

10. The students are collecting food for the local foodbank.

	Social Studies	Not Social Studies	Reason
1.			
2.			
3.			
4.			
5.			
6.			
7.			
8.			
9.			
10.			

You will notice that in all the above situations students are engaged in some sort of activity. But it is not the activity itself that constitutes Social Studies; students could read, act, discuss, draw, and listen in any subject. Rather, it is the content of the activity and the reason(s) for studying the content that lead us to conclude that it is Social Studies. If the goal of reading a story about the life of two children in Japan is to develop students' abilities in phonics, then it is a language arts activity. If the goal is to teach about how children live in Japan, then it probably fits under the Social Studies label.

It is unlikely that everyone in your class has arrived at exactly the same definition of Social Studies. If you look at definitions offered by experts in the field, you will notice that they too cover a broad range.

1. The social studies are the social sciences simplified for pedagogical purposes.[1]

2. Social Studies should furnish the forum for the analysis and evaluation of normative propositions or value judgments about man [sic] and society.[2]

3. Social studies is the integrated study of the social sciences and humanities to promote civic competence. Within the school program, social studies provides

coordinated, systematic study drawing upon such disciplines as anthropology, archeology, economics, geography, history, law, philosophy, political science, psychology, religion, and sociology, as well as appropriate content from the humanities, mathematics, and natural sciences. The primary purpose of social studies is to help young people develop the ability to make informed and reasoned decisions for the public good as citizens of a culturally diverse, democratic society in an interdependent world.[3]

4. Social studies is a composite subject area drawn primarily from (1) the social science disciplines; (2) the findings (or knowledge) that the social disciplines have produced; and (3) the process that the social scientists use to produce their findings.[4]

5. Social studies is the study of human beings.[5]

6. The social studies is that part of the elementary and high school curriculum which has the primary responsibility for helping students to develop knowledge, skills, attitudes, and values needed to participate in the civic life of their local communities, the nation, and the world.[6]

7. The goal of Social Studies … is preparation for and practice of citizenship and involves an integration of concepts in a spiralling scope and sequence taken largely from the humanities and social sciences.[7]

8. Social Studies is the integration of history, the social sciences, and the humanities to promote civic competence.[8]

9. The social studies are concerned exclusively with the education of citizens. In a democracy, citizenship consists of two related but sometimes disparate parts: the first socialization, the second countersocializaton.[9]

10. Social Studies is the school subject in which students learn to explore and, where possible, to resolve social issues that are of public and personal concern.[10]

11. Social Studies is methodological inquiry into social problems.[11]

In spite of their differences, all these definitions either state explicitly that Social Studies includes the study of human beings in social settings using knowledge drawn from (at least) the social sciences or imply that Social Studies requires this knowledge (e.g., to solve social problems). This is the *content* of Social Studies. But a definition of content does not tell us *why* we should teach Social Studies—the goals of teaching the subject. Nor does it tell us what choices we should make from the vast array of possible Social Studies content that we could teach.

The goals we aim at are those thought to be worth pursuing by makers of public policy; we make content decisions on the basis of these goals. Some of the definitions above state what these goals should be. For example, several of them claim that the purpose of Social Studies is education for citizenship. This was identified as the primary goal for Social Studies education by the U.S. National Education Association in 1916—the association credited with the "invention" of Social Studies. It is today espoused by the U.S. National Council for the Social Studies and by most of the ministries of education in Canada. Education for citizenship is thus viewed by most educators as the *raison d'être* for the Social Studies.

This goal has been the traditional one for the subject throughout its history in Canada. Beginning in the western provinces in the 1920s and in Ontario in 1937, Social Studies was the name given to an interdisciplinary approach to the teaching of history, geography, the social sciences, and civics. Canadian Social Studies educators have been strongly influenced by their American counterparts. In the early days of the subject, in the 1930s and 1940s, there was an emphasis at the policy level on "child-centred" or "progressive" educational ideas, with activity-oriented curricula in which children worked together on projects. These ideas relied heavily on the theories of the American philosopher John Dewey. In the 1960s, Canadian educators were influenced by the "structure of the disciplines" movement in the United States. Here, curricula were based on the structures of the various disciplines: students were taught to think and act like historians, geographers, political scientists, and so on. Another influence was that of Hilda Taba (see Chapter 5), whose ideas on organizing curricula around key concepts were accepted by many curriculum developers.

The reliance on ideas from the United States was challenged in the late 1960s, especially by Hodgetts.[12] On the basis of his research, Hodgetts concluded that civic education and the teaching of history needed a great deal of improvement. The Canadian Studies Foundation was created as a result of his efforts in 1970. This organization produced a profusion of curriculum materials. Provincial curricula began to focus more sharply on Canadian content, and Canadian publishers started to produce more materials on Canadian history and geography. Aspects of this movement can still be found in Canadian education, but the "structure of the disciplines" approach has given way to new concerns. In the last twenty years, as Canadian society has awakened to such problems as sexism, environmental degradation, and the demand for native self-government, and has had to face the question of how Canada ought to be governed, new curricula have been developed. Their focus has ranged from values issues to a renewed emphasis on history and geography. New themes such as multicultural, antiracist, global, law-related, human rights, environmental, economic, and Maritime and Pacific Rim studies have been included as the political climate changes at the national and provincial levels. Yet, despite changes over the years, the key concern of the Social Studies—citizenship education—has remained constant.[13]

However, even though we may all agree on the broad content of the Social Studies, we may not agree on what the citizenship goals of Social Studies should be. Should Social Studies education develop passive citizens who do not criticize the existing social order? Or, as Engle and Ochoa state, should its purpose consist of socialization and then countersocialization (by which the authors mean "a learning process designed to foster independent thought and social criticism"[14])? Other Social Studies experts may agree with Engle and Ochoa that education for citizenship should be the goal of Social Studies, but they have very different ideas on what constitutes a "good citizen."

A similar problem arises when we consider other aspects of these definitions. Consider those that include a prescription for teaching history. What are the aims of this teaching to be? Are students to know what great men, and a few women, did in the past? Are they to be taught to understand how historians work? Or is the aim of teaching history to use it as a vehicle to raise important social and political issues and help students understand that "history is an ongoing attempt to make sense of why we are here and what our actions should be"?[15]

In the cases of the last two definitions, we can ask how these social and personal issues should be resolved and how they should be inquired into. Further, we can ask *why* students should explore or inquire into social problems. Is the aim to create effective and rational citizens?

Later in this book you will discover how differing goals lead to different definitions of multicultural, law-related, global, and values education.

As we have seen, we may all agree, broadly speaking, on the content of the Social Studies, but what is actually taught will depend on our goals. And even though most Social Studies educators accept that education for citizenship is the primary goal, we still have to consider what constitutes the "good citizen." Thus, the question that is the title of this chapter—"What is Social Studies?"—might be better rephrased as "What should Social Studies be?"

OTHER ACTIVITIES

1. Look at the Social Studies curriculum guide for your province. How is "Social Studies" defined? Does the definition change according to grade level? What disciplines are included in the curriculum?

2. Look at any other Social Studies curriculum guide and/or Social Studies texts or kits. How is "Social Studies" defined?

3. Ask students in an elementary school, teachers, consultants, parents, professors, or school trustees for their definition(s) of "Social Studies." Differentiate between what people say Social Studies *is* and what they say Social Studies *ought to be*. Compare your responses with those of another person who interviewed a different group of people. How do you account for the similarities or differences? How can you explain the differences between what people say Social Studies is and what they say it should be?

NOTES

1. E. Wesley and S. Wronski, *Teaching Social Studies in High Schools* (Boston: Heath, 1958), p. 3.

2. B. Massiaslas, *Inquiry in Social Studies* (New York: McGraw-Hill, 1966), p. 24.

3. The definition approved by the House of Delegates of the National Council for the Social Studies, 1992. Quoted in *The Social Studies Professional* January/February (1993), 3.

4. D. Welton and J. Mallan, *Children and Their World,* 3rd ed. (Boston: Houghton Mifflin, 1988), p. 15.

5. A. Ellis, *Teaching and Learning Elementary Social Studies,* 3rd ed. (Boston: Allyn and Bacon, 1986), p. 5.

6. J. Banks, *Teaching Strategies for the Social Studies,* 4th ed. (New York: Longman, 1990), p. 3.

7. J. Barth and J. Spencer, "The foundations of the Social Studies and the future," *Social Education* 54:6 (1990), 346.

8. M. Mcguire, "Board seeks members' comments," *The Social Studies Professional* March/April (1992), 1.

9. S. Engle and A. Ochoa, *Education for Democratic Citizenship: Decision-Making in the Social Studies* (New York: Teachers College Press, 1990).

10. Alberta Education, *1981 Alberta Social Studies Curriculum* (Edmonton, Alta.: Alberta Education, 1981).

11. B. Goldmark, *Social Studies: A Method of Inquiry* (Belmont, Calif.: Wadsworth, 1968).

12. A. Hodgetts, *What Culture? What Heritage? A Study in Civic Education in Canada* (Toronto: Ontario Institute for Studies in Education, 1978).

13. G. Tomkins, "The Social Studies in Canada," in J. Parsons, G. Milburn, and M. van Manen, eds., *A Canadian Social Studies* (Edmonton, Alta.: Faculty of Education Publication Services, University of Alberta, 1983).

14. Engle and Ochoa, *Education for Democratic Citizenship*, p. 31.

15. G. de Leeuw and B. Griffith, "An historical approach to human understanding," *History and Social Science Teacher* 25:4 (1990), 187–92.

Given that Social Studies can be defined to include everything that is known about people and their interactions, the following question arises: What should we teach? The answer to this will depend upon how we construe the purposes of Social Studies. What do you think the goals of Social Studies should be?

ACTIVITY 2-A

Indicate your degree of agreement or disagreement with each statement.

	Strongly agree	Agree	Not sure	Disagree	Strongly disagree
The main task of Social Studies is to preserve and transmit the cultural heritage.	✓				
Social Studies should provide learners with an understanding of decision-making processes so that they may become effective decision-makers.		✓			
Social Studies should teach about social phenomena; it should not manipulate students' attitudes and values.		✓			
Social Studies should help students understand the structure of the social sciences.			✓		
Social Studies should develop students' abilities to deal with questions of "What ought to be?" and "What can I do about it?"	✓				
Social Studies should teach children to be good Canadian citizens by being patriotic and obeying the laws of the land.		✓			
Social Studies should provide learners with an awareness of possible futures and the roles they might play in developing these futures.	✓				
Social Studies should teach history and geography so that students understand their place in the world.	✓				

(Table continues on next page.)

	Strongly agree	Agree	Not sure	Disagree	Strongly disagree
Social Studies should teach a body of tested principles and generalizations about human relations and societies.				✓	
Social Studies should teach students to make rational decisions about personal and social issues and to act upon their decisions.					
Social Studies should provide students with the skills necessary to solve problems and to become independent learners.					

You may find that you agree with all the above statements to some extent. If you analyze the beliefs and value judgments that underlie each of the statements, however, you may find that some of them are incongruent. Can you strongly agree both that students should "obey the laws of the land" and "make rational decisions about personal and social issues and act upon their decisions" if a student's decision is to break a law? If you look at other statements to which you agree you may find similar incongruities.

Whether differing aims are a result of differing definitions of Social Studies or different definitions arise from different aims is, perhaps, of little importance. What is important, however, is that each definition and its concomitant aim(s) is embedded in a larger conception of Social Studies. These conceptions must include beliefs about how students learn, what constitutes truth, what values are appropriate to hold, and so on.

According to Barr, Barth, and Shermis,[1] three traditions or conceptions of Social Studies can be identified: Social Studies as Citizenship Transmission, Social Studies as Reflective Inquiry, and Social Studies as Social Science. All share the view that the primary purpose or goal of Social Studies is citizenship education.

Social Studies as Citizenship Transmission

In this conception, the aim is to instil in students the knowledge and values thought necessary for good citizenship. Through the study of history, government, and the students' own community and country, students are to learn the virtues of being responsible, patriotic, loyal, and respectful citizens. The basic instructional approach is didactic: teachers pass on knowledge selected by an external authority (e.g., the ministry of education) through lectures and activities based on student reading of a textbook.

This Citizenship Transmission conception is based on several assumptions: that there are irrefutable societal values (such as respect for authority) that students have to accept; that reality is objective (not based on the subjective views of individuals) and essentially unchanging; and that wisdom from the past must be transmitted to future generations. Presumably, children are born as *tabulae rasae*—their minds are "blank slates" on which are to be written the knowledge and values necessary for citizenship. Alternatively, they are born with a propensity for being "bad" (the idea of "original sin" fits in with this view), and must be taught to be "good." This conception is receiving attention especially in the United States, where E.D. Hirsch[2] is promoting the view that there is a body of content (which he refers to as the "civil religion") that all students must learn if they are to be considered "good" Americans. Similarly, in Canada, various interest groups are calling for more "content" (especially Canadian history and geography) to be taught so that students become "good" Canadian citizens.

Social Studies as Reflective Inquiry

In this conception the aim is to develop rational decision-makers in the social-political context. The focus is on structured and disciplined inquiry into the problems and issues that children face in their day-to-day lives—problems that have their counterparts in the wider world. In this conception it is not assumed that values are finite and absolute. Values can be changed. Similarly, knowledge is also changeable; it is constructed by the learner through the interaction of the content presented and the learner's developing mental powers. Children are not born "bad" or as a "blank slates" but with potential that can be channelled in appropriate directions. Further, this conception assumes that if students are presented with relevant problems they can be taught to use their developing rational powers. They have the right to apply these powers in making their own decisions. This conception is child-centred.

Social Studies as Social Science

The aim in this conception is for students to become effective citizens by acquiring knowledge from the social sciences and the skills of social scientists. Thus, the content chosen for study consists of concepts and research methodologies that students are to apply to problems derived from these disciplines. The focus is on the academic aspect of the Social Studies. It is assumed that the social sciences best explain human behaviour and that students can use these explanations in becoming good citizens. Behind this conception lies the belief that knowledge can be organized into discrete disciplines and that truth can be determined through the use of social science research methodologies.

Social Studies as Critical Reflection

One other recent conception of Social Studies is not listed by Barr, Barth, and Shermis. This is labelled the Critical Reflective approach (see Clarke).[3] Its goal is to empower people so that they can take action to solve societal ills. Clarke argues that students are presently socialized into holding the beliefs and ideologies of the dominant groups in society, and that opposing beliefs are ignored. Thus, students are taught to be noncritical and to accept the existing distribution of power in society. What students need to learn is to be critical, to participate in civic affairs, and to take the actions needed to bring about social justice. This conception assumes that knowledge is constructed by groups who share common interests; what qualifies as truth is relative to a group. However, although some values are relative, underlying moral principles are not. Concerns for social justice, human dignity, and freedom are universal, even though the ways they are conceptualized and applied as a basis for action can be a matter of disagreement and debate.

ACTIVITY 2-B

Now that you are familiar with the differing conceptions of Social Studies, identify the conception that would be congruent with each of the following statements. Then turn to the ANSWERS section.

1. The content to be learned in the Social Studies should be determined by an authority and passed down to students by the teacher. *CT*

2. It is better to evaluate students on how they think rather than on the products of their thought. *RI*

3. By reading stories of great men and women of the past, students will learn the requirements for being good people. *CT*

4. By reading the stories of people who are oppressed or ignored in society, students will realize that there are differing realities. *CR*.

5. Learning how historians arrive at their answers to historical questions will help students solve contemporary social problems. *(RI)*

6. Students should be tested on their knowledge of facts, and their performance should be compared against national norms. *CT*

7. The two most powerful psychological theories are behaviourism (human behaviour is a direct function of the environment, and learning is defined according to the quantity of information acquired) and social learning theory (learning is a gradual accumulation of patterns of behaviour from imitation and modelling). *CS* *CT?*.

8. If students are presented with problems that are relevant, they are more likely to be motivated to learn and to create solutions that are meaningful to them. *RI*

9. All knowledge is shaped by human interests. Dominant groups in society use their self-interested knowledge to subjugate other groups and individuals. *CR*

These four conceptions are "ideal types." Rarely will you find pure examples of each. Rather, Social Studies curricula tend to incorporate aspects of several of them, although there is little evidence that the Critical Reflective view receives attention in curriculum documents or in textbooks. The other three conceptions receive varying amounts of emphasis. All elementary school Social Studies curricula in Canada of which I am aware include the study of history and geography and some of the research methodologies used in these disciplines, such as oral history and field studies. All include the teaching of critical thinking. All incorporate the values thought necessary for being an effective citizen of Canada. Where curricula will vary is in the degree of emphasis accorded history, critical thinking, citizenship, and so on.

Although there are other ways of categorizing conceptions of Social Studies (for example, see Parsons, Milburn, and van Manen,[4] or the research of Goodman and Adler,[5] which found that elementary teachers held six different conceptions), these four—Citizenship Transmission, Reflective Inquiry, Social Science, and Critical Reflection—do provide a useful way of looking at Social Studies. However, to answer our question as to which is the most appropriate conception, we have to develop a rationale. We have to argue that the aims of one particular conception of Social Studies are more appropriate than the aims of another. We must provide evidence that the assumptions on how children learn in one conception are more believable than those in another. We must decide between competing conceptions with respect to the nature of truth and how knowledge is constructed. These questions are not specific to Social Studies; they are relevant to the entire education enterprise. To answer them, you need to develop your own philosophy of education. This is a complex endeavour. The example given below will help you start thinking about the reasons you would use to justify the teaching of a particular topic in Social Studies. Here a teacher is asked questions by a student.

T. I've decided to teach my Grade 4 students about the early explorers in Canada—e.g., the Vikings, Cabot, Cartier.

S. Didn't the native peoples first explore Canada?

T. Of course, and I'll be putting what I teach into the context of the earliest inhabitants and their reactions to explorers.

S. Why do you think students need to know this?

T. Well, I think that having a sense of history—how Canada developed—helps students understand present-day events, like English–French relationships.

S. And understanding present-day events is important?

T. Yes. Unless students realize what is going on around them they can be swept up in things they don't understand and, as a result, feel powerless to do anything.

S. So, you want students eventually to have some control over their own lives.

T. Absolutely. And to do this, they need not only to have information but also to learn to think for themselves.

S. How do you think your study of early explorers will do this?

T. In a number of ways. Students will examine historical accounts of events and see that different points of view exist—for example, how Cartier and the native peoples viewed the claiming of land for the King of France. Further, students will begin to realize that much of history is someone's interpretation of what occurred, and this will help them begin to think about other information in a critical way.

S. Do you think your students can understand this?

T. Oh yes, by this age they can realize that different points of view exist.

S. Have you other reasons for teaching about early explorers?

T. I think students can begin to think about what motivates exploration and to think about such human characteristics as curiosity, greed, courage, and so on. I think they'll find the topic interesting; there are some wonderful stories. I think the way in which explorers and native peoples interacted is important, in terms of both conflict and cooperation. Furthermore, children need to know that it is not just great men (or great women) that history is all about; it is also about ordinary people. It is through their stories that students can gain a sense of their own identity. Without a sense of history, students won't have much of a sense of identity.

S. What do you mean by "a sense of identity"?

T. Well, if we didn't understand our roots as individuals and as a part of a culture or nation, we wouldn't understand ourselves—"me" as a unique individual but sharing much with others because of a common history.

The above dialogue reveals that T has a number of reasons for including the study of early explorers in the Social Studies curriculum. Notice that some of the initial reasons are supported with "higher order" reasons—for example, that understanding present-day events is important because students need to obtain control over events that impinge on them. T might also be able to give reasons for saying that understanding human characteristics such as courage and greed is significant or that stories are important. T is also asked to clarify terms—to say what is meant by a "sense of identity." Finally T is asked whether students are capable of understanding what is to be taught.

What T has done is to present a series of arguments to justify the teaching of a particular topic. For example:

Conclusion I ought to teach about early explorers.

Reason Through the study of early explorers, students can learn about different points of view.

Because T believes the reason to be a good one, T must also believe that learning about different points of view is of significance. When asked to justify this belief, T presents yet another argument. You will find out more about arguments in later chapters.

Now that you have some familiarity with the four conceptions of Social Studies and how to construct a rationale, try the next activity.

ACTIVITY 2-C

A committee has been formed in your school to look at the goals of Social Studies for your school. There are four people on the committee. Choose to be person A, B, C, or D *before* you read the role cards below. Read your role card and play the role. Your task is to persuade the committee to accept your goal and the conception of Social Studies in which the goal lies. Then create a *very brief* outline for a Social Studies curriculum for a particular grade level, listing four major goals and suggesting four topics to be taught, four major skills to be incorporated, and four important values to be stressed.

PERSON A   You believe that Social Studies should teach children to be good citizens. Your goal is to develop children who are patriotic, law abiding, democratic, and knowledgeable about current events. You believe in the Citizenship Transmission conception of Social Studies.

PERSON B   You believe that Social Studies should teach children how to find information for themselves and interpret and evaluate that information so that they can solve problems and make their own decisions. You believe in the Reflective Inquiry conception of Social Studies.

PERSON C   You wish students to study history and geography in a disciplined way. You believe that if students can think like historians and geographers, they will be better equipped to understand their own environment and their own place in it. You believe in the Social Science conception of Social Studies.

PERSON D   You think that the ultimate goal of Social Studies is for students to critique the existing social order and take actions that will lead to equality and justice for all people. You believe in the Critical Reflective conception of Social Studies.

The next activity asks you to develop a rationale for a specific aspect of Social Studies. Even though you will be starting with this straightforward task, you will have to apply "higher order" reasons to justify your decision. Eventually you will be appealing to your own complex philosophy of education.

ACTIVITY 2-D

Choose something—a topic, an ability, an attitude—that you think would be worthwhile to teach to a group of students. List your reasons for teaching it and, where appropriate, try to answer the following questions. (The questions are not in hierarchical order.)

1. What do I mean by "X" (a key term in my reasoning—e.g., What do I mean by "respect," or "co-operation," or "history")?

2. Do I believe that students don't already know what I intend to teach them? Have I any evidence for this?

3. Are students capable of learning what I intend to teach? Have I any evidence for this?

4. What value position am I assuming in giving a particular reason? Is this value defensible?

5. If students didn't learn what I intend to teach, would they be disadvantaged? Why or why not?

6. How is what I intend to teach relevant to students' lives? What does "relevance" mean in this case?

7. Do students really need to know what I intend to teach them? Why?

We must remember that Social Studies is but one subject among many, that education is lifelong, and that the school can't "do it all." Further, although we may formulate what we consider to be a justifiable rationale for a particular goal of Social Studies, we need to keep an open mind because our reasons and reasoning may change as we reflect upon our teaching practices. Rationale-building is complex, but it can't be ignored. We should be able to give good reasons for what we do in the name of Social Studies.

OTHER ACTIVITIES

1. What rationale is presented in your province's Social Studies curriculum? Is it based on the Citizenship Transmission, the Reflective Inquiry, the Social Science, or the Critical Reflective conception of Social Studies?

2. Very often surveys are taken of public opinions on education, or commissions are convened to advise provincial governments on educational matters, or assessments of students' knowledge about Social Studies are carried out by ministries/departments of education. If such information is available, which conception of Social Studies underlies the results of the surveys or commissions, or the interpretations placed on the results? Is this conception consistent with that of your provincial curriculum?

3. Ask students in an elementary school why they think they have to study Social Studies. Compare their comments to rationale statements in your provincial curriculum.

4. According to the latest recommendations of the National Commission on Social Studies in the United States,[6] history and geography should provide the framework for Social Studies; selective studies of the history, geography, government, and economic systems of the major civilizations should receive coverage at least equal to the study of the United States (substitute Canada here for purposes of answering the question below); and integration of other subject areas with the Social Studies should be encouraged. Are these recommendations desirable? Are they feasible to implement?

5. Find out from other professional bodies (e.g., your provincial Social Studies organization) what they think the goals of Social Studies are and/or should be. Compare these goals with those in your provincial curriculum guide. How would you account for the similarities and/or differences?

NOTES

1. R. Barr, J. Barth, and S. Shermis, *Defining the Social Studies* (Washington, D.C.: National Council for the Social Studies, 1977).

2. E. Hirsch, *Cultural Literacy: What Every American Needs to Know* (New York: Vintage Books, 1988).

3. M. Clarke, "A critically reflective Social Studies," *The History and Social Science Teacher* 25:4 (1990), 214–20.

4. J. Parsons, G. Milburn, and M. van Manen, eds., *A Canadian Social Studies* (Edmonton, Alta.: Faculty of Education Publication Services, University of Alberta, 1983).

5. J. Goodman and S. Adler, "Becoming an elementary Social Studies teacher: A study of perspectives," *Theory and Research in Social Education* 13:2 (1985), 1–20.

6. National Commission on Social Studies in the Schools, *Charting a Course: Social Studies for the 21st Century* (Report of the Curriculum Task Force of the National Commission on Social Studies in the Schools, Washington, D.C., 1989).

CHAPTER 3 Curriculum decisions

It is clear that the content of Social Studies includes knowledge from many disciplines. As we can't teach all of this knowledge, we have to make curriculum choices. But how? In the previous chapter, we looked at some broad goals for Social Studies and some different conceptions of Social Studies. These goals and conceptions provide the framework for the development of a curriculum. So, if you view Social Studies as the teaching of the social sciences, then the curriculum you design will reflect knowledge and skills drawn from these disciplines. If you accept the Reflective Inquiry conception, your curriculum will be built around problems for students to resolve. But "knowledge and skills of the social sciences," "problems for students to resolve," and goals such as "becoming a good citizen" are too broad to serve as guides to classroom teaching. How does one translate these into operational terms for a particular group of students?

How you translate goals into practice will depend upon a number of considerations. First and foremost, there are the curriculum guides that every province produces. These either state in quite specific terms what to teach or provide guidelines to follow. In both cases, teachers are contractually bound to follow what the curriculum guide stipulates. There may also be prescribed textbooks or other learning materials. You should become familiar with all the prescriptions of the ministry/department of education in the province in which you teach.

ACTIVITY 3-A

Review the curriculum guide(s) and prescribed curriculum materials (if any) in your province. What MUST you teach? What decisions are yours to make about what and how you can teach?

Even though there are guidelines or specific prescriptions in curriculum guides, student capabilities still have to be considered. If what you intend to teach is beyond students' abilities, then there is no point in teaching it. Thus, we have to take into account the intellectual maturity of elementary students.

What do the following vignettes tell us about the capabilities of students in the early grades of elementary school?

TEACHER: Where's British Columbia?

STUDENT: In Vancouver.

TEACHER: Dinosaurs once roamed the earth.

STUDENT: Were there dinosaurs when you were alive, teacher?

TEACHER: We're going to visit the zoo.

STUDENT: How far is the zoo?

TEACHER: About fifty kilometres.

STUDENT: Is that a long way?

TEACHER: Let's see, it's noon here, so it's 4:30 p.m. in Newfoundland.

STUDENT: How can that be? Did they miss lunch?

TEACHER: Define "climate."

STUDENT: It means how much rain and sun there is.

TEACHER: What about barometric pressure?

STUDENT: Uh?

TEACHER: How do you think this person feels? (*shows a picture of a boy crying at a birthday party*)

STUDENT: He feels happy.

TEACHER: Why do you think so?

STUDENT: Well, I'd feel happy if it was my birthday.

TEACHER: Draw a map of your desk and chair.

STUDENT:

These vignettes demonstrate that young elementary students (and some older ones too) have concepts of time and space that differ from those of most adults, and they have problems with taking the perspective of another person (role-taking). They define words from a limited knowledge and conceptual base.

ACTIVITY 3-B

Obtain examples of students' work in Social Studies or interview students about their knowledge of Social Studies content. What conceptions do they have of the content they have studied? How do they conceive of time and space? What explanations do they have for historical events, for climatic phenomena, for social phenomena, and so on?

In addition to beliefs about what capacities students have, beliefs about student characteristics such as class, ethnicity, and gender affect how the curriculum is developed and then implemented by teachers. There is evidence that children from working-class backgrounds[1] and from minority cultures[2] are viewed by some teachers as having deficiencies, such as low self-esteem and poor attention span. Teachers may also perceive working-class children as having less facility with language than their middle-class counterparts. Further evidence suggests that teacher expectations about the abilities of boys and girls differ,[3] and that teachers reinforce sexual stereotypes.[4] Thus, you should reflect on your beliefs and practices and ensure that you treat *all* students equitably.

Another consideration is how to *organize* the content of the curriculum. The terms "scope" (what is to be taught, and the depth and breadth of what is to be taught) and "sequence" (the order in which knowledge, skills, and attitudes are taught) are frequently used to describe the organizational pattern of a curriculum. It should be noted here that there is ambiguity in the use of the term "scope." Sometimes it is used to refer to the topics (family, community, geography of Canada, etc.) and the skills and attitudes to be taught; sometimes it refers to the depth and breadth of what is to be taught—e.g., the inclusion in Canadian geography of a detailed study of each of the regions and of a section on interpreting topographical maps.

Most elementary school curricula in Canada and the United States organize their Social Studies programs on the basis of *expanding horizons.*

This view of scope and sequence is based on the assumption that children should start with what they know—themselves and then their families—and then move outward in space to the community and eventually the world. Kieran Egan criticizes the expanding horizons view, arguing that what children know best are such concepts as "good" and "bad," "love" and "hate," and that these—and the child's power of imagination—should be the basis for organizing the curriculum.[5] In his book *Teaching as Story Telling*, he outlines how his ideas could be put into practice.[6] Egan's concerns about the rigid and lockstep manner in which the expanding horizons approach has been implemented are valid. For example, Grade 1 children *can* examine events that would be construed as beyond the boundaries of a study of families, and they *can* grapple with abstract ideas, either within a story format or through other activities.

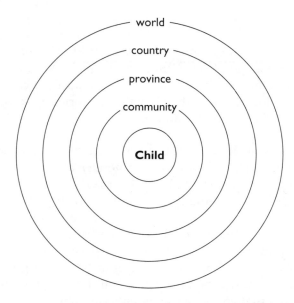

Another way of organizing a curriculum is a scope and sequence based on *spiralling concepts.*

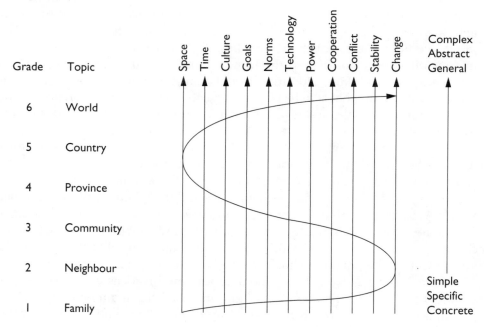

In this approach, chosen concepts are dealt with at increasing levels of sophistication as students move through the grades. Often the concepts are chosen from the scope of the expanding horizons approach; that is, in Grade 1 the concepts are related to studies of families, in Grade 2 to community studies, and so on. When this rigid pattern is chosen, Egan's criticisms of the expanding horizons view apply.

Another way of sequencing, applicable to historical content, is chronology. Starting at Grade 3 or 4, Canadian students learn about the history of Canada in chronological fashion. Study of the first inhabitants is followed by learning about the first European explorers and settlers, and so on. Then, at about Grade 6 or 7, students begin another chronological sequence with the study of the first humans and first civilizations, and continue in Grades 8 through 12 to follow a chronological history, usually of Europe and North America.

A curriculum may be organized by amalgamating a number of different organizational patterns. In Canada, expanding horizons is often melded with spiralling concepts and with chronology, when history is the topic. Further, the scope may consist of topics that pertain to a single discipline or to topics that require a multidisciplinary or integrated disciplinary approach. A recent edition of *Social Education*[7] outlined a number of proposals for organizing Social Studies curricula. For example, Kniep's global education proposal draws on knowledge and skills from many disciplines.[8] It consists of the following sequence based on key concepts:

GRADE 1: Studies of interdependence in the family, school, and community; scarcity—needs and wants; pollution and waste.

GRADE 2: Studies of change in the family and community; culture of self and others in the world; development—hunger and poverty.

GRADE 3: Studies of conflict and economic systems; peace and security.

GRADE 4: Studies of culture of indigenous peoples; the growth of the United States.

GRADE 5: Studies of interdependence, conflict, and scarcity in the United States; human rights in the United States.

GRADE 6: Studies of change, conflict, interdependence, and culture in Latin America, Africa, and Asia.

A very different scope and sequence is presented by Downey,[9] whose focus is on history as a discipline. He proposes the following:

GRADE 1: The study of essentials for living in the past and present, worldwide.

GRADE 2: Studies of living together in the past and the present, worldwide.

GRADE 3: Studies of living well (e.g., creation and enjoyment of the arts) in the past and present and throughout the world.

GRADE 4: The study of early peoples of the world.

GRADE 5: The study of classical and medieval civilizations.

GRADE 6: The study of United States history.

GRADE 7: The study of world history.

ACTIVITY 3-C

How is the scope and sequence of the Social Studies curriculum in your province organized? Are any reasons given for the organizational scheme? Do you think the reasons are good ones?

Whatever organizational pattern is used, it should be remembered that students learn best if the amount of information is (1) limited, (2) structured around and related to a key idea or concept, (3) thought about in a critical way, and (4) applied to new contexts.

In choosing the scope and sequence of a curriculum, logical criteria must be considered. A student may have the capacity to memorize "fifteen degrees of longitude is equivalent to one hour of time," but to *understand* this the student must comprehend, at least, that the earth rotates on its axis every twenty-four hours (approximately) and that there are 360 degrees in a circle. It is logically necessary to know some things before one can begin to know other things. Therefore, in sequencing anything we have to ask, "In order to know X, what do students have to know prior to studying X?" Having ascertained this, then we have to find out whether students actually have this prior knowledge. If they haven't got it, then we will have to teach or reteach it.

These logical and psychological criteria are especially important when skills are sequenced. Most Social Studies curriculum guides, and many Social Studies programs, state when particular skills can be introduced. For example, the British Columbia *Social Studies Curriculum Guide 1–7* describes its Understanding Time and Chronology sequence as follows:[10]

SKILLS	GRADES						
Understanding Time and Chronology	**1**	**2**	**3**	**4**	**5**	**6**	**7**
Develop an understanding of the time system and the calendar:							
1 Use names of the days of the week in order	❏	●	●	✻			
2 Use names of the months in sequence	❏	●	●	✻			
3 Learn to tell time by the clock (including use of the 24-hour clock)	❏	●	●	✻	✻	✻	✻
4 Use calendar to find dates of special events and to determine length of time between important dates		❏	●	●	●	●	●
5 Use the vocabulary of indefinite (before and after) and definite (today, yesterday) time expressions	❏	●	●	●	●	●	●
6 Comprehend the Christian system of chronology — B.C. and A.D.							❏
7 Learn to translate dates into centuries							❏

(Table continues on next page.)

SKILLS		GRADES						
Understanding Time and Chronology	1	2	3	4	5	6	7

Develop an understanding of events as part of a chronological series of events and an understanding of the difference in duration of various periods of time:

	1	2	3	4	5	6	7
1 Learn to put experiences and events in order of time	❏	●	●	✳	✳	✳	✳
2 Recognize sequence and chronology in personal experiences, as the school day, weekly schedule, etc.		❏	●	●	✳	✳	✳
3 Learn to think of the separation of an event from the present in arithmetical terms				❏	●	●	●
4 Understand and make simple time lines				❏	●	●	●

Where ❏ is Introduce; ● is Develop; and ✳ is Test, Reteach, Maintain

Excerpted from *Social Studies Curriculum Guide: Grade 1–7*, rev. ed. (Victoria, B.C.: Ministry of Education and Ministry Responsible for Multiculturalism and Human Rights, Province of British Columbia, 1983). Used with permission.

ACTIVITY 3-D

What skills are emphasized in the curriculum in your province? How are they sequenced? Do you think that the sequence is a realistic one? Is there any evidence that children learn these skills in the sequence outlined in the curriculum guide?

A further consideration is the number of objectives that can be realized through the study of a particular topic. It is usually better to strive for multiple objectives, not just because it is an efficient method (it allows teaching language arts skills through the writing of a report in Social Studies, for example) but also because it is a comprehensive one (allowing students to develop knowledge at the same time as they develop skills and attitudes, and teaching that any particular phenomenon can be viewed from a variety of perspectives).

One of the major ideas in contemporary Social Studies is integration. Of course, Social Studies has always been an integrated subject as it draws on knowledge from many disciplines, which themselves are integrated fields of study (e.g., historians study economic, social, cultural, and political factors). In learning Social Studies, students use skills drawn from other subjects; they put their Social Studies skills to use in still other areas. The debate today concerns the desirable degree of integration and the question of what is to be integrated. Curricular integration can include the joining together of Social Studies and language arts into a humanities course; it can involve the teaching of critical thinking in all subject areas; it can mean the integration of student interests with what they are to learn; or it can consist of the integration of all that is done in the school around a particular "philosophy," such as multiculturalism. The curriculum can also integrate what is learned in one grade with what was learned in previous grades and what will be learned in the next one. Thus, when integration is mentioned, it is necessary to determine what sort of integration is being discussed and, especially, why it is desirable.

The following goals can be identified for integration: (1) to help students deal with a complex and interconnected world, (2) to help them see that subject boundaries are artificial, and (3) to help them learn more efficiently. For example, to understand the situation in 1993 in what was formerly Yugoslavia, one would have to understand (at least) history, geography, economics, religion, and anthropology. The goal of efficiency could be met in teaching about this topic if students also learned and applied map-reading skills.

According to Case,[11] there are four modes of integration. "Fusion" refers to the joining of two elements, as in the example concerning Social Studies and language arts. "Insertion" is the addition of part of another subject into an existing one. An example here would be the teaching of statistics (for purposes of designing survey research and interpreting the results of the research) in Social Studies. "Correlation" refers to drawing connections between elements that are taught separately—for example, learning about Japan in Social Studies and doing origami in art. Finally, there is "harmonization," in which common elements are stressed in all or several subject areas—for example, when all teachers focus on the same critical thinking competencies.

Whatever form integration takes, the results must make sense. More does not necessarily equal better. For instance, many of the so-called integrated units I have seen involve taking a topic and linking everything to it. So, in a unit on bears, students count bears, draw them, write about them, sing songs about them, and so on. This performs no true integrative function. An integrated unit on bears would draw on knowledge needed to understand bear behaviour and habitats, and how humans have reacted, do react, and should react to them. The degree to which the topic is integrated will depend upon the capacities of the students and on the objectives of the study. Integration does not have to be forced onto a topic—an approach that may well be mis-educational.

Integration, like many other educational ideas, is complex and requires careful thought before it is acted upon.

ACTIVITY 3-E

To what extent does the curriculum guide in your province integrate Social Studies into other subject areas? What subjects are integrated into Social Studies? What form does the integration take (fusion, insertion, etc.)?

Your own knowledge, abilities, and interests are important in curriculum development. If you have recently visited another country and the curriculum calls for the study of another culture, you are probably going to be more enthusiastic about studying the country you visited than one you haven't. Moreover, you are likely to have up-to-date information about the culture. Having current information about the topic being studied is another key criterion for choosing to study X rather than Y.

School and community pressures may also be an issue. Does the school administration require you to teach certain topics? Does the community want you to avoid raising particular controversial issues? The mere mention of "values education" may raise people's ire in some communities. Factors such as the social make-up of the community in which you teach and the students you teach have to be considered. If there is prejudice in the community, it has to be dealt with. If a political event occurs—a strike, a government action that divides the community, a war—it has to be dealt with in a way that is sensitive to both educational goals and the needs of students.

Broader public pressures also influence curriculum decision-making. Recently, public concerns have been raised about multiculturalism, the environment, Canada–U.S. relations, trade with Pacific Rim countries, global education, and human rights. Furthermore, the perceived lack of student knowledge about Canadian history and geography has resulted in curriculum changes in some provinces.[12]

You will find that most elementary school Social Studies curriculum guides are based on the Reflective Inquiry conception of Social Studies and that, generally speaking, the same sort of content is taught in all provinces. This is not to say that there will be no differences.

Although most Social Studies curriculum guides start with the content to be learned, there are other ways of organizing a program. We can start with an ability (to solve particular problems; to interpret a map) or a dispositional objective (to be open-minded; to consider others' points of view), and then choose the best *instrumental* content to develop or foster the ability or disposition. Rather than being the objective, learning the content becomes a means to achieve a more important goal. If the objective was to teach students in Grade 1 how to resolve conflicts, then the most relevant content might be a good story, or incidents in the students' own lives, where a conflict had to be resolved. The same objective at the Grade 6 level might be emphasized with content drawn from a recent political event.

ACTIVITY 3-F

1. Your objective is:

To develop decision-making abilities. What instrumental content would be appropriate for a Grade 1 class? A Grade 6 class? Give reasons for your decision.

1 – housing developments & trees? ⇒ integrates with building & environmental concerns, aesthetics

6 "

2. Your objective is:

   To develop respect for cultural differences. What instrumental content would be most appropriate for Grade 3? Grade 5? Why?

   3 – Stories / literature

   5   "

3. Your objective is:

   To teach historical awareness. What instrumental content would be appropriate for Grade 2? For Grade 4? Why?

In this activity you were required to make judgments about appropriate content by considering the factors examined in this chapter. This can be a complex task; often decisions have to be made partly on the basis of the amount and quality of the resource materials available.

ACTIVITY 3-G

No one in Canada, as far as I know, has ever carried out a systematic research study to find out what elementary school students would like to study or think it is important to study in Social Studies. What would you guess that elementary school students would answer?

Now go and ask at least one student. Have a class collection of the findings.

1. Were your original guesses correct?

2. Are there any topics that a majority of students would like to study?

3. Are any of these topics included in the provincial curriculum guide or texts?

4. Do choices change with age—that is, do Grade 1 students make different choices than Grade 6 students?

5. Should topics that students like to study be included?

6. If there is a vast discrepancy between the actual curriculum and student choices, should you do anything about it? Why or why not? If you think something ought to be done, how would you go about doing it?

7. Are resource materials available to teach the topics chosen by students?

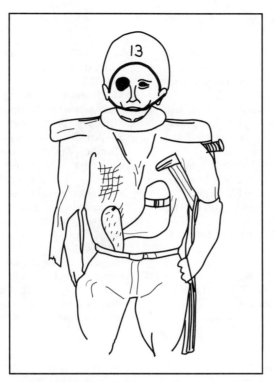

"I think that the impact of contact sports on violent behaviour ought to be taken up in our Social Studies class."

Having looked at the range of factors that need to be considered in deciding what to teach, we will move on to the question "How do I go about teaching?" The rest of this book is devoted to answering this question.

OTHER ACTIVITIES

Choose a particular topic (law, environmental problems, multiculturalism, or the treatment of women) that you believe Social Studies should focus upon. Show how you would modify the existing Social Studies curriculum to include this topic.

NOTES

1. B. Curtis, D. Livingstone, and H. Smaller, *Stacking the Deck: The Streaming of Working-Class Kids in Toronto Schools* (Toronto: Our Schools Our Selves, 1992).

2. G. Gay, "Culturally diverse students and Social Studies," in J. Shaver, ed., *Handbook of Research on Social Studies Teaching and Learning* (New York: Macmillan, 1991).

3. R. Best, *We've All Got Scars: What Boys and Girls Learn in Elementary School* (Bloomington, Ind.: Indiana University Press, 1983).

4. J. Shapiro, S. Kramer, and C. Hunerberg, *Equal Their Chances: Children's Activities for Non-Sexist Learning* (Englewood Cliffs, N.J.: Prentice-Hall, 1981).

5. K. Egan, "What children know best," *Social Education* 43:2 (1979), 130–39.

6. K. Egan, *Teaching as Story Telling* (London, Ont.: Althouse Press, 1986).

7. *Social Education* 50:7 (1986), 484–542.

8. W. Kniep, "Social Studies within a global education," *Social Education* 53:6 (1989), 399–403.

9. M. Downey, "Time, space and culture," *Social Education* 50:7 (1986), 490–501.

10. Ministry of Education and Ministry Responsible for Multiculturalism and Human Rights, Province of British Columbia, *Social Studies Curriculum Guide: Grade 1–7*, rev. ed. (Victoria, B.C.: Ministry of Education and Ministry Responsible for Multiculturalism and Human Rights, 1983).

11. R. Case, "The anatomy of curricular integration," *Canadian Journal of Education* 16:2 (1991), 215–24.

12. For a review of the kinds of changes that occur in Social Studies curricula, see K. Skau, "A curriculum of changes; Social Studies in Alberta," *The History and Social Science Teacher* 23:4 (1988), 214–20.

PART 2

Empirical &
Conceptual Claims &
Questions

CHAPTER 4 Becoming operational

Most beginning teachers of Social Studies start with a topic—my community, China, prairie pioneers. This topic is usually taken from a curriculum guide and, in the case of student teachers, is often assigned by a sponsor teacher. Although there are other starting points—a skill, a concept, or a generalization to be learned; a decision to be made; an issue or problem to be resolved—we will start with a topic.

The first step is to break down the topic into its constituent parts. Suppose you have a Grade 3 class and have been asked to teach about the Inuit. What specifically do you teach? You could examine food, shelter, and clothing, but what else would you need to examine in order to build up as complete a picture as possible of the Inuit?

ask the students what they want to learn? Kids don't

ACTIVITY 4-A

What aspects of Inuit life could be studied? Write down what you think ought to be studied if as complete a picture as possible of Inuit life is to be obtained.

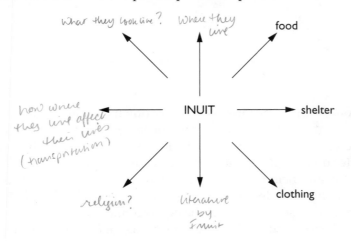

what they look like? *where they live* food

how where they live affect their lives (transportation) ◄——— INUIT ———► shelter

religion? *literature by Inuit* clothing

ACTIVITY 4-B

If your topic is Ancient Greece, what aspects might be covered?

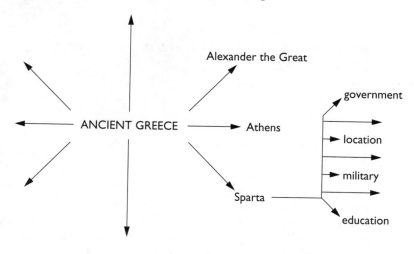

ACTIVITY 4-C

If your topic is The Family, what might you teach?

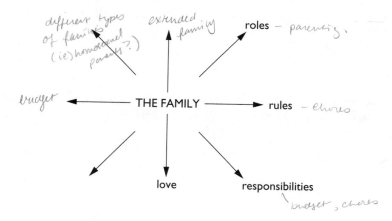

What you have done in these activities is to break down or analyze your topic into its components so that you can see what could be taught. Of course, decisions will have to be made concerning what will actually be taught, especially as any analysis could be quite complex. If we mapped out a complete picture of the forest industry in Canada, it could include everything from chainsaws to types of trees, conservation, or international trade and tariff regulations. Specifically, what you focus upon will depend upon such factors as the age and maturity of students, the time available to teach the topic, suitable resource materials, and so on (see Part 1).

It is useful at this stage to see if there is a theme around which you could organize your study. This might be a concept, a generalization, or a decision to be made. For example, the study of a neighbourhood could focus on how the concept "community" relates to the topic; or how the generalization "People's way of living is affected by the physical and social environment in which they live" applies; or how the question "What would constitute a perfect neighbourhood?" is decided. Whether you choose to teach a survey of the topic or organize it in some other way will depend upon your objectives. But, in each case, a "map" of the territory you wish to cover will be necessary. Without a map you can become hopelessly lost!

This "map" is also useful for students if they are to derive meaning from what they are studying. Constructing meaning is an interactive process in which learners use their existing conceptual schemas (their knowledge and understandings) to make connections between what they already know and new information. Thus, students with rich background knowledge derive more and deeper meanings from new information than do students with poor background knowledge.[1]

One way to help students use their prior knowledge in order to comprehend the new is to use a technique called "semantic mapping."[2] The student draws a visual representation of the relationships between concepts and information that the student already knows. When completed the "map" will look much like the ones shown in this chapter. Carried out at the beginning of a new topic, this activity allows you to find out how much students already know. As the topic is developed in class, students can add to their semantic maps and show how new information is linked to their prior knowledge.

ACTIVITY 4-D

Following is a semantic map on the topic "Immigrants Coming to Canada in the Olden Days" (late 1800s and early 1900s). It was drawn by Elena Lowenthal, a Grade 5 student in Vancouver.[3] What does she appear to know about the topic? What else do you think she needs to know?

OTHER ACTIVITIES

1. Create a map showing what *could* be studied on a topic and at a grade level of your choice. Then decide which of these *would* be studied by your class. Give reasons for your decisions.

2. Have elementary students draw a semantic map on the Social Studies topic they are studying in school. What concepts and information do they provide? How are they different or similar? Compare them in order to determine whether students give the same meaning to the topic.

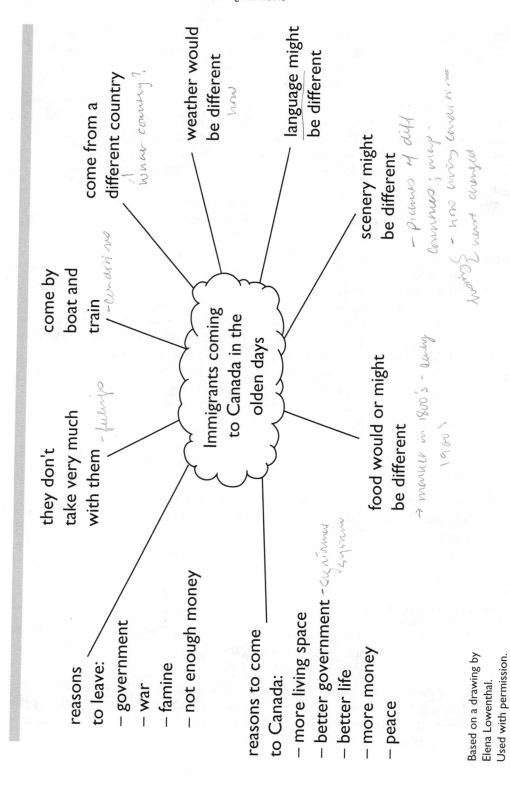

reasons
to leave:
– government
– war
– famine
– not enough money

they don't
take very much
with them

come by
boat and
train

come from a
different country

weather would
be different

reasons to come
to Canada:
– more living space
– better government
– better life
– more money
– peace

food would or might
be different

Immigrants coming
to Canada in the
olden days

scenery might
be different

language might
be different

Based on a drawing by
Elena Lowenthal.
Used with permission.

NOTES

1. See K. Camperell and R. Knight, "Reading research and Social Studies," in J. Shaver, ed., *Handbook of Research on Social Studies Teaching and Learning* (New York: Macmillan, 1991).

2. P. Antonacci, "Students search for meaning in the text through semantic mapping," *Social Education* 55:3 (1991), 174–75/194.

3. Used with permission of Elena Lowenthal.

CHAPTER 5

Concept teaching & learning

In Chapter 4 you analyzed a topic in terms of its component parts, many of them concepts such as "role," "food," and "government." Concepts are classification devices we use to bring order to the myriad objects, ideas, and events that surround us. They are crucial to the understanding of any statement or question. You cannot answer the questions, "Is the yurt well made?" and "Was that a fair decision?" unless you have the concept "yurt" and have a concept of "fairness." You would also need, of course, to have the concepts "well made" and "decision."

We always need to be clear about the concepts we are using. In our own writing, we want to use words clearly so that our readers know what we're trying to say. Suppose I want to write about the benefits of teaching decision-making to students. In order to communicate with my readers, I have to be as clear as possible about "decision-making," since it is a term that can be applied to the making of any choice—from what to eat for breakfast to how native land claims should be settled. So, if I want to discuss the making of *any* choice, then I should say so; but if I want to focus only on socially significant decisions, then I should stipulate this meaning.

Clarity is also needed when we have to interpret what someone else means in a statement or question. Suppose the headline in the newspaper reads "Toronto to grow over the next ten years." I have to read the article to know whether the headline is referring to growth in population, in land area, or in something else before I can understand it.

To demonstrate understanding of a concept, it is not always enough for a student to be able to speak the word or even to use it in a sentence. Neither of these means that the student has grasped the concept. I used to teach about the "customs" and "traditions" of various peoples and had a vague idea that these two terms were somehow different, but it was not until one of my student teachers was asked to differentiate between these terms in teaching about the customs and traditions of people in Mexico that I seriously contemplated these concepts. You will see the result of the student's and my own deliberations later in this chapter. Although the difference between custom and tradition may not strike you as significant, in many contexts meaning is of crucial importance. Disagreements about what is fair, whether or not X was a case of cheating, or whether certain people are poor or not often revolve around the meaning attached to the terms.

How words are used affects actions. For example, if certain human beings are regarded as "non-persons," then they will be treated differently from "persons." (Witness the Holocaust.) If taking candy from the local convenience store is not defined as "stealing," then the action may not be deemed wrong by the taker. If someone is deemed to be "not poor," then we may not think the person deserving of aid. This is one important reason for the focus placed on the teaching of concepts.

In the classroom, teaching any discipline requires us to introduce students to the key concepts of that discipline. For example, to understand history students need to grasp concepts such as "causation," "time," "change," "continuity," and "chronology." To understand anthropology we need to comprehend and apply such concepts as "culture" and "ethnic." We must remember, too, that different disciplines often use concepts in a technical way. People who are immersed in a particular discipline will have a common understanding of terms that are used somewhat differently in everyday language. For instance, we may use the word "valid" to mean "true," but logicians use it to denote an argument in which the conclusion necessarily follows from the premises. So, in teaching concepts that are relevant to a particular discipline, we have to be aware of how a specific concept is used in that discipline and whether that use differs from the concept's use in everyday language.

Finally, it is crucial to understand that unless we have some understanding of the concepts used in our language, we would be unable to communicate with one another. In that sense, the teaching and learning of concepts is as vital in the Social Studies as in any subject area.

ACTIVITY 5-A

Note the concepts that are emphasized in the curriculum guide in your province. To which disciplines are these concepts related? Are the concepts listed vital to the understanding of a particular discipline? Can you tell whether these concepts are supposed to be used in specialized ways? If so, what are these specialized ways?

Before we can teach concepts we have to know what they are. Concepts are mental constructs that provide the rules for giving meaning to a word. They are, in one sense, definitions. Thus, if I say, "By 'school' I mean a place where it is intended that learning occurs," I am saying that one of the rules for saying that X is a school is that learning is intended to occur there.

Suppose, however, that I'm not sure what a school is. Then two tasks face me. First, I have to find out what the attributes or characteristics of "school" are, and how this term relates to other concepts, such as teaching and learning. Second, I have to know that the building on the corner of the street is a school and not a factory, or a store, or a house. Not only do I have to know what the word means, I also have to be able to point out examples of the word.

Now, imagine a young child who is told by a parent that the building on the corner is a school. What does the child know? All she knows is that this building of a certain shape and size is called a school. She may notice that it has other characteristics, such as a playground, or that children go there, but how does she know it's a *school*, rather than a community centre, or a church, or any other building that has a playground and children? She has to learn that certain activities go on in a school that differentiate it from other buildings. Eventually, as her knowledge of the concept "school" becomes broader, she will realize that a school's key characteristic is not its particular structure (one can have a school under a tree, in an open field, or in the basement of a home), but rather the activities that take place there. So, in teaching a concept, we have to teach students the attributes that give a term its meaning. Sometimes this is fairly easy. For example, all the shapes below are examples of the concept "triangle."

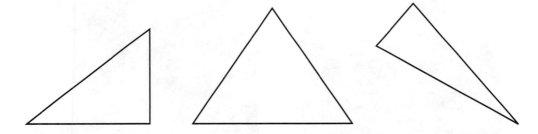

Even though each shape differs in some respect, they all share the same "triangle rules"—closed plane figure, three straight sides. These characteristics or attributes are necessary for the pictured geometric shapes to be called triangles. Whether the triangle is blue or has a dot in it are irrelevant attributes. A triangle must be a closed plane figure with three straight sides. Three sides alone do not make a triangle, nor does a closed plane figure alone. A triangle must have both attributes. These are the necessary and sufficient conditions of a triangle.

Unfortunately, most concepts in Social Studies are not this easy. It is not always possible to determine specific necessary and sufficient conditions. There may well be fuzzy boundaries between one concept and a closely related one, even for seemingly simple concepts such as "family."

ACTIVITY 5-B

Which of these would qualify as examples of the concept "family"? How do you know? What would you need to know if you are not sure whether the picture depicted a family? What does "family" mean?

When you have answered these questions, refer to the ANSWERS section.

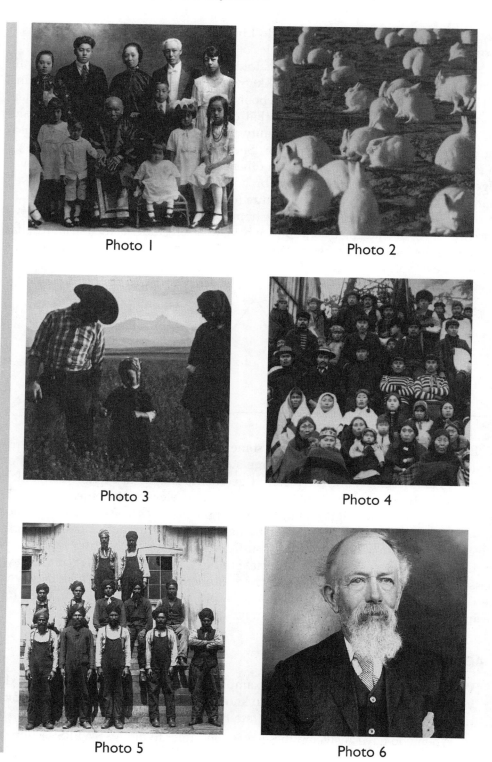

Photo 1

Photo 2

Photo 3

Photo 4

Photo 5

Photo 6

From these activities, you have probably gained some idea of the difficulty that exists in teaching concepts.

The idea that pointing at something and saying, "That's an X" is *all* that is needed to teach a concept is inadequate. In the "family" example, merely pointing to a picture of a group of people or animals and saying "That's a family" would not be enough. Students have to learn that the concept is a complex one and can refer to different groups within which certain sorts of relationships exist. Different relationships pertain in different contexts. In some cultures a family is always an extended one. In our society a family can refer to a single parent and child; in the future, gay and lesbian couples may constitute a family for legal purposes in Canada. In other contexts "family" can refer to all members of a group, such as the cat family or the human family.

The context in which a concept is used is significant. A colleague of mine provides an example here. His son had learned the word "no" as a command, so "No, don't touch" made sense to him. When he began to read he could point out the NO at the start of certain signs, and when the rest of the sign was read to him, a message such as NO PARKING made perfect sense. NO THROUGH ROAD, however, was incomprehensible. While the words were no problem, the change in function from "no" as a command to "no" as information giving was something he didn't understand.

Another issue is raised by the distinction between concrete and abstract. Educators often make the point that there are concrete concepts (like "chair") and abstract ones (like "learning"). However, there is no such thing as a concrete concept. There are concepts that refer to concrete things, and there are concepts that refer to abstract ideas. The view that concepts referring to concrete objects are easier to teach and learn than those referring to abstract ideas is also mistaken. Teaching children the concept of "computer," a concrete object, is probably more difficult than teaching them "obey," a rather complex and certainly abstract idea. True, children can become more sophisticated at using particular concepts as they acquire more experience with them, but this does not mean that concepts come in levels, with some more "simple" than others. The fact that some concepts must be taught in advance of others does not necessarily make the prerequisite ones simpler. And it must always be remembered that a new concept is easier to learn when students are familiar with concepts closely related to the new one and with the context in which the concept is being used.

As noted earlier, unlike "triangle," many concepts cannot be defined in terms of specific necessary and sufficient conditions. It is difficult to determine specific attributes of even seemingly simple objects like "table" or "chair." Suppose that upon replying to an advertisement that reads "Chair for sale: 50¢," you discover the "chair" to be an old wooden crate. When you complain, the seller responds that the crate has been used to sit on—therefore, it is a chair. Has the seller used the concept "chair" inappropriately?

Additional difficulties arise with value-laden concepts. As with other concepts, it may not be possible to define these in absolutely specific terms. The context in which they are used is crucial. The concept "good," for example, means different things when you are referring to a good person or a good painting. Although "good" is clearly a value term, not all value concepts are as easy to pick out. Concepts like "cheat," "discriminate," or "manipulate" are also evaluative. In using them, we evaluate events, actions, and policies. We will examine value concepts in more depth in Chapter 18.

How then do we teach concepts? There are basically two methods—one in which students discover meaning for themselves, the other in which students are directly taught or guided by a teacher.

CONCEPT DEVELOPMENT

This procedure, developed by the late Hilda Taba,[1] consists of six steps that eventually lead to the testing of generalizations. We will concentrate on the first three steps and leave the last three until we discuss generalizations in Chapter 14.

ACTIVITY 5-C

1. List about twenty items from these photographs.

2. Do any of the items seem to belong together? Draw up a chart grouping items into categories.

3. What would you call the groups (categories) that you have formed? Explain why you have assigned each category a particular label.

	Label	Label	Label	Label	Etc.
Items					Etc.

Look at your chart.

4. Can any of the items in one group be placed into another group?

5. Can you classify your items in any other ways?

6. Get together with one or more of your peers and ascertain whether you agree on the labels. Does it matter if you disagree? Would different labels be equally useful for your purposes?

This may appear to be a simple-minded activity, but, as we'll see later in this chapter, the way items are classified differs according to the purposes of the classifier. Whether items are classified appropriately also depends upon the conceptual sophistication of the classifier.

THE CONCEPT DEVELOPMENT PROCEDURE IN THE CLASSROOM

Children will need items to classify. Young children can classify actual objects or can be given pictures to manipulate physically. Older children can use pictorial or printed material. Children can form their own categories, or you can begin by asking the children to state what items they see, and list these on the blackboard. Initially, limit the number of items to between fifteen and thirty, depending on the ability of the class. Then, having listed items, ask the class to group and label them. You may have ideas as to how the items should be classified. Your students, however, may have different ideas.

ACTIVITY 5-D

Below is a list of foods. In how many ways can you classify them?

Peach	Cheese	Pea
Egg	Meat	Milk
Melon	Eggplant	Carrot

1. If you were teaching beginning consonants, what classification scheme would be most appropriate?
2. If you were teaching about Canadian imports and exports, what classification scheme would be most appropriate?
3. If you were teaching about supermarkets/colours/vowel sounds/processed foods/vitamin content/foods I like, what would be the most appropriate classification schemes?

The classification scheme chosen will depend upon the purpose of the lesson and the perceptions of your students. If, using the above list of foods, your purpose was to teach the concepts of "vegetable," "meat," "fruit," and "dairy," but your students want to classify according to colour, your job is to encourage students to see that there are many ways of classifying—and then help them understand the one that is useful in the context of your lesson.

When using the *Taba concept development procedure* it is important to remember that, even though the labels are concepts that are used to organize and classify information, the listed items are not necessarily *attributes* of the concept label. Clearly, in the above activity, a peach is not an attribute of the concept "fruit." A peach is an *example* of "fruit." The distinction should be kept clear. Students often give an example of the concept when asked for a definition.

ACTIVITY 5-E

In order to fully grasp a concept, what must one be able to do? Read the following dialogue and try to ascertain what the teacher is doing to help the student fully grasp the concept of "(hot) desert."

TEACHER: Tell me, what is a desert?

STUDENT: A desert is a place where there is sand and it's hot.

TEACHER: Is this a desert? (*shows a picture of the Sahara*)

STUDENT: Yes.

TEACHER: Is this a desert? (*shows a picture of a beach*)

STUDENT: Yes.

TEACHER: What about this? (*shows a picture of the Sahara in a rainstorm*)

STUDENT: No.

TEACHER: How is that (*beach*) different from this (*Sahara in a rainstorm*)?

STUDENT: This (*beach*) has sand and it's hot and the other one isn't hot.

TEACHER: Is the sandbox in the playground a desert?

STUDENT: No, it isn't big enough. A desert has to be big.

TEACHER: All of these are deserts. (*shows pictures of deserts*) Tell me what is the same about all of them.

STUDENT: They are all big and have sand in them. It is hot.

TEACHER: So, could this (*beach*) be a desert?

STUDENT: No, it's not big.

TEACHER: And this one (*Sahara in a rainstorm*)?

STUDENT: There's sand, but it's not hot.

TEACHER: Could it be hot when it is raining? Like a shower in your bathroom?

STUDENT: Guess so.

To understand a concept, students must be able to define the term (state the attributes that give the concept its meaning) as well as to give examples of it (state what would qualify as an example of the concept). Consider the concept "island." Students must know that it is a body of land entirely surrounded by water, and that Madagascar and Jamaica are examples of the concept.

In using the Taba procedure, students may list items under a concept label when the items are not really examples of that concept label, but are related in some way. For example, if "climate" were the concept, items like rain and snow fit. Umbrella doesn't, even though umbrellas are linked to climatic conditions—one can make inferences about the climate of a place if one sees people using umbrellas.

When teaching concepts, therefore, it is important to teach the attributes of the concept so that the student can recognize correct examples of it.

CONCEPT ATTAINMENT

Dictionaries can define words in their ideal form, but they may be inadequate for the purposes of teaching concepts because: (1) It is often the case that definitions are circular (value = evaluation: evaluation = judging on the basis of a value); (2) meanings in normal language are ambiguous or vague, and dictionaries cannot point out many of the complexities; (3) dictionary definitions often lack precision. Using concept attainment methods can help avoid these problems.

ACTIVITY 5-F

Below are two examples of a particular concept. What might the concept be?

1. Jane Smith wanted to live in Canada. She went to the Canadian Embassy in London, England, to apply to live in Canada. As she had the appropriate qualifications, she was accepted. Eventually, she became a Canadian citizen. Jane is an example of a/an _____.

2. Liu Chan came to Canada as a graduate student. While he was in Canada, he was accused of political crimes in his own country. As he knew he would be arrested and possibly executed if he returned to his own country, he applied to stay in Canada. His case was heard and he was allowed to live in Canada. Liu is an example of a/an _____.

Here is another example of the concept, and one non-example. After you have looked at them, refer to the ANSWERS section.

3. In the late 1880s, many families came to Canada to escape persecution and economic hardship in Eastern Europe. They intended to stay in Canada and create new lives for themselves. These families are examples of _____.

4. Rajender Singh and his family came to Canada to visit friends and relatives. The family lived in Canada for nine months and then returned to India. Rajender Singh and his family are not examples of _____.

The steps for you, as teacher, to follow in this method are these:

1. Having decided on the concept to be taught, you must be able to define the term and know what would qualify as examples of the concept and what would count as non-examples. The non-examples should be items that are closely related to the example. It would be pointless to contrast "immigrants" with "skyscrapers"; rather, that concept should be contrasted with examples of other people who come to stay in Canada—tourists, visitors, diplomats—but who have no intention of settling here or becoming Canadian citizens. It would also help if, where possible, you could find a range of examples of the concept, some of which are more concrete than others, or more familiar to students. Examples and non-examples can be in print, picture, or actual object form. You will also have to consider whether your students understand the concepts related to the one you plan to teach. If these are not understood, then you will have to teach them.

2. Show examples of the concept, and ask children if they can use one word

(the concept) to describe all the examples (a guessing game). Ask "Can you think of one word that would describe all these?" Non-examples can also be displayed and children told that these are not examples of the concept. This may help make the game more interesting and may help children make more reasoned guesses.

3. When children have guessed the concept name, ask them to state *why* the examples can be called by that name. This will lead children to note the attributes of the concept. Here, it is important to relate the concept to other concepts that are part of the students' prior experience.

4. Show children additional examples and non-examples of the concept, and have them differentiate between them and state why they are examples or non-examples.

5. As an evaluation procedure, children could list the attributes of the concept, find examples and non-examples of the concept, and state why they are examples or non-examples.

A variation on this procedure is to display the examples of the concept and state that these are examples of concept X. Ask children what is similar about all the examples and have them identify the attributes of the concept. Then, carry out steps 4 and 5 above.

EXAMPLE: *Concept "Rural"*

Show children pictures of rural scenes. Ask "Can you think of a word that would describe all these pictures?" As guesses are given, introduce some non-examples (a city park, city scenes) and tell children that these are not examples. When children have guessed the concept, show some more pictures of rural and non-rural scenes and ask them to identify which are rural and which are non-rural. Have children tell you their reasons. Then children should list the attributes of the concept "rural." Finally, they could be given old magazines and asked to cut out examples and non-examples of "rural" and paste them onto paper. Or, using a textbook, children could tell you on which pages pictures of rural scenes occur. Reasons for believing these pictures to be examples of the concept could be discussed.

For more sophisticated students you could introduce examples of "suburbs." Point out that the term "urban" has been modified in order to describe a phenomenon that is neither urban nor rural, but somewhere in between. You could ask students to think of other words that have been modified to describe situations in which the original word was not quite appropriate. Examples might include "war" and "civil war," or "book" and "booklet."

There are a few key guidelines that should be followed in concept-attainment activities. First, research evidence indicates it is better to present examples of the concept first and to have them remain in view (either in pictorial form or as printed statements) during the activity.[2] Second, the optimal number of examples presented simultaneously should be about four. Third, concepts having few critical attributes are easier to learn than those that have many. Finally, presenting examples and non-examples in verbal form increases the ease of concept attainment. This is because critical properties can be emphasized more easily through verbal than through pictorial means.

To help you clarify the meaning of the concept you wish to teach, you can ask yourself and your students the following sorts of questions:[3]

1. With what terms is X (the concept you wish to teach) synonymous?

2. Can X be classified as a kind of _____?

3. How does the meaning of X differ from the meaning of _____ (which seems to be similar in meaning)?

4. What are the attributes of X? Is _____ a characteristic of things to which X refers?

5. What different kinds of X are there? Is _____ a kind of X?

6. If I say something is an X, am I ascribing positive or negative value to it?

Two major problems occur in concept learning: one is overgeneralization, the other is overdiscrimination. Although young children may overgeneralize ("Anything that flies is a bird"), they are more likely to overdiscriminate ("That's not a bird, it's a sparrow"). There is evidence to suggest that a child's ability to determine differences among concepts develops earlier than the ability to determine similarities. While the tendency to overdiscriminate tends to decline with age, the tendency to overgeneralize does not. The Wisconsin Model attempts to explain the development of concept learning.[4]

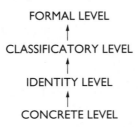

FORMAL LEVEL

↑

CLASSIFICATORY LEVEL

↑

IDENTITY LEVEL

↑

CONCRETE LEVEL

Concrete — the object is discriminated from other objects.

Identity — the object is generalized to two or more forms of the same thing that look similar.

Classificatory — the objects, although they may look different, are seen to belong to the same class of things.

Formal — the object can be fully defined, and inferred from examples.

Although the ability to understand and use concepts increases with age, this does not mean that young children cannot deal with abstractions. Young children do use words like "fair," "good," "cheat," and so on. They understand "climate" in terms of hot/cold and wet/dry. Older children may be able to discuss wind force and air pressure. They understand these terms at their own level and can be helped to develop conceptual abilities and knowledge through concept-attainment activities. What follows are some variations on these activities.

ACTIVITY 5-G

What one word could be used in each of the blanks? For a discussion of the answer see the ANSWERS section.

It is a _____ in this culture to make reed baskets. For centuries, mothers have taught their daughters to weave. When it appeared that modern technology would lead to the loss of this ancient craft, a revival of interest in this _____ occurred.

There has been a longstanding _____, based on a strong belief in male supremacy, of excluding women from important roles in Iranian society. When this _____ is flouted, there are serious repercussions.

Every year on October 3 the Smith family has held a birthday party for Grandma Smith. There is always a cake and presents. This family _____ has been practised for eighty-two years and is part of a larger cultural _____ of having parties on birthdays.

Every night John watches the television news. He does not expect his wife or children to do this, and he knows that he can change his behaviour at any time. This practice is not a _____.

ACTIVITY 5-H

Which are examples of the exercise of "power," and which are examples of the exercise of "authority"? When you have decided, turn to the ANSWERS section.

1. The teacher tells the students to line up.
2. The captain of the baseball team says that Catrina can't pitch because she isn't as good as Rachel.
3. Some older children tell Billy to get out of the park.
4. Joel says, "If you don't give me your chocolate bar, I'll get you after school."
5. Mrs. Chan tells her daughter to take out the garbage.
6. A police officer tells Mr. Brown to pull his car off to the side of the road.
7. The school principal says that the teacher must attend the workshop on the new Social Studies curriculum.

From this activity you can see that, although we and our students may use such words as "power" and "authority" in our speech and may recognize them in print, mere use or recognition does not necessarily mean that the concepts are understood. As teachers, we have to ascertain whether our students have grasped necessary concepts, and teach them if they have not. To help young students learn key concepts we can pose the following sort of questions:

1. Can you name a kind of _____?
2. Can you give an example of a/an _____?
3. How are a/an _____ and a/an _____ alike?
4. How are a/an _____ and a/an _____ different?
5. How are _____ all the same?

ACTIVITY 5-1

Design an activity to teach a primary or intermediate level class a concept that you consider to be important to learn in the context of the Social Studies. State your reasons for choosing this particular concept. State in what context you will be teaching the concept and list the examples you will use and the questions you will ask. Try out your activity on a partner.

There is one final point. Words have different connotations for different people. Returning to our "school" example from the beginning of the chapter, even though it merely describes a place where certain activities occur, to some people "school" may have a positive or negative emotive force, evoking pleasurable memories or feelings of loathing. So, in clarifying meaning, we have to be on the lookout for words where the meaning is surrounded by emotional reactions— and the actions we take are based on these reactions. Even if I loathed my school, it was still a "school"; I do not wish to get rid of "schools" just because mine was an awful place to be.

We must also be on the lookout for words that can fool us. For example, advertisements that promise something for "free" may not give you anything that is really free. You may remember that during the Gulf War, we were informed that the dropping of bombs on Iraq had caused "collateral damage." This piece of jargon was meant to take our minds off the fact that civilians had been killed or injured. The most powerful tool of humankind is its language. We use words to communicate information, to control others, to praise and condemn. We shape words, and words shape us. This is one reason why sexist terms must be eliminated, as their power demeans women. Words are meant to affect us. We must teach students to recognize when words are being used in unsupportable ways.

OTHER ACTIVITIES

1. Formulate a lesson plan to teach the concept "ceremony" to a primary grade class.

   (a) Define "ceremony."

(b) Choose examples that would be meaningful to primary grade students.

(c) State how you would use these examples and how you might differentiate between "ceremony" and such closely related concepts as "celebration" and "ritual."

2. Write a lesson plan for a grade of your choice on a topic or concept that uses the Taba concept development procedure or a concept-attainment model. Include:

(a) A rationale: Why teach concepts?

(b) Objectives: What specifically do you want students to know and do?

(c) The materials you will use.

(d) How you will begin the lesson.

(e) The main body of your lesson. What you and the children will do, in what sequence. How children will be organized (at individual desks, in groups).

(f) How you will end the lesson.

(g) How you might evaluate student learning.

(h) How you would follow up on your lesson; what you'll do next.

3. A teacher is using the Taba concept development procedure to introduce a unit on Japan. The students have viewed a videotape on the life of a boy and girl in Tokyo and have listed what they saw. In groups, students are now grouping and labelling the items. The teacher is working with one group. Critique the teacher's approach. For an assessment, see the ANSWERS section.

TEACHER: I see you have *fish, noodles* and *chopsticks* in one group. What is similar about these?

STUDENT: They all have to do with eating.

STUDENT: They're all food.

TEACHER: Well, what is the best label?

STUDENT: I think fish and noodles should go under *food* and the chopsticks should go somewhere else.

TEACHER: *(to another student)* What do you think?

STUDENT: Guess so. I wouldn't want to eat chopsticks.

TEACHER: So, what's similar about the food grouping?

STUDENT: They are all things you eat. They're good for you.

TEACHER: Where will the chopsticks go?

STUDENT: We've got a group here of pots, pans, knives, and stuff like that. It could go with them.

TEACHER: Do you remember in the videotape that the chopsticks had beautiful designs on them? Could they go with the group of items labelled *art*?

STUDENT: They could, but I think they fit better with the pots and things. They aren't like paintings.

TEACHER: Do you think your labels are OK?

STUDENT: I think so. If I was in Japan, I'd want to know about their food, how they cooked and ate it, their art …

STUDENT: I think so too. If a Japanese person came here, she'd want to know what we ate.

NOTES

1. H. Taba, M. Durkin, J. Fraenkel, and A. McNaughton, *A Teacher's Handbook to Elementary Social Studies* (Reading, Mass.: Addison-Wesley, 1971).

2. P. Martorella, "Knowledge and concept development in social studies," in J. Shaver, ed., *Handbook of Research on Social Studies Teaching and Learning* (New York: Macmillan, 1991).

3. Adapted from J. Coombs, "Critical thinking and problems of meaning," in I. Wright and C. LaBar, eds., *Critical Thinking and Social Studies* (Toronto: Grolier, 1987).

4. H. Klausmeier and F. Hooper, "Conceptual development and instruction," in F. Kerlinger and J. Carroll, eds., *Review of Research in Education 2* (Itasca, Ill.: Peacock, 1974).

CHAPTER 6

Exposition, narrative & the teaching of history

The task of teaching concepts is not complete unless students know how to apply them in a variety of circumstances. For example, we would not want to say that students had learned the concept "food" if they thought that it included only what they liked to eat. Concept learning, as discussed in the previous chapter, is deepened as students acquire more knowledge. Obviously, a significant part of teaching is to help students acquire worthwhile information. We shall use "information" to refer to knowledge that is basically empirical in nature. Empirical information describes what is, was, or will be the case. Its validity is tested through the observation of oneself and of others. The statement "The Haida used to eat whale meat" is an empirical claim because its accuracy could be checked through historical sources. The claim that people in India eat rice could be found to be true or false by going to India and looking at what people eat, or relying on the observations made by others. The claim that taking vitamin C will prevent people from getting colds can be checked through "observing" the results of experiments. While many empirical claims are easy to verify, others are not. We will discuss the assessment of empirical claims in more depth in Chapter 8. Needless to say, the information that you impart to students should be accurate.

There are two main ways students can obtain information. Either you can impart it to your students (exposition) or the students can locate it on their own. We'll first look at how you can make exposition interesting and worthwhile.

For reasons of brevity and efficiency, or because resource materials are not available, you might "lecture" to students. This does not mean that you stand up in front of the class and read from a prepared paper for thirty minutes. In the elementary classroom, you might spend some time lecturing to students, but you intersperse this with questions, discussion, blackboard notes, and audio-visual presentations. Here are some guidelines:

1. Make sure that students know the objectives for your "lecture." A good idea is to tell students at the beginning of the class what your talk is about and what, in particular, they are to listen for.

2. Organize your talk so that it contains the main points in a logical order.

3. At the end of the talk, summarize the main points.

4. Make your talk interesting by asking questions of students, encouraging discussion, and using audio-visual materials.

5. Prepare an activity in which students have to use the information contained in your talk.

6. Speak in a clear, interesting manner.

7. As you speak, maintain eye contact with the students.

8. If you notice that interest is slipping, ask questions or give students an activity to do.

ACTIVITY 6-A

Prepare a ten-minute talk on a topic of your choice. Decide what the main points are and in what order they will be presented. Choose suitable audio-visual aids. Prepare an activity for students to do after your talk.

Here is an example of a lesson plan using this expository approach. It is but one example of this kind of approach.

GRADE 3. RATIONALE FOR USE OF AN EXPOSITORY APPROACH

Exposition is a highly economical way of presenting information. It can synthesize quantities of information, eliminate the irrelevant, concentrate on the significant, and present data in a structured way. The presentation can be highly entertaining and interesting. It can include a variety of visual and other aids that reinforce significant details. Changes in the level of abstraction can be included so that all students, whatever their cognitive capacities, can learn something.

OBJECTIVES

Students will be able to list three basic needs of people (food, shelter, and clothing) and state how the Hutterites fulfil these needs.

INTRODUCTION

Picture of Hutterites eating a meal in the communal dining room.

Looking at this picture, we can see that, like you and me, these people need food. What else do they need? At the end of this lesson, I'll want you to be able to tell me who these people are, what needs they have, and how they go about fulfilling their needs.

MAIN BODY OF THE EXPOSITION

These people are Hutterites *(writes word on board)*. This group lives in Alberta *(shows Alberta on map—relates to where students live)*. Like you and me, they have certain needs.

(The needs are listed and explanations given as to how the Hutterites fulfil these needs. Students are questioned about the ways in which their own needs are fulfilled and how these compare to the Hutterites' ways. Pictures of Hutterites farming, building, sewing, and so on are shown.)

SYNTHESIS

So we have seen that, like you and me, Hutterites need food, clothing and shelter. They obtain them in ways that may be similar to, or different from, the ways in which we obtain them.

EVALUATION

Each student is given the following.

1. Name of people talked about _____.
2. They live in the province of _____.
3. Fill in this chart.

Need	How I obtain	How Hutterites obtain

Each student should correctly answer questions 1 and 2, and correctly identify how the Hutterites obtain food, shelter, and clothing.

The objective of exposition is for students to learn a body of information. Another way to achieve this objective is to use a cooperative learning activity employing the "jigsaw" technique. For more information on cooperative learning, see Chapter 9. In the "jigsaw" technique, each student is assigned to a study group and a learning group. In the study groups, each member becomes an expert on a particular body of information. Students then go to their learning groups and teach the rest of the group the content they learned in their study group. Finally, all students are tested on all the information. The steps in this procedure are as follows:

1. The teacher prepares materials so that the content to be learned is divided into separate parts.
2. Students are placed into learning groups and each student is assigned a

number. All the number 1's receive one body of information, all the number 2's receive a different body of information, and so on.

3. All the number 1's meet in a study group, all the number 2's meet in another study group, and so on.

4. Members of each study group teach and test one another on the information until they are all experts on it.

5. Students return to their learning groups, and each member teaches the others the content learned in the study group.

6. All students are tested on all the content.

7. Grades can be assigned on the basis of the average of each student's individual score and the team's average score. For example, if Rita's individual score was 90 and the learning group's average score was 86, then Rita would receive a score of 88. If students are informed at the beginning of this activity that their scores will be partially dependent on the score obtained by the rest of their group, they are more likely to stay on task and ensure that the content is really understood.

A variation on this activity is to have study groups read different parts of a textbook, become expert on the parts assigned to them, and then teach the content to their learning group. What is to be learned can be phrased in question form so that student attention is focused on the relevant content. Another technique, which can be used by pairs of students who are studying written materials, is labelled SQ3R. This stands for:

Survey—read headings.
Question—create question(s) from the heading(s).
Read—orally to find answers.
Recite—discuss answers to questions.
Reread—to check answers and write them down.

In pairs, one student acts as reader, the other as recorder. The latter asks the questions and listens as the reader reads the relevent materials. Answers are then discussed and the recorder writes down the agreed-upon ones. Roles are then switched for the next section of the materials.

THE STORY-TELLING APPROACH

Another way in which information can be imparted is to use Egan's story-telling (narrative) approach.[1] Narrative can be fiction or nonfiction; the term refers to writing that is shaped in story form. If the content is fiction, then students should be apprised of this. A brief example follows, but you should study Egan's book for a full grasp of the theoretical basis of his approach and how best to apply it in your teaching. Egan recommends that any Social Studies topic can be approached as a good story to be told, as well as a set of objectives to be attained. He suggests certain questions be answered so that a story unfolds.

1. Identifying importance

What is most important about this topic?
Why should it matter to children?
What is affectively engaging about it?

Suppose the unit was "Multiculturalism" and the focus was on Japanese Canadians. In answering the above questions, we could argue that multiculturalism is vital to Canada (see Chapter 20), that it matters to children because they interact with people from a variety of cultural backgrounds, and that the stories of immigrants—their sorrows, their triumphs—can engage children.

2. Finding binary opposites

What powerful binary opposites best catch the importance of this topic?

A number of significant binary opposites could be used: prejudice/tolerance; freedom/oppression; survival/destruction; cooperation/conflict; unity/diversity. Given that many groups come to Canada to escape oppression and that young children find "oppression" to be a powerful idea (my children were always complaining that they were being oppressed!), the binary opposites "freedom/oppression" will be used here.

3. Organizing content into story form

What content most dramatically embodies the binary opposites in order to provide access to the topic?
What content best articulates the topic into a developing story form?

Many incidents could be used to show how "freedom/oppression" applies to the history of the Japanese Canadians. They were denied the right to vote, excluded from certain jobs, and discriminated against in the fishing industry. But the most telling content concerns their evacuation from the British Columbia coast during World War II. One of the best ways of telling this story is through the eyes of Naomi, in Joy Kogawa's *Obasan*,[2] who with her family experiences the evacuation and subsequent internment. Students could carry out a number of activities based on the story: role-playing particular incidents; discussing the rightness or wrongness of the internment; writing a diary from the point of view of one of the internees.

4. Conclusion

What is the best way of resolving the dramatic conflict inherent in the binary opposites?
What degree of mediation of these opposites is it appropriate to seek?

In the story, there is a resolution. When the Canadian government ordered the deportation of Japanese Canadians, a decision which was upheld in the courts,[3] the resulting public outcry led to the repeal of the deportation orders on January 26, 1947. Recently, the survivors of the evacuation were granted both financial compensation and a formal apology from the Canadian government.

To extend this activity, we could clarify the two concepts to show, for example, that freedom does not mean licence, and that having to do what you're told does not necessarily mean oppression. We could show how oppressed people have taken political actions and sometimes have gained particular freedoms (e.g., Eastern Europe in 1989). We could look at the lives of immigrant groups and find out how they attempt to get control over their own lives. We could discuss relevant incidents in children's lives in which they see a conflict between freedom and oppression.

5. Evaluation

How can one know whether the topic has been understood, its importance grasped, and the content learned?

One of the best ways to evaluate student learning would be to have students write a story from the perspective of a member of the Japanese-Canadian community in 1941, telling of the evacuation, life in an internment camp or on a farm, and the deportation orders. Finally, students could state what their feelings are about "freedom" and "oppression" in this context. Other evaluation techniques can be found in Chapter 15.

ACTIVITY 6-B

Create a lesson plan using Egan's story-telling approach on a topic and grade level of your choice. The lesson should contain your objectives, an "opener," a brief description of what you will say, activities students will carry out, and a method of evaluation.

1. Identifying importance

What is most important about this topic?
Why should it matter to children?
What is affectively engaging about it?

2. Finding binary opposites

What powerful binary opposites best catch the importance of this topic?

3. Organizing content into story form

What content most dramatically embodies the binary opposites in order to provide access to the topic?
What content best articulates the topic into a developing story form?

4. Conclusion

What is the best way of resolving the dramatic conflict inherent in the binary opposites?
What degree of mediation of these opposites is it appropriate to seek?

5. Evaluation

How can one know whether the topic has been understood, its importance grasped, and the content learned?

THE TEACHING OF HISTORY

Egan's story-telling approach is a powerful one for teaching history, as it builds on students' experiences with stories, fairy tales, and myths. The major themes in these are typically conflicts between bravery and cowardice, good and evil, and so on. Students are already familiar with these themes from watching television and movies; this makes it an easy task to capture their imagination and impart some historical information. As stories consist of causes and effects within a temporal sequence, children can also begin to develop their concepts of historical time and causation.

There are other ways of teaching history. If you accept the Reflective Inquiry or Social Science conception of Social Studies, you will want students to inquire into historical events and act like historians. One way to do this is through oral history projects. Some very successful work has been carried out in which students interview people who have lived in the community for a long time.[4] For guidelines on how to conduct these interviews, see Chapter 9. From interviews and from other activities such as visiting historic sites and museums, and studying old maps, letters, newspapers, and other documents, students could create a history of their community. Students could also collect artifacts and create a classroom museum, watch some of the excellent movies and documentaries made about historical events, or role-play the characters in particular historical incidents.

Students should also be taught some of the criteria for judging evidence (Chapter 8). They can be presented with two or more conflicting accounts of the same event and begin to consider questions of historical interpretation. Many textbooks now present these sorts of accounts—describing, for example, how the native people viewed European explorers as well as the reactions of explorers to native people. The realization that different points of view exist is an important lesson for elementary students. In this kind of activity, students should be encouraged to project themselves into earlier times and try to understand the point of view of historical characters. Young children find this difficult, as they tend to view the world from their own egocentric point of view, but older students can begin to empathize with historical characters (see Booth[5]). This can be done through drama and role-play in situations where students have some background information and thus some idea of how a character might react given the tenor of the times. Understanding a historical character's point of view is best carried out by telling the story of the character's life from childhood to adulthood within the environment in which she or he lived. Showing that people in the past had the same sorts of needs as students do today, and that they experienced the same sort of emotions, makes it easier for students to identify with them. One excellent way to do this is through historical fiction. Students could read, or have read to them, some of the stories written about children in past times.[6]

In teaching any historical topic, it is necessary to locate it in time. The concept of "time" is a difficult one for children to grasp, but research indicates that young children can and do understand historical time in several ways (see Downey and Levstik[7]). Young children conceive of time not only in terms of their daily lives—

going to bed, watching cartoons on television on Saturday—but also in terms of "dinosaur times" or "when people lived in caves." They recognize the passage of time by identifying a number of discrete points that they put in a sequence—for example, events in their own lives such as birthdays; important cultural festivals such as Christmas, Hanukkah, or Divali; and such events as when they were in hospital or when a sister or brother was born. Thus, one way to teach children about historical time is to have them create a personal time line and to use this as a reference for the sequencing of historical events. For other ideas on the teaching of time, see Muir[8] and Burlbaw.[9]

ACTIVITY 6-C

Create a time line for your own life. Compare your time line to that of a peer. Did you mention the same sorts of events? Why or why not?

Underneath your time line, create another one listing important events that occurred in Canada during your lifetime. Again, compare this with a peer's. Did you mention the same events? Why or why not?

If possible, create time lines for your parents and grandparents. Relate their lives to events in Canada and the rest of the world.

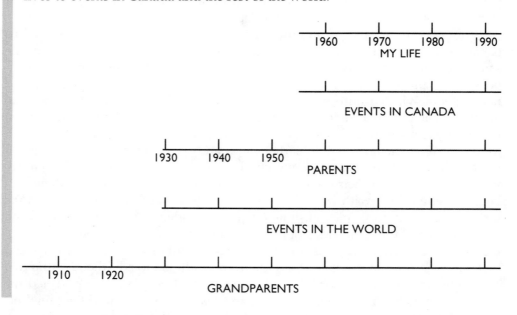

Not only do time lines help students locate events in sequence, they also help them "see" duration. Children have difficulty in understanding how long a year is, let alone a century or a millennium. Time lines can show duration in spatial terms: in Near Eastern and European prehistory, the Stone Age (approximately 1 million B.C. to 3000 B.C.) takes up more space on the time line than the Bronze Age (approximately 3000 B.C. to 1000 B.C.), so therefore it lasted longer. To help students understand the concepts of "B.C." and "A.D.," it is necessary to tell them that in many Western cultures A.D. (Anno Domini) dates from the time that it is believed Christ was born. So in the 1st century A.D. (there is no zero century) are the years 1 to 100, in the 2nd are the years 101 to 200, and so on. The publication date of this book is 1994, in the 20th century. If this idea has been grasped, then the idea of B.C. becomes more understandable. Again, there is no zero century B.C.; we have to count backwards from 1 B.C. To find out how long ago something occurred "Before Christ," we have to add the A.D. and B.C. figures. Thus, if it is correct that the first people came to North America around 10 000 B.C., then that was approximately 12 000 years ago.[10]

OTHER ACTIVITIES

1. Choose a historical character with whom you are familiar and create a time line for that person's life. Underneath this time line create another one that shows what other events were happening in the world during that character's lifetime.

2. Have elementary students of different ages construct time lines of their own lives. Compare results and explain why there are differences or similarities among the time lines.

3. In outline form, suggest what sources of information elementary students could use to write a history of a community with which you are familiar. What activities could students carry out in order to obtain this information?

NOTES

1. K. Egan, *Teaching as Story Telling* (London, Ont.: Althouse Press, 1986).

2. J. Kogawa, *Obasan* (Harmondsworth: Penguin, 1981).

3. See I. Wright, "Social Studies and law-related education: A case study of the Japanese in British Columbia," *The History and Social Science Teacher* 22:4 (1987), 209–14.

4. See M. Hickey, "And then what happened, Grandpa? Oral history projects in the elementary classroom," *Social Education* 55:4 (1991), 216–17.

5. M. Booth, "A critique of the Piagetian approach to history teaching," in C. Portal, ed., *The History Curriculum for Teachers* (London: Falmer, 1987).

6. For sources of such stories see I. Aubrey, *Notable Canadian Children's Books*, 1988 and 1989 Supplements (Ottawa: National Library of Canada, 1992). You might also look at reviews of children's books that appear periodically in newspapers such as *The Globe and Mail*. Chapter 4 of S. Egoff and J. Saltman, *The New Republic of Childhood: A Critical Guide to Canadian Children's Literature* (Toronto: Oxford University Press, 1990) is another useful guide.

7. M. Downey and L. Levstik, "Teaching and learning history," in J. Shaver, ed., *Handbook of Research on Social Studies Teaching and Learning* (New York: Macmillan, 1991).

8. S. Muir, "Time concepts for elementary school children," *Social Education* 54:4 (1990), 215–18/247.

9. L. Burlbaw, "An unfolding timeline," *Canadian Social Studies* 26:4 (1992), 158–60.

10. However, there is purported evidence from Brazil that human habitation was much earlier—50 000 years ago. See Isabel Vincent's Science and Archeology column, *The Globe and Mail*, January 1, 1994.

In the previous chapter we discussed various ways teachers could provide information to students. There are also many ways to help students acquire information for themselves. One way is for you or the students to pose questions that require them to carry out research. For example, if the question "What do people in country X eat?" arises students would have to locate appropriate resources (a book, a person who has lived in X) to answer the question. This chapter attempts to help you identify and use questions in the classroom.

ACTIVITY 7-A

List ten questions that could be asked about the photos below.

Presumably, you are familiar with what?, why?, where?, when?, and how? questions. But in your list above, did you include any of the following types of questions?

TYPES OF QUESTIONS

EMPIRICAL

Answers are in the form of statements about what is, was, or will be the case. This does not mean that the statements will *necessarily* be true or correct. We may never know the truth (where it exists) about some matters.

1. **Descriptive**

   What is happening? What are those people doing?
   How many of them are there? Is it raining?
   How does S use the term X?
   What is the dictionary definition of X?
   What does S value?

2. **Comparative**

   How are they similar/different?
   Has X changed?

3. **Historical** (as descriptive but concerning the past)

   When did the first people inhabit North America?

4. **Causal/Correlational**

   What caused that? Why did X happen?
   What has the climate got to do with the vegetation?

5. **Predictive**

   What will happen next? What will it be like in the future? What would happen if ...?

6. **Methodological**

   Where can we locate the answer? How can we tackle this problem?

7. **Relevance**

   What has this got to do with me? How does this relate to my life?

CONCEPTUAL

Answers are statements about what X means.

- Does A mean the same as B? (Does taiga mean the same as northern forest?)
- Is A an example of B? (Is this landscape an example of a prairie?)
- Is A an attribute of the term B? (Is a peak an attribute of a mountain?)

VALUE

Answers are in the form of a judgment.

- Is X good?

- Is A better than B?
- Should S do X?
- What should be done about X?
- Are our observations reliable?
- Is the datum believable?
- Is concept X used appropriately?

ACTIVITY 7-B

Pose one question for each of the above categories using the picture below.

The point of asking questions is not only to get students to state what they know already but also to stimulate further learning and thinking. This next set of questions focuses on this latter aspect.

Questions to introduce discussion:

What do you see here? Who would like to say something about this? Who would like to ask a question?

Questions to help analyze human behaviour:

What are these people doing? Why are they doing this? Have you done anything like this? How is it done?

Questions to help identify human feelings:

How do these people feel? Why do they feel this way? Have you ever felt this way? When? Do all people have the same feelings?

Questions to provoke further research:

What questions could be asked? How could answers be found? Is there a problem here? What could be done to solve it? What will we need to know? If you had this problem, what would you do? Why? Are some problems easier to solve than others? Why?

Questions to encourage geographic inferences:

What can we say about the location? Is it hot or cold? wet or dry? Is it like our own neighbourhood, province, or country? How have people adapted to the environment? How have people adapted the environment to suit themselves?

Questions to encourage historical inferences:

What do you think it was like in the past? Would people have done things differently one hundred years ago? What events in the past caused this situation/scene to be as it is today?

Questions to introduce sequential relationships:

What happened before? What do you think will happen next? Why?

Questions to broaden understanding and encourage summarization:

What conclusions can we draw from this? What has _____ got to do with _____? Can you make up a sentence to summarize this? If _____ occurred, what might happen? What does this tell us?

You will notice that not only are there different types of questions, but also that different sorts of reasoning are required to answer various questions.

ACTIVITY 7-C

Go back to your list of questions in Activity 7-B.

1. Which questions would be easiest to answer? Why?

2. Which questions would be most difficult to answer? Why?

3. What types of thinking abilities (reasoning skills) would be required to answer the easiest and most difficult questions? (Reasoning skills consist of inferring, analyzing, evaluating, interpreting, conceptualizing, and the like.)

4. Would these thinking abilities be necessary to answer all the other questions? Are other thinking abilities necessary also? If so, what are these abilities?

Clearly, those questions to which you already know the answers are easy. If you want to find out what students know, then questions of recall are important. But these questions don't require any of the reasoning skills identified above. If we want students to evaluate information, to infer, to analyze, and so on, then we have to ask questions that involve more than the recall of information.

Many educators use Bloom's taxonomy[1] to identify different levels of questions and the thinking abilities necessary to answer questions at each level. Sanders,[2] who adapted Bloom's taxonomy, lists the following categories. (I use Sanders's classification because it divides Bloom's Level 2 into two separate categories, and I find it useful to differentiate Translation and Interpretation. Bloom places both of these under Comprehension.) A typical question is included for each of the categories.

KINDS OF QUESTIONS

1. Memory
  – the student recalls previously learned information.
  "Who is the Prime Minister of Canada?"

2. Translation
  – the student changes information into a different symbolic form or language.
  "What is the point the artist makes in the cartoon?"

3. Interpretation
  – the student discovers relationships among facts, generalizations, and concepts. Interpretation involves a reordering or rearrangement of material. It makes use of comparative and cause-and-effect relationships.
  "What are the differences and similarities between the standards of living in Australia and Canada?"

4. Application
  – the student performs a task or solves a problem that requires the application of previously learned skills.
  "Use your inquiry skills to answer the following question ..."

5. Analysis
  – the student solves a problem by analyzing it into its constituent parts.
  "Is the reasoning in the following quotation sound or unsound?"

6. Synthesis
  – the student solves a problem that requires original, creative thinking. Synthesis is the assembly of elements and parts so as to form a whole. Synthesis questions encourage students to engage in imaginative, original thinking.
  "How would you solve the problem of litter in the school playground?"

7. Evaluation
  – the student makes a judgment of good or bad, right or wrong, according to particular criteria or standards such as:
  (a) Empirical accuracy

(b) Conceptual appropriateness
(c) Logical relationships and internal consistency
(d) Value principles, or standards

"Should Canada give aid to people who are starving in Somalia? Give reasons for your answer."

ACTIVITY 7-D

State whether each of the following is an empirical, conceptual, or value question. Specify its level according to Sanders's categorization. Answers are in the ANSWERS section.

1. In what year did Cartier build a settlement in what today is Quebec?

2. What are the major recommendations, and the reasons for them, of the recent report of the National Commission on Social Studies in the Schools, *Charting a Course*?

3. What caused World War II?

4. What is the population of Toronto? (Use the graph provided to answer the question.)

5. What is a harbour?

6. Is unity the opposite of diversity?

7. How should you solve the problem of starvation in Somalia?

8. Should First Nations people have the right to operate their own schools?

9. Should you hit someone whenever you feel like it?

10. If you believed killing was wrong and that capital punishment was a form of killing, then would you believe that capital punishment was wrong?

Whereas Sanders's adaptation of Bloom's taxonomy can be useful in focusing attention on different levels of questions, there are some problems with it. First, it should not be assumed that it is more difficult to answer "higher level" questions than "lower level" ones. The question "Should you hit someone whenever you feel like it?" is an evaluation question, yet is easy to answer for anyone with any moral sensitivity.

Second, recall questions can vary in level of difficulty. Some require recall of a specific fact; others require recall of complex bodies of information.

Third, merely stating that a question is at a particular level says nothing about the significance of the question. In my view, rather than relying on Bloom's taxonomy or Sanders's adaptation of it to tell you something about what will be required to answer a question, you should ask yourself the following:

QUESTION CHECKLIST

1. Is the question significant enough to be asked?

2. Can the question be answered in a satisfactory way by the students who will be attempting to answer it?

3. What type of question is it (empirical, conceptual, value)?

4. What information will be needed to answer the question?

5. Is this information available? Where?

6. What concepts will have to be understood in order to answer the question (concepts included in the question statement and in the information needed to answer it)?

7. What sorts of procedures could be used to answer the question? Do the students know how to carry out these procedures? Which is the best procedure?

8. What sorts of thinking tasks will students have to perform? Will they have to infer, generalize, hypothesize, etc.? Are they capable of performing these tasks?

9. What would qualify as a good answer?

The last question will involve a lot of thought by you and by your students. Students should be introduced to some of the criteria that pertain to evaluating the truth, believability, or acceptability of various types of claims. For example, some of the ways in which you can judge the appropriateness of the use of a concept appear in Chapter 5. In following chapters, you'll find standards relevant to judging the accuracy of empirical claims. In Part 3, some standards for justifying value claims are discussed.

ACTIVITY 7-E

Apply the Question Checklist to a question of your choice or to one or more of the following questions, all of which have been taken from recent provincial Social Studies curriculum guides.

1. Why do families need rules? (Grade 1, B.C.)

2. What services and facilities show that individual initiative and/or cooperation are/is valued in a particular community? (Grade 2, Alta.)

3. What are the distinctive geographical features of the prairie region? (Grade 3, Man.)

4. To what extent did native peoples make wise use of their physical environment? (Grade 4, B.C.)

5. What is meant by "government"? (Grade 5, N.S.)

6. How do people use the natural environment of Atlantic Canada in order to make a living? (Grade 6, P.E.I.)

7. Should a people, in order to satisfy their needs, be allowed to alter the physical environment of people in other parts of the world? (Grade 7, B.C.)

There are several other important points to be made about questions and questioning. It is clear that the sort of questions you ask will depend upon your objectives. If you want students to recall specific information, then a clearly worded recall question is needed. If you want students to generate a lot of different information, or pose many specific questions, then a broad general question is appropriate. For example, asking the question "What was life like in a fur fort in 1750?" may lead not only to information being given by students but also to questions such as "Where did drinking water come from?" or "Where did people go to the bathroom?" (a serious question asked seriously by a Grade 5 student).

You should be aware of the possibilities of expanding upon both specific and broad questions. You may have to rephrase a question so that it is understandable, or provide prompts to get students on track. It may be necessary to ask for clarification of a particular answer, and you may wish to redirect a question if a particular student is unable to provide an answer. You should also encourage students to ask questions. A correctly answered question does not mean that you and your students should not pose further questions.

ACTIVITY 7-F

Take any question you might ask in the study of any topic and expand on this question.

Look at your "expansion" questions and put a checkmark against those you consider important. Give reason(s) for your choice(s).

In oral question/ answer classroom situations, there are basically two ways of operating:

Individual designated:	Saul, what is _____ ?"
Group designated:	(a) "Class, what is _____ ? Saul, please answer."
	(b) "Class, what is _____ ?" (student who is not designated by the teacher spontaneously answers)
	(c) "Class, what is _____ ?" (whole class responds *en masse*)

Each of these procedures has its advantages and disadvantages.

Individual

The advantages are that the whole class is alert, as nobody knows who is going to be called upon to answer the question, inattentive students are engaged, and a student who is likely to know the answer can answer. The disadvantages are that favouritism can prevail if only some individuals are called upon by the teacher (this can be insidious if the favouritism is based on ethnicity, gender, class, or the presumed mental or physical capabilities of a student). When the student's name is called, the rest of the class may not pay attention to the question or the answer, and shy children may be overlooked entirely. Exclusion of students in a question-and-answer session should be avoided at all costs unless there is a compelling reason for it (such as in a case where a student is experiencing some emotional upset and needs to be left alone for a while).

Group

The advantage is that the entire class is involved initially—every student has the opportunity to answer. The disadvantages are that once a student is chosen to answer the question, the rest of the class may not pay attention to the answer given, and, if an answer is to be given spontaneously, those who know the answer immediately will foreclose on those who need time to think.

Keep these points in mind when you are engaged in question-and-answer sessions and, whichever procedure you adopt, always try to involve as many students as possible. You can achieve this by sharing a single question among several children or by posing further questions related to the original one to other students.

EXAMPLE:

TEACHER: Raoul, when did Jean Chrétien become prime minister of Canada?

RAOUL: In 1993.

TEACHER: Susan, is Raoul correct?

SUSAN: Yes.

TEACHER: Fred, are you sure it wasn't 1994?

FRED: I don't think so ... I'm not sure.

TEACHER: Who in the class is sure? Marie?

MARIE: It was in 1993.

TEACHER: Good, we've got the answer.

EXAMPLE:

TEACHER: Dorothy, what's the capital of British Columbia?

DOROTHY: It's Victoria.

TEACHER: Lea, is Victoria the capital of British Columbia?

LEA: Yes.

TEACHER: Claude, what makes it the capital?

CLAUDE: The premier lives there.

TEACHER: Is that why Victoria is the capital, Sanjit?

SANJIT: No, it's because Parliament is there.

FIONA (*spontaneously*):   It's the legislature. Parliament is in Ottawa.

TEACHER: Well, class, who is right?

Note that in these exchanges, four or more students can be quickly involved. This "quick-fire" strategy is appropriate only when students do not need time to think about their answers. When time is required for students to reflect, then the teacher should provide adequate "wait-time."

Another way in which students can be involved in a question-and-answer activity is to use a cooperative learning strategy in which the class is divided into groups of three to five and each group member is given a number. Each group should be representative of the composition of the class (in ability, gender, ethnicity, etc.). Each group discusses the answer to a question. The teacher then calls upon all students with a particular number (e.g., all number 3's), and designates one of them to provide the answer. This procedure has several advantages. Higher achievers are willing to share their knowledge, as they want their group to do well, and lower achievers are likely to listen carefully, as they might be called upon to give the answer. Cooperation among students is also enhanced.

Children need rewarding when their answers are correct. Avoid saying "good" or "O.K." after every answer—it will become meaningless. Also avoid "No, you're wrong." Instead, say "That's not quite right; can you clarify that a little more?" or ask another student "Can you help?" When the correct answer is ascertained, ensure that the student who gave the wrong answer knows and understands the correct one.

OTHER ACTIVITIES

1. Ask a number of questions about your classroom or a local parking lot, street, or other location. Take one particular question and list the ways in which this question could be extended. Evaluate your questions for their clarity and importance.

2. Take a particular question from any Social Studies curriculum material and complete a thorough analysis of it.

(a) What sort of question is it (empirical, conceptual, value)?

(b) What concepts would students have to grasp in order to answer the question?

(c) What information would students need to answer the question?

(d) What sorts of thinking abilities would students have to demonstrate?

(e) What would qualify as a reasonable answer?

NOTES

1. B. Bloom, ed., *Taxonomy of Educational Objectives: Handbook 1—Cognitive Domain* (New York: David McKay, 1956).

2. N. Sanders, *Classroom Questions: What Kinds?* (New York: Harper and Row, 1966).

As stated in Chapter 6, there are two ways in which students can obtain information. One way is for you to impart it to them, the other is for them to discover it themselves. The focus of this chapter is on ways in which answers can be found to questions that are posed either by students or by a teacher. The major strategy to be discussed will be *inquiry*.

In the Social Studies literature, inquiry sometimes refers to any procedure whereby students find answers to questions. Thus, looking up the answer to a simple and specific question to which the answer is known would constitute inquiry. In this case, the defining attributes of inquiry are that the question is beyond the recall level, according to Sanders's taxonomy (see Chapter 7), and that the student has to find the answer. This is a worthwhile activity at times. In this chapter, however, inquiry will be used to denote a procedure in which students generate hypotheses and test them by locating, interpreting, analyzing, and evaluating information. The term "hypothesis" will refer to two different kinds of statements:

1. A guess about the answer to an empirical question that would require a fairly complex answer from students—that is, many answers are possible and the answer cannot usually be found in one source. (For example, "What toys did Canadians who lived during the early 1900s play with?" Or "Why did Egypt become a dominant power during the New Kingdom, 1552–1070 B.C.?")

2. Statements about the predicted outcome to questions that demand a survey or experiment be performed. (For example, "What are students' attitudes to litter in the playground?" Or "If there were more garbage cans in the playground, would the amount of litter decrease?")

Suppose you are interested in finding out how many of your peers, or students in your class, have parents/guardians whose native language is not English. In that case, the following questions need to be asked as the inquiry procedure is implemented.

ACTIVITY 8-A

Question. How many of the students/peers in my class have parents/ guardians whose native language is not English?

Is the question clear? Do you know what the terms used in the question mean?

Hypothesis. What do you think the answer is?

Organization and data collection. How will you find out whether or not your hypothesis is supported? What information will you need? Where do you think you could obtain this information? Will you work alone or would working in a group be more efficient? If you work with others, how might various tasks be shared?

Data analysis. How might the information be classified, interpreted, and evaluated? What skills and abilities would you need to make use of the data?

Checking the hypothesis. Is the hypothesis supported by the information? What will you do if (a) your hypothesis is not supported? (b) your conclusion is so tentative that you can neither accept nor reject your hypothesis?

Conclusion. How might you report your conclusion?

In this inquiry procedure there are several important factors to consider.

1. **The question.** Make sure students understand the question, especially the concepts contained in it. For example, in the question "What motivated the first Europeans to explore North America?" students would need to clarify "motivation" and understand that various sorts of mental states—fear, greed, curiosity—can motivate human behaviour. Without this clarification, the next step would be pointless.

2. **Hypothesizing.** Once the question has been clarified, students should hypothesize as to what they think the answer will be. Hypotheses should be listed by you and/or the students. Accept all hypotheses, even if you know they're wrong. One of the reasons for using inquiry strategies in the classroom is that students find it more interesting and challenging to test hypotheses than to merely look up answers to a question in a book—or to rely on the teacher.

   Hypothesizing depends upon students' previous knowledge and experiences. It would be pointless to have students hypothesize about Mongolian lifestyles if students had never heard of Mongolia, just as it would be pointless for them to hypothesize about "motivation" if they did not understand the term. The next activity is designed to show that the quantity and quality of background knowledge make a significant difference to the hypotheses that are generated.

ACTIVITY 8-B

Refer to the accompanying map. Place a dot on the map to indicate each place where you think a settlement is located. When you are done, turn to the ANSWERS section.

What previous knowledge did you use in order to arrive at these hypotheses?

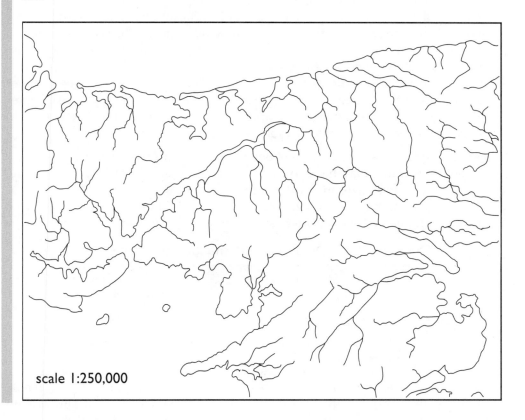

scale 1:250,000

In order to make sensible hypotheses you had to have some ideas why settlements are located in particular places—for example, proximity to a water supply, location that offers a sheltered harbour, etc.

3. **Data gathering.** Ask the students how they are going to find out whether their hypotheses are correct. Ensure that they explore all possible sources. Depending upon the number of resources available and on the skills of the students, you can work with them in the library or you can provide all the material in the classroom. All students could use the same material, or groups could be formed (for example, one group could look at a video, another look at pictures, and a third read print material). In cases where some sort of survey or experiment has to be conducted, ensure that it is feasible.

Students will need to be taught the skills necessary to use the materials or conduct a survey. They should learn how to locate references in the library and how to use indexes, chapter headings, and subheadings in order to find specific information. By the intermediate grades, students should be able to use most reference sources and compare sources to see if they agree.

The reading level of resource materials may pose problems. Those students who have difficulties reading can be given simple print material, or they can be helped by another student. Providing pictorial sources is another option for younger readers. Even in the intermediate grades, it may be necessary for you to paraphrase some reading material. Historical documents, for example, are often difficult for even very able students to read.

The answers to some questions may involve taking surveys (see Chapter 11), or interviewing people (see Chapter 10), or interpreting maps (see Chapter 13), or going on a field trip (see Chapter 12). In each case, students will have to be taught how to collect information by these means.

4. **Analysis.** Once information has been collected, students have to test their hypotheses. They may have to be taught how to classify, interpret, analyze, synthesize, summarize, and evaluate the information.

How the information is organized will depend on the question posed. One way information can be recorded is on an inquiry "worksheet."

Question: What Did Pre-European-Contact Haida Eat?

Hypothesis	Data supporting	Data rejecting and additional data
Fish	Yes, salmon	Ate shellfish also.
Beef		Didn't have cattle.

5. Checking the hypotheses. The conclusions derived from the information must be checked against the hypotheses. Are the hypotheses supported? Can we be sure we are right? Are the hypotheses rejected? Again, can we be sure we are right? Perhaps the evidence to support or reject a particular hypothesis cannot be found. In this case, we may be able to arrive at a tentative conclusion, or we may have to search further to see if we can find an answer. For example, if on the Haida question recorded on the worksheet (see above) students hypothesized that seagulls were eaten and no evidence could be found that the Haida either did or did not eat seagulls, then this will have to remain a hypothesis.

6. Presenting the conclusion. Once students have checked their hypotheses and decided which ones are supported, they can present their conclusions. These can be written, drawn, graphed, modelled, or diagrammed, depending upon the type of question posed. For a hypothesis about food, the conclusion might be presented in the form of a menu. See Chapter 10 for ideas on presenting information.

How will we know whether the conclusion is true or believable? What qualifies as a reasonable answer to an inquiry question? The next activity is designed to focus attention on the accuracy of claims presented in reference materials.

ACTIVITY 8-C

Use at least three different sources to find out the date of Christopher Columbus's birth. Do these sources agree? If not, which source is correct? Carry out the same procedure for the question "Where did Columbus first set foot in the New World?"

Generally, we rely on authorities to provide us with information. We accept that the information in a textbook is accurate; we believe what experts tell us. Most students will believe what you tell them. I think it is obligatory for us to tell students why we believe that the information we impart to them is accurate; we should have reasons for saying that something is true or believable. We should teach students how to evaluate empirical claims. One way to do this is to focus on the types of information students are exposed to, not only in school but also in their daily lives, and help them judge which would be the most reliable.

ACTIVITY 8-D

Suppose you had to teach the topics listed below. If you had to choose *one* reference, which would you consider to be the best? Why? When you have decided on your answer, refer to the ANSWERS section.

1. **Topic:** Life in China today.

   (a) A *National Geographic* movie about life in China, produced in 1992 by two people who spent six months touring the country.

   (b) A book published by the Chinese government extolling the virtues of life in the country.

   (c) Slides taken by a friend who recently spent two weeks in Beijing and Canton.

   (d) A 1992 CBC documentary about student unrest in China.

2. **Topic:** The internment of the Japanese during World War II.

   (a) A recent high-school textbook on the history of Canada in the 20th century.

   (b) The memoirs of a former politician who was instrumental in setting up internment camps.

   (c) A television documentary about six families who were interned during the war.

   (d) The autobiography of a Japanese Canadian who, as a child, was interned.

For the above activity, you should really choose more than one source because, if authorities agree on something, there is a greater likelihood that it is accurate. However, by forcing you to choose *one* source, my intention was to compel you to think seriously about the criteria you would use to determine what sources of information are likely to be the most reliable. According to Ennis,[1] the following criteria should be applied: The authority/expert (1) has a good reputation; (2) is making statements that lie in his/her field; (3) has studied the matter using acceptable procedures; (4) is aware that his/her reputation could be affected by his/her statements.

Applying these criteria is necessary not only when reading textbooks and other sources of information, but also when people are trying to convince you to believe something or buy something. Suppose you see a commercial in which a famous film star is telling you to buy Brand X toothpaste. While the star may be an expert on acting, there is little reason to accept the star's views on dental hygiene. If we did buy Brand X toothpaste *because* the star told us to, then we would be committing the fallacy of "appeal to authority."

Of course, we do not rely on authorities for all our information. The other major source of information is observations made by ourselves or others. These too need to be evaluated.

ACTIVITY 8-E

Which of the following would you consider to be a reliable observation? Why? After justifying your choice, turn to the ANSWERS section.

1. **(a)** The umpire in the baseball game said that Rachel was out.

   (b) Rachel's mother said she was not out.

   (c) The captain of the opposing team said that Rachel was out.

2. **(a)** The driver of the car that hit the bus said the traffic light was green when he went through the intersection.

   (b) The driver of a car that arrived at the intersection ten seconds after the incident said he thought the light was red when the car went through the intersection.

   (c) A cyclist who had stopped at the intersection said the car went through a red light.

3. **(a)** Using a measuring tape, the police measured the skid marks of the car that crashed and said, "The car skidded for twenty metres."

   (b) A witness to the crash paced out the skid and said, "The car skidded for fifteen metres."

   (c) Another witness to the crash, who had narrowly avoided being hit by the car, said, "The car skidded for at least thirty metres."

In assessing observation statements, the following criteria should be applied:[2]

The observer

1. Does not allow emotion to interfere.
2. Has no conflict of interest.
3. Has senses that function properly.
4. Has a good reputation.
5. Uses appropriate observation instruments.
6. Was in a suitable position to observe.
7. Makes statements that are confirmed by others, or are confirmable.

Students in the elementary school can begin to grasp some of these criteria by carrying out the following sorts of activities:

1. Compare two or more sources of information for answers to a particular question, or compare two or more newspaper, radio, TV, textbook, etc., accounts of a particular event. For example, ask students to find out the present-day population of Canada. Ask them to present their answers along with complete details about the source they used.

Population	Title of reference	Author	Where published	Date of publication
Source of population figure	Date of source of population figure			

2. Have students witness a given event and write a description of it. Compare the descriptions using the observation criteria listed above.
3. We all have our own biases. Thus, it is important that students recognize their own and others' biases and judge when a bias leads to unfairness, distortion, prejudice, or closemindedness. Which of the following accounts are biased in any of the above senses?

(a) "Slugger" Smith hit 32 home runs for the Torpedoes in the 1992 season. "Hits" Wood of the Sharks hit 30, placing him second in the year's standings.

(b) "Slugger" Smith was extremely lucky to hit 32 home runs last season. If you remember, most of these came against pretty poor teams and lousy pitching.

Without doubt, the player to praise is "Hits" Wood, who scored all his runs against top league teams and top pitchers.

(c) "Slugger" Smith, who hit 32 magnificent homers last season, is probably the greatest ballplayer the Torpedoes have ever had. It was he, and he alone, who took the pennant away from the Sharks. He is so far ahead of "Hits" Wood in home runs that he is in a class all by himself.

4. Help students distinguish between primary and secondary sources: Write the letter P beside those items that you think should be classed as primary sources, and S for those you think are secondary sources.

(a) The Canadian Charter of Rights and Freedoms.

(b) *Obasan* by Joy Kogawa, a novel about the internment of Japanese Canadians in World War II.

(c) *Hansard.*

(d) Adolf Hitler's autobiography, *Mein Kampf.*

5. Encourage students to answer the following sorts of questions:

Where was the evidence found?
When was the evidence found?
Who reported the evidence?
How was the evidence found?
Can the evidence be *checked*? If so, *how*?

6. If inferences are made from information, then ask students whether there is evidence for their inference or whether other inferences can be made that are just as plausible. For example, if a picture is shown of people lining up outside a store before it opens, it is plausible to infer that there is a sale; it is also plausible, however, to infer that there is a shortage of goods and people are lining up to ensure that they obtain them. To discover which inference is true, we'd need more information.

ACTIVITY 8-F

Observe the following picture. Which of the statements that follow are inferences? Of these inferences, which do you think are plausible? Answers are given in the ANSWERS section.

(a) The colour of the car is black with white lettering.

(b) The lettering on the car says John D. Smith, M.D.

(c) Someone is ill in 4122.

(d) The car belongs to John D. Smith, M.D.

(e) The car is parked outside 4122.

(f) John D. Smith lives at 4122.

(g) John D. Smith is a doctor.

(h) John D. Smith is economically well-off.

7. Help students avoid making some common fallacies in reasoning. One widely used fallacy is overgeneralization—arguing that if one example of something has a particular characteristic, then all similar examples have the same characteristic. For instance, we cannot state that because one doctor is well-off, therefore all doctors are well-off (see above). Neither can we claim that because something is true of a group, then it is necessarily true for individual members of the group. The fact that Canadian doctors, on average, are near the top of the earning hierarchy doesn't mean that every single doctor is well-off.

Another common mistake is to see things only in black and white, ignoring all the shades of "grey" (e.g., "Either we stop all immigration or there will be no jobs left for people who already live here").

Other common fallacies include appeals to tradition ("We did X in the past, so we should do X now"); appeals to large numbers ("If the majority of people believe X, then X must be right"); and reasoning that because one event preceded another, then the first must have caused the second. This assertion of a causal link between events in sequence when there is insufficient evidence is labelled *post hoc ergo propter hoc* ("after this, therefore because of this").

An excellent way to draw student attention to these fallacies is to evaluate advertisements. Have students compare advertisements for similar products. Comparisons should be made about the intended audiences of each, the images they create, the fallacies (if any) committed, the language used, the amount of information conveyed, and possible negative aspects of the product that are not mentioned.

Thinking critically about information takes time and effort, and depends upon having background information. Encouraging students to ask questions and gradually teaching them some of the standards of critical thought are important throughout your teaching, and essential when students are engaged in inquiry procedures.

Unless the information we use is as accurate as possible, we are likely to make serious mistakes that can affect our own lives and those of others. Consider the "simple" matter of being taken in by false advertising—and the far more serious consequences of hateful propaganda for innocent minorities.

The activity that follows is designed to encourage you to think critically about the data you collect.

ACTIVITY 8-G

Carry out an inquiry procedure to answer the question "What rules govern the interactions in this classroom?"

1. Is the question clear? What would qualify as a "rule"?

2. Generate a hypothesize about what rules you think govern the interactions in the classroom. Write down your hypothesis.

3. How will you test your hypothesis? How will you observe whether a rule is or is not being followed? For how long will you observe? How will you ensure that you observe all the likely situations in which your hypothesis could be tested? How will you record your data?

4. Collect your answers according to the decision made in 3, above. Decide what you're going to do with the answers—list all of them, classify them, graph them, or tabulate them in some other way.

5. Decide whether your hypothesis is supported by the evidence. Are you sure your results are reliable? Did you observe for a long enough period? If your hypothesis was not supported, can you explain why? What conclusions can you draw?

Questions about the reliability of information can be raised with young students as well as older ones. In the example below, primary children are encouraged to clarify concepts and judge the reliability of data.

Question	What is the most popular pet of students in the class?
Hypothesis	The teacher has pictures of animals on the blackboard and she asks children to state which of them are pets. She helps children clarify the concept by introducing other examples and non-examples. She then asks the class to guess which

pet is the most popular one among class members. Each child then draws a picture of the pet that he or she thinks is most popular.

Data collection Each child is given a sheet of paper with the names of the pets included and space to note down the number of children who own each type of pet.

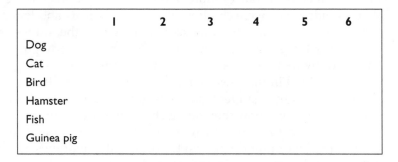

	1	2	3	4	5	6
Dog						
Cat						
Bird						
Hamster						
Fish						
Guinea pig						

Each child asks the other children in his or her row or table what pets they have, and checks the number on the sheet. Each row or table checks that each student has the same answers.

Hypothesis check The information from each row or table is collected by the teacher and a master chart is made on the board. The teacher asks questions about the data collected. Are they reliable? How could we find out? If there is an animal in a house, does it mean that the animal is a "pet"? A decision is made about whether or not the hypothesis is supported.

Conclusion A simple block graph of class results is constructed by students, or each student could draw and label the most popular pet.

Here is another example, for students in Grades 3 and 4.

Major question: "What was life like when my grandparents were children?"

Background: The class has started by constructing a time line commencing with when they were born and ending with the present. They have photos and drawings showing themselves at various stages in their lives. The time line has been extended to display information about the lives of their parent(s) and grandparent(s). The class is using old Sears and Eaton's catalogues and has noted and discussed the type of houses their grandparents might have lived in, the clothes they wore, and the type of jobs they might have had. Some children have interviewed their parent(s) and grandparent(s), and photos and artifacts have been collected for a classroom museum.

LESSON

Question: "What toys did my grandparents play with?"

The teacher asks the class what a "toy" is. Answers are discussed and examples of "toys" are given. The children are asked to guess the answer to the question. As guesses are forthcoming, they are written or drawn on the board or on chart paper. Students then draw one or more of the items they think children played with when their grandparents were children. They use old Sears and Eaton's catalogues to test their hypotheses. If a hypothesis is supported, the student puts a check mark against the toy. A student who finds a toy that nobody guessed was played with should draw that toy. Finally, the students share their findings. Other toys that students identified in their research are added to the list. If no evidence can be found for a toy listed by a student, students are asked whether it might have been a toy fifty years ago, and how they might check their hypotheses.

The teacher then may provide extra information and/or have students ask their parent(s) or grandparent(s) to confirm the hypotheses. As grandparents may come from different ethnic backgrounds, it would be interesting to compare toys. Do they differ from those shown in the resource materials? If the family members can provide confirmation of a toy's use, a picture of the item is mounted along with the other correct items. If the guess was wrong, then the reasons why it was wrong are discussed.

If actual toys can be obtained, children can play with them and discuss such things as the level of technology involved in producing the toys; whether they would be "good" toys; whether there were fewer toys available fifty years ago, and why; how economic status influenced the type and number of toys available to a child; whether there are, and should be, female and male toys; and how advertising has been carried out in the past and the present and how it influences what children want. This topic could culminate in a toy fair in which work done by students is displayed and other students in the school are invited to come and see the display and play with the toys.

Here is an idea for an upper elementary grade class that is studying ancient civilizations. Students should be divided into two equal groups. Each group is given one ancient civilization and told to work independently. Each group should prepare models, collect pictures, or illustrate artifacts that archeologists use to describe the civilization. Artifacts should be presented to the other group (even better, they could bury the artifacts in a sandbox and have the other group dig them up), and the other group should respond by describing the civilization. This group's interpretation can then be checked against the original group's information.

Inquiry procedures have to be taught to students. They need help so that they can:

1. Identify a problem that is testable and suitable for their level of maturity.
2. Clarify the question by clarifying the words used in it—i.e., by defining words and/or by giving examples.

3. Hypothesize possible conclusions.

4. Select appropriate research techniques: survey, interview, library research, field work, actual experiment.

5. Select information pertinent to the question and show willingness to look at all points of view. Locate information using card catalogues, bibliographies, on-line data retrieval systems.

6. "Read" sources of information—skim read to find specific information; use headings, topic sentences, and summary statements to select between main and subordinate ideas; draw inferences from information; use and interpret maps, surveys, graphs, historical documents, and pictures.

7. Evaluate information—identify bias and faulty reasoning.

8. Organize information—use main and supporting evidence; formulate suitable classification schemes; create tables of contents; use appropriate bibliographic formats.

9. Synthesize information—formulate generalizations and cause-and-effect relationships; summarize main ideas; identify information that supports and does not support a hypothesis; recognize the need to change a conclusion when new evidence warrants it; show willingness to re-inquire if necessary.

10. Present conclusions in a variety of forms: written and verbal reports, graphs, models, charts, diagrams, models, and so on.

Although the inquiry procedure has many major advantages, it also has potential pitfalls and problems. These include:

Lack of time	Inquiry can be time-consuming; adequate time must be given so that students can explore on their own.
Lack of resources	Often resources are lacking, and teachers and students will have to search for pertinent materials.
Teachers who want to be "in charge"	You will have to be receptive to students' ideas, supportive, and willing not to impose your "answers" on students.
Questions that are too difficult	Questions must be within the cognitive capacity of students.
Rigidity	Despite its many guises, if inquiry is the only method of teaching/learning, it can become boring for students.
Particular student characteristics	If students can't find answers or can reach only tentative conclusions, inquiry can have a paralyzing effect on them. Students need to know that there are some questions to which we can find answers, while also realizing that there are some things we don't know. Inquiry has to be introduced gradually to students who are unfamiliar with it. You might start with finding answers to specific questions in one

source, then advance to posing questions requiring research using many sources. This could be followed by posing more complex questions and finally by group inquiry in which various questions are answered by groups of students, who locate their own resource materials and make decisions about how the inquiry is to proceed.

Possibility of male bias

The questions inquired into may be of more import to males than females; insistence on a particular answer may exclude other viewpoints, including feminist ones (see Maher[3]).

All these pitfalls can be avoided by careful teaching, and by recognizing and taking into account possible negative biases. They should not dissuade you from using inquiry procedures, which are exciting ways for children to learn. Inquiry procedures actively engage students and teach them many valuable skills. Students are more likely to remember what they learned through inquiry procedures than through more passive methods. Their motivation is enhanced when it is their own questions that are the subject of inquiry. Students discover some of the joys of learning on their own and in the company of others. They can have fun. I enjoy using inquiry methods because they keep me actively engaged with children. They often teach me.

Throughout this discussion the term "inquiry" has been used as if the meaning were clear. In the Social Studies literature you may find the inquiry procedure labelled as "problem-solving" or "reflective thinking." Sometimes you will find the term "inquiry" used to describe any procedure used by students to answer questions whose answers they do not know.

ACTIVITY 8-H

Given how inquiry is defined in this chapter, which of the following would qualify as inquiry? When you have made your choice, turn to the ANSWERS section.

		INQUIRY		
	Yes	No	Not sure	Reason
1. The teacher asked, "When was Columbus born?" Students went to the library and then reported their answers to the teacher.	___	___	___	___
2. The students brought an election poster into class. They asked the teacher to explain it. The teacher sent the students to election headquarters to find out answers to their questions.	___	___	___	___

	INQUIRY			
	Yes	No	Not sure	Reason
3. The teacher gave a lecture on communism. Students were then given a worksheet and were required to identify examples and non-examples of communism.	___	___	___	___
4. The class became interested in capital punishment. Students hypothesized as to whether or not hanging should be retained for convicted murderers. Students collected, classified, analyzed, and evaluated information and debated reasons until finally each student reached a conclusion.	___	___	___	___
5. To discover some of the effects of overcrowding, half the class worked in a broom closet for thirty minutes.	___	___	___	___
6. The teacher asked the class to sit silently for ten minutes and meditate on the meaning of life.	___	___	___	___
7. In order to verify hypotheses made regarding the lifestyle of the contemporary Inuit, students went to various resources and collected, classified, and interpreted data. On the basis of their evidence, they decided whether or not their hypotheses were supported.	___	___	___	___
8. The class was divided into groups. Each group had five questions to answer and resource materials from which to answer them.	___	___	___	___
9. In order to discover how many vehicles used the road outside the school, the students conducted a traffic census.	___	___	___	___
10. The Grade 1 class was shown a yurt and were asked to identify it by asking questions of the teacher and by guessing.	___	___	___	___

As with all teaching methodologies, underlying the use of inquiry procedures are beliefs about how children learn, what constitutes knowledge, and what the aims of education should be. In the next activity you are asked to identify those beliefs that underlie inquiry procedures.

ACTIVITY 8-I

If you use inquiry procedures, which of the following assumptions might you be making? When you have chosen, refer to the ANSWERS section.

(a) All knowledge is absolute.

(b) Children learn best when they are finding out their own answers.

(c) In a democracy, people have to make decisions. This entails the analysis and evaluation of conflicting evidence.

(d) Children learn best when they are told the answer.

(e) Children learn self-confidence when discovering knowledge for themselves.

(f) Children "by nature" are problem-solvers.

(g) Children learn to think by being taught how to think.

(h) Knowledge is a product of continuing inquiry and experimental test, hence open to re-examination, renewal, and change.

(i) Children remember what they've discovered for themselves better than what they've been directly taught.

(j) Children are "naturally" curious.

OTHER ACTIVITIES

1. Write a lesson plan on one of the following questions:

(a) Who works in my school and what jobs do they do? (Grade 1)

(b) What part, if any, did the building of the Canadian Pacific Railway play in the history of Canada? (Grade 5)

Include the following components:

Opener—How will you motivate interest?

Hypothesis(es)—How will you organize for hypothesis-making?

Organization and data collection—How will you organize the class? What data will you use?

Data analysis—How will students use the data?

Hypothesis check—How will this evaluation be carried out?

Conclusion—How will students present their findings?

Finale—How could you continue on this topic?

2. During a class discussion on clothing, the girls claim that they dress better than boys. They say that boys wear dull-coloured clothing, whereas girl wear bright colours. The question arises, " Do boys in the school wear dull-coloured clothing, whereas girls wear bright colours?" How would you use an inquiry approach to help students arrive at a conclusion to this question?

3. There are billions of questions that could be inquired into. Below are some problems for you and your students to solve.

(a) You are stranded on the island pictured below. You have heavy-duty, cold-weather, waterproof clothing, a pocketknife, a watch, and some rope—nothing else. You know that a ship will visit the island in a month's time. What problems will you have in surviving for a month? How will you solve these problems?

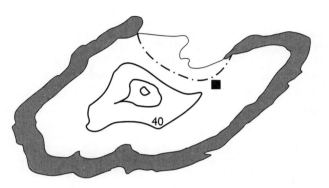

Scale: 1 cm : 1 km
Legend: ▨ steep rocky cliffs
     — · — beach
     ■ stone hut – no roof

Flora: grass and low shrubs, fruit bushes
Fauna: seabirds, seals, goats
Climate: heavy rain, very cold nights, cool days
Contour interval = 20 m

(b) How have I changed?

Get a picture of yourself as a small child (2-year-old) and as a 10-year-old. Formulate hypotheses for ages 2 and 10 for each of the characteristics listed on the chart. Check your hypotheses by asking parents, relations, and friends.

	2-year-old	10-year-old	Today
Height			
Weight			
Usual dress			
Hair colour			
Eye colour			
Food eaten			
breakfast			
lunch			
supper			

	2-year-old	10-year-old	Today
Favourite food(s)			
Favourite game(s)			
Best friend(s)			
Favourite TV or radio show			
Favourite book			

(c) In the year A.D. 3000 a time capsule (3 m^3) will be opened. The capsule will contain artifacts that will help archeologists reconstruct your life and times. What will you place in the capsule? Why? What do you think archeologists will need to know?

NOTES

1. R. Ennis, *Logic in Teaching* (Englewood Cliffs, N.J.: Prentice-Hall, 1963), p. 393.
2. S. Norris, *The Dependability of Observation Statements: Rational Thinking Reports, Number 4* (Urbana, Ill.: Illinois Rational Thinking Project, 1979).
3. F. Maher, "Inquiry teaching and feminist pedagogy," *Social Education* 51:3 (1987), 186–93.

In the last chapter, our discussion focused on how students could go about finding answers to questions using inquiry procedures. Sometimes an inquiry is best carried out by individual students; at other times it is better to have groups of students working together in cooperative learning groups. The term "cooperative learning" is used to describe a variety of activities in which students work together on a task. These activities are designed with several objectives in mind: to develop communication skills; to create trust, acceptance, and sharing within the classroom; to lower fear of failure; to develop a commitment to learning; and, especially, to foster individual and group accountability. Proponents of cooperative learning also point out that it can help prepare students to work effectively with the variety of people with whom they will interact in their day-to-day lives.[1] These activities are premised on the beliefs that students can learn from each other, that students perceive their success as being linked to the success of others, and that cooperation is better than competition.[2]

Research evidence indicates that the objectives of cooperative learning can be realized. Students improve in achievement and gain in self-esteem and social skills; they develop more positive attitudes toward school in general and particular subjects, and more positive attitudes toward other ethnic groups.[3] It has also been found that teachers who used cooperative learning activities were more positive about their work than those who did not use them. They also saw less need to discipline students.[4] Because these conclusions are derived from a compilation of results from different studies, it should not be assumed that any one cooperative learning activity will lead to these outcomes. Nevertheless, there are many advantages in the use of cooperative learning activities. In whole class instruction, a student has an approximately one-in-thirty chance of speaking. Every student in a group has an approximately one-in-four chance. Students are able to help one another and learn from one another. In their lives both inside and outside school they will find themselves in group situations; they need to learn how to interact well. Good group relationships are rewarding and enjoyable.

Before launching into cooperative learning activities, you should ask yourself the following questions:

1. Is the topic appropriate? Cohen[5] suggests that questions posed should have more than one answer, that the task should allow different students to make different contributions, and that a variety of information should be required to carry out the task.

2. How will I ensure that all students can and do contribute? How will I avoid situations in which the high achievers either do all the work and learn more, or decrease their efforts so they are not perceived as "suckers"?

3. What behaviours should students exhibit, and how will I monitor these behaviours?

4. How will the group monitor its own progress?

5. How long should the activity last?

We cannot always expect students to be able to work together without some initial preparation. Students have to be helped to realize the benefits of cooperation. We may have to start off with simple partner activities and progress to more substantial group tasks. According to the activity, groups may be formed on the basis of prior friendships, common interests, common abilities, or on a random basis. Groups should be small in size: three to five members is best. Rules for group learning should be followed: students should help one another; students should not "put down" anyone's contribution; students should encourage each other; students should monitor and evaluate their individual contributions and the overall group effort; there should be equal participation. You might like to start with small-group activities in which children get to know each other, followed by activities that rely on the participation of all the group members (creating a collage, building a model). Carefully consider group membership. Ideally you want a fairly equal distribution on the basis of gender, ethnicity, and ability. However, you might want to avoid putting certain students together, at least initially, if you know that they do not get on well together. And you will have to deal with the problems that arise when students work together. Some of these, such as "bright" students putting down "less bright" children, can be avoided by assigning roles to each group member (see the ideas presented later in this chapter).

The following activities are designed to help students begin to work together.

PRODUCTION LINE

Divide students into groups of six. Give each student a sheet of paper and give each group a pair of scissors, a red crayon, a blue crayon, a green crayon, a coin, and a pencil (for drawing a circle), and a ruler with a pencil. Each group is to produce six of the following products.

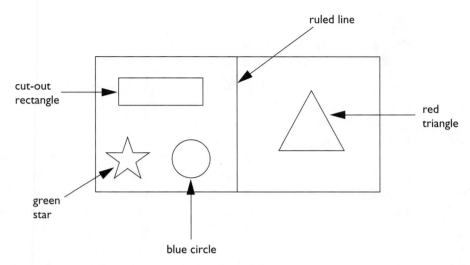

The first group to produce six such products is the winner.

Usually, each student in each group will attempt to make his or her own item and will "fight" for the materials. The quickest way to produce six items is for each student to have one of the materials (that is, crayon, ruler, scissors), and as the six pieces of paper are passed from student to student, to draw a red triangle on each, or draw a ruled line on each, etc. Specialization is required, with each specialist cooperating with the others to produce a finished product.

PARTNER GAME

Cut out the following shape:

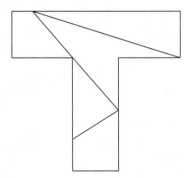

Divide up the class into pairs, and give one member of each pair the cut-out shapes. The other person tells the person holding the shapes how to put the shapes together in the form of the T. Try it—it's not easy.

ANIMAL MAKING

Divide the class into groups of four. Give each person a pair of scissors, a coloured sheet of paper, and the following directions:

PERSON A The name of the animal the other three group members are to make
(Leader) *together* is a _____. Do not tell the group members the name of the animal. Answer all questions with *yes* or *no*.

PERSON B Cut out a body of an animal. Ask your leader questions about the size and shape. You may only ask questions that require a *yes* or *no* answer. Attach the body to the parts being made by other group members.

PERSON C Cut out the legs of an animal. Ask your leader about the shape and size. You may only ask questions that demand a *yes* or *no* answer. Attach the legs you made to the parts being made by other group members.

PERSON D Cut out the head, neck, and tail of an animal. Ask your leader about the shape and size. You may only ask questions that demand a *yes* or *no* answer. Attach the head, neck, and tail to the parts being made by other group members.

There are a variety of ways in which cooperative learning activities can be implemented in the classroom. All those listed below can be used when carrying out inquiry procedures as well as in other teaching/learning activities.

1. Students in a group are given a topic and are to identify questions that they think are worth investigating. These questions are ranked from most interesting to least interesting, then shared with the whole class, rank-ordered again, and classified. Groups are then created to hypothesize answers to particular questions and test the hypotheses.

2. Within a group, certain students perform particular tasks—one acting as scribe, another as researcher, another as illustrator.

3. Broad questions on which a group is working can be broken down into more discrete questions and hypotheses, with one member of the group becoming a specialist on a specific question. The specialist then teaches the rest of the group, and the information is used to answer the broad question. If several groups are working on the same broad question, then specialists on a particular question from each group can work together. This "jigsaw" technique can also be used when students are required to learn bodies of content (see Chapter 6).

4. If a group is working on a particular question, each member can use different resources to test their hypotheses, and findings can be shared. A final answer is then formulated by the group.

5. If a group is working on a particular question, each member of the group can be given information that provides only part of the answer. The information is then synthesized into a final group answer.

6. If a group product is required (a report, a chart, a model, a mural), each student can choose to make a particular contribution.

7. If groups are working on different aspects of the same broad question, each group can teach the rest of the class about their particular topic, so that a class answer to the broad question is formulated. For example, if the broad question is "What motivated the first Europeans to explore Canada?" each group tests their hypotheses about a particular explorer. Each group then shares its findings with the rest of the class and the broad question is answered.

8. If there are students who need help on a particular aspect of an inquiry procedure, then peer teaching can be used. For instance, if a student needs to be able to read the scale on a map, a student who knows how to do this can teach that student.

ACTIVITY 9-A

Design a cooperative learning activity for either a primary or intermediate class that is studying conservation. Choose one particular aspect of this topic that you consider to be appropriate for the grade level. Develop a lesson plan that includes your objectives and a detailed description of how the cooperative learning activity would be organized.

It should not be assumed that cooperative learning is designed to stifle conflict. Rather, conditions can be created in which conflict is dealt with in rational ways. The following activity for upper elementary students illustrates one way to do this. It is consistent with Paul's belief that critical thinkers are able to present arguments for all sides of an issue and are able to enter sympathetically into someone else's point of view.[6]

1. Groups of four are formed and then divided into twos. Each group of two is given a different side of an issue. The pairs then prepare a case to defend their side of the issue. Pairs can meet with other pairs on the same side of the issue to ensure that they've got a strong case.

2. Each pair presents their case to the other members of their group of four; then, each pair can challenge the others' arguments.

3. Each pair then presents the strongest argument for the side opposed to the one they were previously defending.

4. Finally, assigned positions are abandoned and the group of four works together to produce a report that summarizes the group's position. Consensus is not required. Each group member should be prepared to justify his or her individual decision to the rest of the class.

Before embarking on cooperative learning, you should carefully consider your objectives and the appropriateness of any particular strategy. Keep in mind that some educators advocate the use of cooperative learning activities for purposes of competition with other groups; others find this unacceptable. Is there any contradiction, for instance, in using cooperative activities in Social Studies and then emphasizing individual competition in spelling lessons? If cooperative activities are used for purposes of competition, will children believe that cooperation is just another way of getting ahead?

Whatever your answers are to the above questions, it is clear that group activities are worth pursuing in the classroom. Coupled with inquiry procedures, cooperative activities can provide valuable learning experiences for students.

OTHER ACTIVITIES

1. Within a group of four, choose a partner and then choose to defend one side of the following issue.

   A You believe that there should be no competition in Social Studies classes. You think that the social aspect of Social Studies should be emphasized, that working together will encourage respect, and that social problems should be solved through cooperative endeavours.

   B You believe that competition should be emphasized in Social Studies because competition creates challenges for students that motivate them to work hard. Further, you know that to succeed in the world you have to be competitive.

2. Get together with your partner and write down the three strongest arguments you can think of to support your position.

3. Within your group of four, argue your case and try to refute the other side's position.

4. With your partner, write down the three strongest arguments you can think of that support the other side's view, and present these to the other members of your group.

5. See if your group of four can agree on a position. If you cannot agree, what is the basis of the disagreement? Is there any way it could be resolved if more evidence were available (e.g., on the effects of cooperation or competition on students)?

NOTES

1. J. Myers, "Co-operative learning in history and social sciences: An idea whose time has come," *Canadian Social Studies* 26:2 (1991), 60–64.

2. H. Margolis and P. McCabe, "Using co-operative learning to facilitate mainstreaming in the Social Studies," *Social Education* 54:2 (1990), 111–14.

3. R. Slavin, "Research on co-operative learning: Consensus and controversy," *Educational Leadership* 47 (1990), 52–55.

4. S. Sharon, ed., *Co-operative Learning: Theory and Research* (New York: Praeger, 1989).

5. E. Cohen, *Designing Groupwork: Strategies for the Heterogeneous Classroom* (New York: Teachers College Press, 1986).

6. R. Paul, *Critical Thinking: What Every Person Needs to Survive in a Rapidly Changing World* (Sonoma State University, Calif.: Center for Critical Thinking and Moral Critique, 1990).

C H A P T E R **10** Finding, using & presenting information

Students need information with which to test hypotheses. Although texts and other books suitable for elementary school children exist, you may find that schools don't have many resource materials, or that available ones are out of date or unsuitable on other grounds. Thus, it is often necessary to locate recent information. Much of this is "fugitive"—that is, you won't find it all in libraries. It includes information published by museums, industries, government agencies, chambers of commerce, tourist bureaus, or private organizations. In this chapter, you will find some of these sources of information. What is included here is only a beginning, however; you should also be on the lookout for the many excellent sources of information that are put out at the local level. In most cases you will have to write a letter stating that you are a teacher requesting that information be sent to you for use with your class(es). Some organizations will send materials only to a school address, so, if you are a student teacher, you'll have to find a friendly school librarian or teacher to act as a go-between.

A. Bibliographies. There are several useful bibliographies to which you should refer when looking for particular resource materials. These include:

I. McDonough. 1980. *Canadian Books for Young People*. 3rd ed. University of Toronto Press: 10 Saint Mary Street, Suite 700, Toronto, Ontario M4Y 2W8.

M. Cariou, S. Cox, and A. Bergman. 1985. *Canadian Selection: Books and Periodicals for Libraries*. Toronto: Ontario Ministry of Citizenship and Culture; and Centre for Research in Librarianship, University of Toronto. A selective annotated bibliography of books and periodicals about Canada.

Books in Canada. Canadian Review of Books Ltd.: 366 Adelaide Street East, Suite 432, Toronto, Ontario M5A 3X9. Nine issues per annum. Occasionally reviews children's books.

P. Maidstone and D. Taylor. 1989. *Guide to Sources on Asia and the Pacific*. Victoria, B.C.: Camosun College. Lists newspapers, journals, books, films, videos, and the addresses of organizations useful for teaching about Asian and Pacific countries.

N. Corley. 1984. *Resources for Native Peoples Studies*. Ottawa: National Library of Canada. An extremely comprehensive listing of materials by and about native peoples.

Educators' Progress Services. 1991 *Elementary Teachers' Guide to Free Curriculum Materials*. Randolph, Wis.: Educators Progress Service. An annual compendium of materials classified by subject and by type of medium (print, video, etc.). Also available is an annual guide to free materials for Social Studies.

L. Hendrikson. 1989. *Data Source Book of Social Studies Materials and Resources*. Boulder, Colo.: Social Science Education Consortium. Contains an analysis of elementary curriculum materials, simulation games, and teacher resources.

Public Focus. 1990. *Environmental Resource Directory*. Toronto: Public Focus. An evaluation of materials for teaching about ecology, pollution, wildlife, and other environmental topics.

National Library of Canada. 1991. *Notable Canadian Children's Books. 1987 Supplement*. Ottawa: Ministry of Supply and Services.

Canadian Children's Book Centre. 1992. *Our Choice*. Canadian Children's Book Centre, 35 Spadina Road, Toronto, Ontario M5R 2S9.

Also check your library's reference section for other indexes, your province's curriculum guides for references, and teacher magazines for advertisements on recent publications.

B. School boards often have resource centres and publish catalogues. Find out if your school district has one, and locate the catalogue (each school should have one). To order materials, you have to use an authorized form, and must have the materials sent to your school.

C. School libraries. Libraries vary in quality. Some contain not only books but also audio-visual resources (filmstrips, audiotapes, videotapes, pictures, records), and files of newspaper and other clippings. Conduct a thorough search of the library and ask the librarian to help you. Often librarians, on request, will collect material on a given topic and will have it located in a particular place so that students may use it.

D. Teachers' organizations. These often produce journals and newsletters and may have professional libraries. In British Columbia, the B.C. Teachers' Federation also has a Lesson Aids Service.

E. Museums. These often provide services to schools—resource materials (pictures, booklets, pamphlets), guided tours, and workshops for teachers and students. Contact your local museum(s) to discover what is offered.

F. Government (federal, provincial, local). Governments produce a host of documents, some of which are suitable for elementary school use. When you require information, contact the appropriate office. Refer to the *Canadian Almanac and Directory* (Toronto: Canadian Almanac and Directory Co., Ltd.) for addresses and, in your local area, refer to the telephone directory.

G. Telephone directories. A great source of information. Use them to find out the number of industries, businesses, and services in a particular area.

H. Magazines and journals. The list of magazines useful for Social Studies is huge. Only a few are highlighted here. For children, there are *Owl* and *Chickadee* (publications of the Young Naturalist Foundation), *Highlights for Children, Cricket, Ranger Rick, National Geographic World*, and *Sesame Stree*t. For a list of available magazines from *Advertising Age* to *Zoonooz*, see S. Richardson (1984) *Magazines for Young Adults* (Chicago: American Library Association). Another excellent guide is by B. Katz and L. Katz (1991) *Magazines for Young People* (New Providence, N.J.: R.R. Bowker).

For your own professional development, the Canadian Social Studies journal is *Canadian Social Studies*, formerly called *The History and Social Science Teacher* (Publication Services, 4-116 Education North, University of Alberta, Edmonton, Alberta T6G 2G5). Many provincial teachers' organizations have Social Studies professional groups that publish their own journals or newsletters.

The North American Social Studies organization is the National Council for the Social Studies (3501 Newark Street, N.W., Washington, D.C. 20016). The NCSS publishes *Social Education, Social Studies and the Young Learner*, as well as *Bulletins, Newsletters*, and other publications that you receive as a member of the NCSS. Another journal is *The Social Studies* (Heldref Publications, 4000 Albermarle Street, N.W., Washington, D.C. 20016).

Other teacher education journals also contain articles about Social Studies. These include *The Instructor, Educational Leadership, Child Education, Junior Education*, and *Young Children*.

I. Embassies. Embassies often provide information to schools. Quantity and quality vary, so contact the embassy or local consulate (see the telephone directory) to discover what materials, if any, are available.

J. Tourist offices. Each province has its own tourist agency and each publishes advertising material. Some provinces produce very high quality booklets, brochures, and maps. Some towns and cities also produce tourist literature. For a list of these, consult the *Canadian Almanac and Directory* (Toronto: Canadian Almanac and Directory Co., Ltd.).

New Brunswick	Tourism New Brunswick, P.O. Box 12345, Fredericton E3B 5C3.
Prince Edward Island	Department of Tourism, Parks and Recreation, P.O. Box 940, Charlottetown C1A 7M5

Nova Scotia	Department of Tourism and Culture, P.O. Box 456, Halifax B3J 2R5.
Newfoundland	Department of Tourism and Culture, P.O. Box 8700, St. John's A1B 4J6.
Yukon	Tourism Yukon, P.O. Box 2703, Whitehorse Y1A 2C6.
Northwest Territories	Department of Economic Development and Tourism, P.O. Box 1320, Yellowknife X1A 2L9.
British Columbia	Tourism B.C., Parliament Buildings, Victoria V8V 1X4.
Alberta	Alberta Tourism, 3rd Floor, 10155 102 St., Edmonton T5J 4L6.
Saskatchewan	Tourism Saskatchewan, 1919 Saskatchewan Drive, Regina S4P 3V7.
Manitoba	Travel Manitoba, 155 Carlton Street, Winnipeg R3C 3H8.
Ontario	Ministry of Tourism and Recreation, 7th Floor, 77 Bloor Street West, Toronto M7A 2R9.
Quebec	Tourisme Québec, C.P. 20,000, Quebec G1K 7X2.

K. Newspapers. There is a wealth of information here. Have students collect information on current events and, where possible, on topics being studied in Social Studies. Try to obtain newspapers from the area being studied. Two useful publications about using the newspaper in the classroom are:

W. Heitzmann. 1986. *The Newspaper in the Classroom*. Washington, D.C.: National Education Association, and

A. Gunn. 1982. *Teaching with Newspapers*. 3rd ed. Vancouver, B.C.: Faculty of Education, University of British Columbia.

Here are just a few ideas for using the newspaper:

1. Look at advertisements. Have students prepare a list for a week's groceries for a family of three with a budget of $50 and $100. How easy or difficult is it to feed a family on these amounts?

2. Compare the same news story in two or more newspapers. How are they similar or different? Why? Trace the same news story over a period of time in several newspapers. Compare the amount of space devoted to the story, the headlines used, any evidence of a positive or negative bias, and a list of empirical and value claims. Decide which of the latter are supportable. Students could also compare two newspapers to ascertain how much space in each is devoted to different types of stories—crime, disasters, politics, etc.— and if both newspapers report on the same major stories in similar ways. Editorials can also be compared. The same comparisons can be applied to radio and television news.

3. Read aloud a newspaper story about a particular event and have students make a picture of it. Compare pictures. Why are there differences? If a photo-

graph was taken of the event, what might the photographer want to show? Would another photographer want to show the same thing? Why or why not? How could a photograph influence people to think in a certain way about an event?

4. Collect pictures of prominent people. Quiz students to check recognition.

5. Graph weather information.

6. Make up headlines for pictures. How could a headline influence how you felt while viewing the picture? How could the use of emotional words make a difference to your interpretation of the picture?

7. Make a class newspaper.

8. Obtain newspapers from other counties and compare them. What is reported? How is a story about one's own country handled by the foreign press?

L. Videotapes and films. A useful source guide is *The Video Source Book*, Tenth Edition (Detroit: Gale Research Inc., 1988), which lists videotapes classified by country and by discipline (e.g., history, geography, sociology). Another source is D. Green (1989) *Guide to Videocassettes for Children* (New York: Parent's Choice Foundation and Consumers Union of the United States), which has a section on Social Studies. In Canada there is the Canadian Association for Children's Libraries (1987) *Films for Children and Young Adults* (Ottawa: Canadian Library Association), which lists films alphabetically for preschool, primary/elementary, older children, and young adults. Also check the National Film Board of Canada's (1988) *Film and Video Guide* (Montreal, NFB). Their local offices have more recent listings of what is available for loan.

M. Computer software. Two guides to what is available are: R. Bowker (1987) *Software for Schools*, 1987–88 (New York: R.R. Bowker) and S. Neil and G. Neil (1989) *Only the Best: The Annual Guide to Highest-Rated Educational Software* (Carmichael, Calif.: Education News Service). M. Blank and L. Berlin (1991) *The Parent's Guide to Educational Software* (Redmond, Wash.: Tempus Books) provides evaluations of software.

N. Speakers and interviews. Many organizations will provide speakers for schools. Contact the relevant agencies to ascertain if one is available. Sometimes, you might wish to invite someone in the community to come and talk to your class, or you might have your students interview someone away from the classroom. Interviewing people on a particular topic is a valuable activity for students. It can teach them how to structure questions, listen carefully, collect firsthand information, and interact responsibly with others. These are necessary skills for oral history projects (see Chapter 6).

Interviews have to be planned carefully.[1] Students need to prepare sufficient background information, know what the purpose of the interview is, and to formulate appropriate questions in advance. Teachers have to set up the interview and ensure that the person being interviewed is suitable and will be comfortable with the sorts of questions students ask and with the way in which students record the responses (e.g., tape recorder, written notes.) When the interview is over, students should thank the person and then send a written letter of thanks.

O. Other sources of free information. Flyers, free magazines, pamphlets, mail-order catalogues, calendars from banks and businesses, newsletters, etc., can provide information useful for Social Studies. So, collect all the materials you can and file them. You'll be surprised at how much of it can be used.

PRESENTING INFORMATION

Sometimes it is possible to obtain only one copy of a piece of information, yet you want the whole class to see it or read it. You could:

1. Copy it or have it typed and duplicated. This allows each child to have a copy, but it can be expensive. Also, copyright laws may preclude the duplication of thirty copies.

2. Read the information to the class, or paraphrase it, and put notes on the board. If it is a picture you wish to show, it could be displayed at the front of the class, or you could walk around the class showing it to everyone.

3. With some pictures it is possible to make black-and-white or colour transparencies on a copying machine and show them on the overhead projector. This is usually quite expensive. A cheaper method is to "lift" the picture. The way to do this is:

(a) Buy some transparent MACTAC from your local hardware store.

(b) Cut out the picture you want to display. The picture *must* come from high-quality, clay-based paper. (You can tell it's clay-based if, when you scratch a corner with a wet finger, a white substance comes off on your finger.) *National Geographic* works extremely well; experiment with other magazines, also.

(c) Cut out a piece of MACTAC slightly larger than the picture. Put the MACTAC on the picture and *press down firmly*—use a rolling pin or rub with a soft cloth. It is very important that this be done well or you will get unsightly air bubbles on the finished product.

(d) Soak the whole thing in a bowl of warm, soapy water for about a minute.

(e) Peel off the picture—it will now adhere to the MACTAC, and your paper will be blank. Carefully clean the clay from the MACTAC—don't scratch it.

(f) You will now have a transparency. You can mount it on clear plastic, frame it, and put it on an overhead projector so that the whole class can see it on the screen.

You might like to get your students to make their own transparencies using this method. Students can present what they have learned in a variety of ways. These include:

- Writing a diary, letter, poem, newspaper, or report.
- Creating a diorama, model, mural, or collage.
- Creating a play, or a radio or television show.
- Creating a filmstrip in a shoebox. (Cut a window out of a shoebox; insert one dowel through the box above the window and one below, with a long strip of paper attached to them on which there are individual pictures that can be displayed through the window one at a time by turning the dowels.)
- Preparing a drawing, table, chart, diagram, graph, cartoon, painting, or computer graphic.
- Assembling a booklet.
- Taking a photograph, or making a video or audio recording.
- Displaying a collection of actual objects.

USING PICTURES

Pictures must be "read." Children have to note not only the major details but also the small items. Probably because of television viewing, children tend to skim pictures very quickly, failing to observe important details. Children will also tend to concentrate on what is important to them. Therefore, using pictures requires skilful questioning and teaching. For example, from a picture of a particular community we may be able to infer the climate, the level of economic development, the relationship of work to the environment, the population density, and the culture of the people.

The following activities focus attention on the ways in which pictures can be used.

ACTIVITY 10-A

For what purposes could each of these pictures and/or picture activities be used? You might like to carry out the activities for pictures (1) and (2). The full picture for (1) can be found in the ANSWERS section.

1. Draw in the missing half of the picture at the top of the following page.

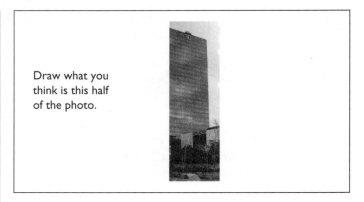

Draw what you think is this half of the photo.

What did you think was in the missing half of the photo? Why? When you saw what is actually there, were you surprised?

2. Where do you think this picture was taken? What is happening?

3. What could be taught/learned by comparing the picture below with the one at the top of the following page?

4. Who do you think these people are? Why do you think they look happy?

Here are some ideas for using pictures:

1. When introducing a new topic, place pertinent pictures around the room. Use these to raise questions and develop hypotheses about the topic.

2. Ask children to describe orally what is happening in a picture. Have children write captions for a picture.

3. Ask inference questions:
What do you think the climate is like? Why?
Are these people similar to or different from you? Why?

What would it be like to live in the area? Why do you think this?
Would you like to visit or live in the area? Why?
How do the people feel?

4. Have children make up sentences about pictures by displaying a picture and giving them key concept words. The student has to make up a sentence that uses information contained in the picture as an example of the concept word. For example, have children use the concept "interdependent" in a sentence using information gleaned from the picture. Another idea is to give students unfinished sentences that they have to complete, for example, "These people feel _____." "The house is made of _____." "If I lived here, I would _____."

5. To teach the differences between a descriptive claim, an inference, and a value judgment, you could play this game.

(a) One player (the leader) is given a picture and a number of statements identified as descriptions, inferences, or value claims.

(b) The other players are each given three cards. One card has "description" written on it, another has "inference," and the third has "value" written on it.

(c) The leader displays the picture and reads a statement about it.

(d) At a given signal from the leader, each player displays the card that she or he thinks correctly identifies the type of statement read.

(e) Players with the correct card receive a point or a token.

(f) The player with the most points becomes the winner and the next leader.

For each sentence, decide which is a description (D), which is an inference (I), and which is a value claim (V).

(i) The girl is wearing a headband.

   (ii) She is happy.

 (iii) There are four teepees in the background.

 (iv) The girl is going to participate in a traditional ceremony.

  (v) The girl is 8 years old.

 (vi) Girls should be accorded equal treatment.

6. Concepts can be taught using pictures (see Chapter 5). Students look at a series of pictures that are examples of a particular concept. The teacher asks what the pictures have in common (what word would describe them all). Non-examples of the concept are also shown. Students have to differentiate examples from non-examples by defining the concept (listing the characteristics of the concept). For example, the teacher displays series of pictures of harbours: pictures with non-examples show a beach, a dock, and a boat.

FILMSTRIPS, MOVIES, VIDEOTAPES, AND TELEVISION PROGRAMS

Visual and audio-visual resources are extremely useful aids in Social Studies. They can show places, events, and people and make them "real." There are thousands available: filmstrips and movies; commercially produced videotapes and videotapes of television programs; television programs viewed "live" in the classroom. Many excellent television programs can be found on the U.S. Public Broadcasting System (PBS) and on the Learning Channel. Our own CBC often has programs that are useful in the context of the Social Studies. One of many examples is *The Nature of Things*. (If you tape any program, ensure that you are not breaking copyright laws when you broadcast it in your classroom.) There are also provincial educational television networks that provide some useful programming for Social Studies classes.

    All these visual aids can be used in a variety of settings—by an individual when studying a particular topic, by a group of students, or in a whole class setting.

1. Always preview. Is this resource the best way of presenting the information? What sorts of things ought students to look for? What activities could students perform after having viewed the resource?

2. Make sure the machinery works and that you have an extension cord, if one is required. There's nothing quite so embarrassing as wheeling a video machine into a classroom and then finding out that the machine doesn't work or that in order for the machine to be located in a suitable viewing spot for the whole class you need an extension cord, and there isn't one available. Even more upsetting is loading a movie upside down. Try watching a movie with your back to the screen and your head between your legs!

3. Ensure that the room is dark enough for viewing.

4. Introduce the resource. Tell students what they should be looking for. Pose questions for students answer.

5. If using a filmstrip with captions, then:

(a) Ask for volunteers to read captions; call on others, in no obvious order, to keep students alert.

(b) If some captions are long or difficult to read, read them yourself or paraphrase them.

(c) Some filmstrips are too long if you show every frame. Show them in instalments or use only a few frames. But tell students what you are going to do, because they may feel cheated if you don't show the entire filmstrip.

(d) Pick out a few frames and discuss them at length. Ask students what they see and why that is important. Then ask, "What else do you see?"

(e) Cover up the caption on a filmstrip so that students see only the pictures. Ask them to suggest captions.

(f) If you stop for discussion, turn off the machine so that it does not overheat, and so that students can be heard.

(g) Speak a little louder than usual because of the noise of the machine. Encourage students to speak up, too.

(h) If a filmstrip is out of date or the captions are poor, have students "rewrite" the filmstrip.

COMPUTERS AND COMPUTER PROGRAMS

Computers have become an important aid in the classroom, and many elementary children are familiar with their use. Social Studies teachers can use computers to enhance instruction in four basic ways.

First, students can create and edit their own writing and, if the software is available, they can use graphics and desktop publishing programs to produce their own reports.

Second, there are hundreds of programs available for use as instructional resources, including tutorials designed to present factual information and to teach rules, principles, and problem-solving strategies. The usual format of these programs is (1) an introduction to outline the objectives, (2) the presentation of information, (3) the posing of a question which, if the student answers correctly, allows the student to proceed to the next lesson. The student can enter or exit these programs at any point. There are also drill programs that provide repeated practice in learning a specific rule, skill, or set of facts. The most popular programs are simulations and games. These include simulations of how particular things work (e.g., how a glacier is formed and how it moves; games such as *Battleships*; and simulation games). Some recommended ones are:

- *The Sea Voyagers*—for Grades 4 to 8. Simulates the voyages of such explorers as Columbus and Cabot. Available from Mindscape, 3444 Dundee Road, Northbrook, Illinois 60062.

- *Cross Country Series*—for Grades 4 and above. In the role of a truck driver, students learn about the geography of the areas in which they make their deliveries. Available from Didatech, 3812 William Street, Burnaby, British Columbia V5C 3H9.

- *The Market Place*—for Grades 3 and up. A simulation designed to teach students about basic economic concepts such as supply and demand. Available from Minnesota Educational Computing Consortium, 3490 Levington Avenue, N., St. Paul, Minnesota 55126.

- *Archaeology Search.* A simulation in which students in teams decide where to dig on an archeological site (T. Synder, 1982, New York: McGraw Hill).

Third, students can use database programs to obtain information and, with some programs such as *PC Globe* or *World Atlas for Macintosh*, students can manipulate data to create their own graphs and charts.[2] Given that much statistical information in textbooks is out of date, database programs are an important source of current information.

The fourth way in which computers can be used is related to their communication potential and is a modern version of having pen-pals. Through electronic mail, your students can communicate with students in other locations and trade information at the same cost as a phone call.

Teachers can also use computers to keep student records and to store questions for tests or quizzes. Test banks allow teachers to choose the most appropriate questions for a particular test.

The most recent additions to the field are CD-ROMs and Interactive Video Systems. CD-ROMs can store encyclopedias; users of some programs can even listen to famous speeches, music, and animal sounds to augment printed and pictorial information. An Interactive Video System consists of a computer connected by a modem to a videodisc player and video monitor. The computer can then access data from any location on the videodisc. Data can be in print or pictorial form and questions or messages can be superimposed on the video material to draw student attention to particular information. The menu on the computer allows fast and easy access to information on the disc; you do not have to search through an entire videotape for a particular piece of information. Another advantage of Interactive Video Systems is that they allow an individual picture or frame to be shown on the screen without the picture eventually wearing out or appearing fuzzy, both of which occur when a videotaped picture is "frozen." Teachers can produce their own interactive video system,[3] but this takes time, expertise, and money. It is expected that more and more videodiscs will become available, although their cost may represent a significant problem for schools.

The computer should be an object of inquiry by elementary students. Raise questions such as the following: What impact are computers having in society? What are the advantages and disadvantages of widespread computer use? Who has most access to computers? Do computers pose a threat to people's privacy? Should everyone be required to be "computer literate"?

Research evidence[4] suggests that computer-based instruction holds a very small advantage over other methods in the teaching of particular knowledge and skills. This evidence, however, is based on numerous studies whose points of reference may not be comparable. As students learn in various ways and as computer programs vary in quality, it should not be assumed that computer-based instruction is always more effective than other means of instruction.

EVALUATION

Although it is clearly advantageous to have a vast range of resources, it is always important to evaluate them before they are used. Below is a list of factors that should be taken into consideration:

- Is the reading level suitable?
- Are the pictorial items clear and bright?
- Is the print size appropriate?
- Are the index and glossaries useful and easy to use?
- Is the information accurate and up to date?
- Is the information biased in an inappropriate way?
- Is the information logically sequenced?
- Is the information representative of the topic?
- Is the language even subtly sexist or racist?
- Are any stereotypes presented?
- If there are student activities, are these appropriate?
- Is the material interesting?
- Do students have the necessary prerequisite knowledge and skills to use the material?
- Can the material be used by students with differing abilities?
- Is the material easily available?
- Will the material stand up to student use?

If you are evaluating a computer program, you should also consider whether the directions are easy to follow, how effective the displays are, how effective feedback is to the student, and how much control students have in using the program.

OTHER ACTIVITIES

1. Select a book, filmstrip, movie, videotape, or software for an instructional program and apply the above questions. Is the material suitable for your purposes?
2. Select a particular topic you are likely to teach and locate ten different resources: textbook, novel, computer software, newspaper article, magazine, etc.

NOTES

1. A. Sears, "Enriching Social Studies through interviews," *History and Social Science Teacher* 25:2 (1990), 95–98.

2. H. Riggs, "Computer data base activities in upper elementary school Social Studies," *History and Social Science Teacher* 25:3 (1990), 145–50.

3. P. Martorella, "Harnessing new technologies to the Social Studies curriculum," *Social Education* 55:1 (1991), 55–57.

4. S. Alessi and S. Trollip, *Computer-Based Instruction: Methods and Development*, 2nd ed. (Englewood Cliffs, N.J.: Prentice-Hall, 1991).

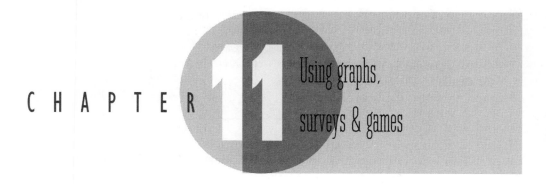

CHAPTER 11

Using graphs, surveys & games

We have already seen that students can obtain information from many different print and pictorial materials, and can present information in many different forms. This chapter focuses on graphs, surveys, and games as tools for learning important content and for presenting information to others.

If you look at nearly any newspaper or textbook you will find graphs. Because graphs can display a great deal of information in a more understandable form than a list of numbers (young children can "see" how big numbers are and can "see" relationships among sets of data), they are important tools in Social Studies.

BLOCK GRAPHS

The simplest form of graph is a block graph. Young children can actually construct these using objects like wooden blocks or coloured stickers. For example, each rectangle in the graph below would have a picture of a cat, dog, or rabbit.

Number of Pets Owned by Grade 1

Number of Students

	5		
	4		
	3		
	2		
	1		

Cats   Dogs   Rabbits

Another way of building the graph is to use student names. Here is an example:

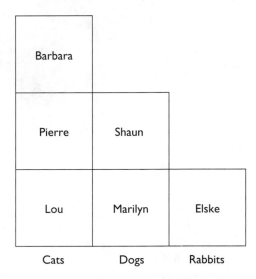

Pets Owned by Grade 1

Once students can make graphs and can use equal intervals, they can draw the intervals/measures on graph paper with large squares.

ACTIVITY 11-A

Construct a block graph using the following information:

Population of cities, 1991 (to nearest thousand)	
St. John's	104,000
Halifax	114,000
Montreal	1,018,000
Toronto	635,000
Winnipeg	617,000
Regina	179,000
Edmonton	617,000
Vancouver	472,000

LINE GRAPHS

When children can "read" points on a line, line graphs can be introduced. The same information on a block graph can be used to show how a line graph is constructed. Here is an example:

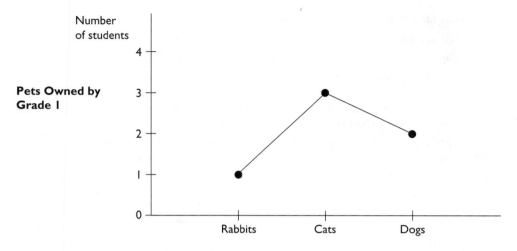

Once students can construct graphs (this can be done by integration with math lessons), they can learn to interpret them. Interpretation involves translating (reading) the data, as well as using data to draw inferences and create hypotheses. These can then be checked by recourse to other information.

ACTIVITY 11-B

Interpret this graph.

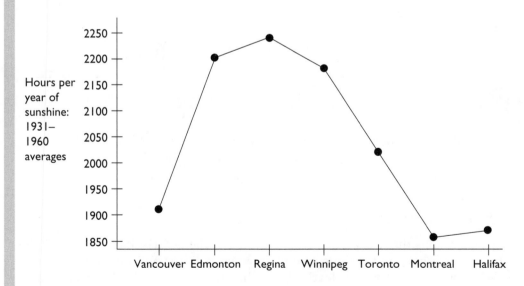

1. Which city has the most hours of sunshine per year?
2. Which city has the fewest hours of sunshine per year?
3. What is the difference in hours of sunshine between Montreal and Regina?

4. What factors account for Regina having the most hours of sunshine?

5. What accounts for Montreal having the least hours of sunshine?

6. If 1960–1993 averages were graphed, do you think the graph would be different from the one above?

Graphs can be created using any numerical data—temperatures in various cities in Canada, favourite television shows of the class, population figures, results of traffic surveys, different kinds of products in a supermarket, and so on.

When interpreting line graphs, it is important to remember that you may not be able to "read" between the lines.

ACTIVITY 11-C

Interpret the graph below.

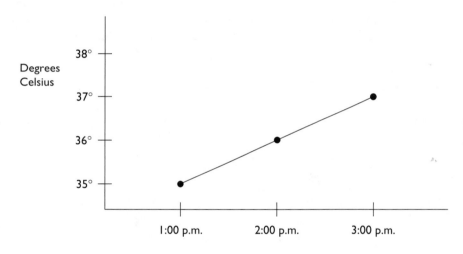

1. What was the patient's temperature at 1:30 p.m.?

2. What was the patient's temperature at 2:30 p.m.?
Could it have been 35.5°, or 38° or more, or 35° or less?

SCATTER GRAPHS

Scatter graphs differ from bar graphs in that variable quantities are scaled along both axes. They are very effective in showing patterns and relationships among data. The following graph clearly shows that, for this Grade 5 class, there is a relationship between the number of hours students spend reading books and how well they perform on language arts tests.

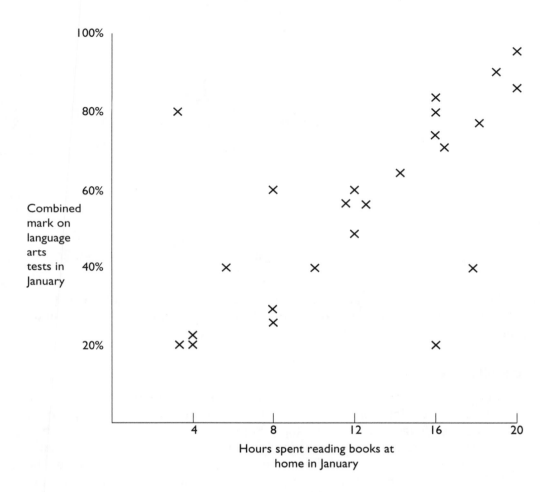

CIRCLE GRAPHS

Circle graphs are the most complicated for children to comprehend, as they must first understand angles in a circle. Once they can comprehend the clock face, it is possible to construct simple circle graphs, but more complicated ones have to be left until the intermediate grades.

A simple circle graph might consist of information about how children spend their time in a twelve-hour period.

Complex circle graphs may involve showing percentages. If this is done, children have to divide a 360° circle into 100 parts. Because this is fairly complex, it has to be left until ratio skills are mastered.

Because they can display a lot of information, are more easily read than columns of figures, and show data in spatial terms that children can understand, graphs are an important tool in elementary Social Studies.

OPINION SURVEYS

Opinion surveys are not only an important source of information but also a means of finding out new information. Surveys are used to discover people's opinions, beliefs, or knowledge of a particular topic. Suppose you wanted to find out what your peers' attitudes were toward the teaching of Social Studies in the elementary school. First, you would have to determine what question(s) to ask. Respondents could be asked an open-ended question such as "How do you feel about teaching Social Studies?" or they could be asked to choose from a list:

"I feel _____ about teaching Social Studies."

☐	☐	☐	☐
Happy	Nervous	Frightened	Confident

Another format that could be used is a scale.
"I feel confident about teaching Social Studies."

☐	☐	☐	☐	☐
Strongly agree	Agree	Undecided	Disagree	Strongly disagree

Once the question(s) have been posed and are judged to be clear and unambiguous, then you have to decide how to conduct the survey. This could be done by conducting individual interviews or by using a questionnaire. In both cases, you have to decide who is to be given the questionnaire or who is to be interviewed. If there are only a small number of potential respondents available, everyone could be questioned. However, if the population is large, you'll have to use a sample. To choose a *random* sample, you can put all the names of potential respondents in a hat and draw out as many names as you think it is feasible to survey. You might also wish to find out information about the persons surveyed. For example, age might be important, or gender, or whether respondents are in the first, second, third, or fourth year of university. Once you have determined what demographic data you require, the survey can be conducted, responses collected and classified, and results interpreted.

ACTIVITY 11-D

Conduct a survey to determine the favourite TV show, or movie, or book, or hobby of your peers. Design a questionnaire, collect and graph results, and interpret the results. Design your survey to answer the following questions:

1. Do males and females differ in their preferences? Can you explain the difference or similarity?

2. Is age a significant variable in explaining preferences? Why or why not?

3. Do you think the results are representative of people who share the same characteristics as you (that is, as a student teacher or practising teacher)? Why or why not? How would you find out?

When students are conducting surveys, they should learn how to make sure that questions are understandable and do not contain ambiguous words like "some" and "many." They should divide complex questions into smaller, more specific ones and decide the best way of obtaining responses. After conducting the survey, they should interpret results. Make sure that students realize the limits of their data. For example, ensure that they understand that people who volunteered to fill out their survey form do not represent the entire population of their community, or even of their school.

ACTIVITY 11-E

Design a lesson plan to teach students how to conduct a survey. State what the survey question would be. Describe how you would get students to design a questionnaire, carry out the survey, tabulate the data, and interpret the results.

GAMES

Games can be used to stimulate student interest in a topic and help them recall important information. They can also help children learn important skills such as those involved in decision-making. Because games are social activities, they allow students to develop positive attitudes toward others and develop the abilities necessary for creating and maintaining good group relationships. And playing games is usually a pleasurable activity.

ACTIVITY 11-F

Imagine you are a member of the British army in Canada in 1818. You are considering settling in Canada, but you'll need the help of the British government to do so. From the following list, decide what you think you will need and put a check mark in the "needs" column. If you think the British government will give you this item, place a check mark in the "individual choice" column. In a group, decide what you think the government would give you and, *if you all agree on the item*, place a check mark in the "group choice" column.

What the British government would provide

I would need		Individual choice	Individual score	Group choice	Group score
	Free transportation				
	Radio				
	Land				
	Axe				
	Broadaxe				
	Money				
	Mattock				
	Bible				
	Pickaxe				
	Furniture				
	Spade				
	Shovel				
	Hoe				
	Scythe				
	Drawknife				
	Hammer				
	Handsaw				
	Scythe stones				
	Panes of glass				

(List continues on next page.)

(Continued from previous page.)

What the British government would provide

I would need		Individual choice	Individual score	Group choice	Group score
	Putty				
	Nails				
	Kettle				
	Bed tick (mattress)				
	Blanket				
	Cooking utensils				
	TOTALS				

Check your responses with the answers in the ANSWERS section at the end of the book, add up your individual and group scores, and consider these questions:

1. Were the individual and group scores the same or were they different?

2. If the scores were the same, what does this tell you about group decision-making?

3. If the scores were different, what does this tell you about group decision-making?

4. What could you learn from playing this game?

5. "Groups are more likely to arrive at better solutions to a problem because there will be more information available." Is this generalization warranted?

This game format can be adapted in several ways. For example, the question could be, "What would you expect to find if you visited X (another country, a museum, a farm, an industrial site, etc.)?"

The following are examples of other games that can be played by groups of students or by the whole class.

ACTIVITY 11-G

For each of the games introduced below, determine what curriculum objectives could be realized.

1. CONSEQUENCES

Players have to imagine the consequences of a given event.

(a) A number of cards are prepared, each describing a particular event: wolves are introduced into an area where deer now live; native people eat mercury-contaminated fish; a forest is burnt out; Kevin broke a window with a baseball; Kevin got up late; Kevin forgot to feed the dog, etc.

(b) Players sit in a circle and one card is displayed.

(c) The first player suggests a possible consequence of the event. If the consequence is seen as reasonable (by the teacher or a student leader), the student is given a point.

(d) The next player states a possible consequence of the first player's consequence. If this is thought to be reasonable, the student is given a point.

(e) This continues until no more consequences are forthcoming or a previous consequence is repeated.

(f) A new situation card is displayed.

(g) The person with the most points wins.

2. EVENTS

Four players combine three clues to describe specific events. These events could be ones discussed in a Social Studies unit—for example, events in traditional Haida culture: potlatch, fishing, raising totem poles, etc.

(a) Each player receives six cards, each of which has a single clue on it. An extra six cards are placed in the middle of the playing area.

(b) In turns, each player attempts to describe a specific event, using three of the cards.

(c) If the player can describe an event that is acceptable to the other players, he/she discards those three cards.

(d) If the player cannot describe an event, he/she picks up a card from the centre pile and discards one of his/her own cards.

(e) The winner is the first player to correctly describe two events, thereby discarding six cards.

Examples:

Canoe is launched.
Lines are baited.
Lines are put over the side (fishing).
Tree trunk is carved.
Hole is dug in the ground.
Lines are attached to tree trunk (totem-pole raising).

3. OCCUPATIONS

Players must identify occupations from clues. A player is chosen to represent an occupation. He/she is given a list of characteristics of this occupation, which he/she reads out one at a time. At any point, the other players may attempt to guess the occupation.

Examples:

I ride on a truck.
I wear a helmet.
I have a dangerous job.
I sometimes carry an axe, etc. (firefighter)

4. GUESS WHAT

Players guess the answer that a person representing a particular culture, group, or occupation would give to specific questions.

(a) A person is chosen to represent a given culture, occupation or person (e.g., Chinese, teacher, Cartier).

(b) Another person is chosen to represent a reporter.

(c) The reporter asks a question of the interviewee (e.g., of Cartier: How did you get to Canada? What did you least like about Canada?).

(d) The interviewee waits for one minute before answering the question. During this time, the other players write down what they think the response of the interviewee will be.

(e) The interviewee answers the question.

(f) Players who have a similar answer to the one given by the interviewee score a point.

(g) When a player has scored three points, he/she becomes the new interviewee and plays a new character. A new reporter is also chosen.

5. TWENTY QUESTIONS

The object of this game is to teach students to begin with broad questions, and then use the answers to narrow the focus. A person chooses an "object" and the class tries to guess the object. For example, a game might proceed as follows: "Is it animal, vegetable, or mineral?" "Animal." "Is it a person?" "Yes." "Is it someone we've studied in Social Studies?" "Yes." "Is it an explorer?" "Yes." "Is it David Thompson?" "No." Etc.

6. BINGO

Make "bingo" cards with key Social Studies concepts, people, events, etc., on them. Give each student a card and squares of cardboard or counters with which to cover the bingo card squares. Then give the questions. If the student has the answer on the card, he/she covers that square. The first to cover a vertical, horizontal, or diagonal line wins. Here's a simple example.

COMMUNITY WORKERS

firefighter	storekeeper	janitor
police officer	doctor	city engineer
teacher	librarian	mayor

Questions could be:

I patrol the streets to keep them safe for people.
I mend the roads and sidewalks.
etc.

7. PICTURES

Two or more players identify examples of a concept drawn from the study of a particular culture or area of the world. Pictures provide the information.

(a) Players receive a matrix card with concepts identified at the top and letters of the alphabet down the side.

(b) Players view a picture or series of pictures and attempt to place examples of the concept that begin with the letters of the alphabet listed on the matrix card.

(c) The winner is the player who can correctly complete the most matrix boxes. Here is an example:

SOUTH AFRICA

	Animals	Landforms	Industry	Vegetation
M				
B				
T				
D				

8. TRUE OR FALSE

Players must identify a statement made about an object or event as being true or false.

(a) An item is displayed.

(b) Two teams are formed, A and B.

(c) One member of team A makes a statement about the item.

(d) One member of team B identifies the statement as being true or false.

(e) If the response is correct, team B obtains a point.

(f) If anyone in team A challenges the response and is proved right, team B loses a point. If the challenger is proved incorrect, team A loses a point.

9. PICTURE QUIZ

Teams study a picture and ask and answer questions about it.

(a) Two teams are formed, A and B.

(b) A picture is displayed.

(c) When the picture has been scrutinized for one minute, it is removed.

(d) Each member of team A, in turn, poses a question that can be answered from details shown in the picture.

(e) Each member of team B, in turn, attempts to answer the questions.

(f) If the response is correct (the teacher can be the judge), team B obtains a point.

(g) Challenges can be made by team A. If the challenger is correct, team B loses a point; if incorrect, team A loses a point.

(h) When all team A members have had their turns, a new picture is shown and team B poses the questions.

10. YES/NO

A picture of an unknown object is displayed. Students have to guess what the object is by asking questions that demand a *yes* or *no* answer of the teacher. (See Chapter 22 for an example.)

II. CATEGORIES

The teacher states a topic and a concept name. Students have to give an example of the concept; the example must be related to the topic. For example:

TOPIC:	Canada	
CONCEPTS:	Continent	(North America or America)
	River	(St. Lawrence)
	Mineral	(gold)

12. SCRAMBLED WORDS

Give students lists of scrambled words to sort out.

Places in British Columbia

o l m k s o p a   _____

t v a i i r c o   _____

To create the sorts of games presented above, you first have to determine what your objectives are. You then decide the sort of format that is most appropriate (many of these formats are displayed in this chapter), the rules of the game, the number of participants, and how the outcome will be decided. An idea worth trying is to have students make up their own games based on the content that they are studying.

What follows is a simulation game. How these are constructed is explained in Chapter 19.

13. THE MARKET GAME

This is a simulation game, in that it simulates reality. Players make decisions within an economic system where their actions model what could occur in the real world. Through playing this game, students can gain an appreciation for such concepts as supply, demand, profit, and loss.

Market

$5	$5	$5

$1	$1	$1	$1	$1

BUYER	BUYER	BUYER	BUYER
With $20, buy	With $20, buy	With $20, buy	With $20, buy
Paper clips 1	Paper clips 2	Paper clips 2	Paper clips 1
Erasers 2	Erasers 1	Erasers 1	Erasers 2
Pencils 3	Pencils 3	Pencils 1	Pencils 1
Crayons 0	Crayons 0	Crayons 2	Crayons 2

SELLER	SELLER	SELLER	SELLER
Paper clips	Erasers	Pencils	Crayons
Sell six clips	Sell ten erasers	Sell five pencils	Sell four crayons
Cost Price = $2 each	Cost Price = $1 each	Cost Price = $2 each	Cost Price = $2 each

You will need to cut out the money and the "buyer" and "seller" cards. A collection of paper clips, erasers, pencils, and crayons will also be required.

(a) Divide the class into four equal groups of buyers and four equal groups of sellers.

(b) Each group of buyers takes one buyers' card and collects $20 in money. Their objective is to purchase all the items listed on their card.

(c) Each group of sellers takes one sellers' card and the requisite number of paper clips, erasers, pencils, and crayons. Their objective is to sell their product at a profit. Each sellers' group should set up a table and list the price of the products. Prices can be changed at any time.

(d) When the game is started, buyers go to the sellers' tables. Bargaining is permitted.

(e) The game ends when a buyers' group collects all the items on their card. That buyers' group, and the sellers' group that makes the most profit, are declared winners.

When the game is over, ask the following questions:

Sellers
- How did you decide what price to set for your products?
- Did you change the price during the game? Why or why not?
- Did you sell all your products? Why or why not?

Buyers
- How did you decide what price you were willing to pay for each product?
- Did you bargain with sellers? Did bargaining result in lower prices?
- Did you obtain all the items on your list? Why or why not?

How could this simulation be adapted so that concepts of monopoly, inflation, competition, and cooperation are introduced? To what experiences of students could this game be related?

OTHER ACTIVITIES

1. Using one of the ideas outlined above, design a game for a particular group of students and a particular context.

CHAPTER 12 Field research

So far we have been focusing on finding answers to empirical questions within the confines of the classroom. Most of what we teach about, however, occurs outside of the classroom. Although we bring in books, pictures, and maps that represent the world outside, whenever possible we should give students the opportunity to see for themselves whatever phenomenon is being studied. We do this by carrying out field research.

Collecting data firsthand and getting a "feel" for a place are two of the major objectives of field studies. Other important aims are to develop certain skills, such as map reading, and to motivate interest in a topic. Field studies can also act as a catalyst for further research. They should be undertaken whenever possible, because they (1) reflect what geographers and social scientists do, (2) are interesting for students, (3) provide an ideal learning situation, especially for teaching research and map skills, and (4) broaden students' horizons.[1]

Field trips have to be as carefully planned as any lesson. Read the following paragraph, and identify what the teacher has failed to do in preparing a field trip. The answer can be found in the ANSWERS section.

ACTIVITY 12-A

A teacher has organized a trip to a local industrial site. Transport has been arranged. The site has been visited by the teacher and full arrangements made (tour guide, time, safety precautions, location of washrooms, lunch facilities). Safety concerns have been addressed. Students have been given background information, a list of questions to answer, and activities to do while going to the site and when actually there. Rules have been laid down. Parent volunteer supervisors have been contacted. Each student has brought 25¢ for transport costs and has been told what to bring on the trip (appropriate clothing, lunch, writing materials). As the teacher teaches all subjects to the class, there are no timetable problems. The principal has given permission for the trip.

Once a suitable field trip location has been identified and logistical arrangements made, relevant activities have to be prepared for students. Below is a list of activities that could be carried out and questions that could be asked at various field trip locations. The activities carried out will depend upon the objectives of the field trip.

1. Identify examples of different forms of land use: industrial, agricultural, residential, commercial, recreational. Why are particular areas used for particular purposes? Is this the best use of the land in question?

2. Note different physical landform features. Locate a cliff, lake, valley, etc. Note the climatic conditions. How do these affect the area and the people living in it?

3. Observe the transport networks. Do power lines, roads, and railroads follow the best route? Why or why not?

4. Note where boundaries are. Where are the political boundaries? What are the reasons for their location? What other sorts of boundaries are there—property, cultural, ethnic, etc.? How do these affect the movement of people or goods?

5. Compare house and house lot sizes in Place A and B. Are they different or similar? Why?

6. Find out the reasons for the location of buildings, roads, and other features. Why is this (industry, farm, store, etc.) built there?

7. Find out the history of the area. Is this an old (building, farm, industry, etc.)? How can you tell? Why was it built? Where did the materials used in its construction come from? Do we build like this now? Why or why not? What did the area look like 100 years ago? Was it better or worse then?

8. Account for the differences in vegetation between Place A and B.

9. Identify examples of natural and human-created hazards. Where has erosion occurred? Why did erosion occur? Was it caused by natural or other means? Could it be prevented? Should it be prevented? What other natural hazards affect the environment? Can these be prevented? How? At what cost?

10. When studying an industry or business, find out about the site, the raw materials, the products and the markets for them, the source of power used, the transport used, the ownership of the industry or business, and the impact it has on the environment. Find out as well about the workers: any health hazards they face; how much input they have into how the business or industry is operated; how they are treated (for instance, if there is discrimination on the basis of sex, ethnicity, or class); whether they are unionized; how much they earn; what hours they work; etc.

11. Draw a picture of Y (building, landform feature).

12. Sketch a map of Place Y.

13. What do you think the area will look like in ten years' time? Will it be better or worse than it is now? Why? Draw a map showing how you would like the area to look in ten years' time.

14. List all the sounds you can hear and smells you can smell. Where do they come from?

15. Write descriptive words or sentences about how you feel at the site. Does it make you feel happy, sad, angry?

16. Collect some items (small rocks, vegetation); label and display them.

17. How are people using the environment? Are they harming it in any way? Are there any indications of conservation in the area?

18. Carry out an environmental appraisal. Create a score sheet like the one below, pose appropiate questions, and use the sheet to evaluate an area.

ENVIRONMENTAL ASSESSMENT

Location _____ Date and time of assessment _____

	+3	+2	+1	0	–1	–2	–3
1. Overall appearance							
2. Architecture							
3. Condition of natural environment (trees, etc.)							
4. Condition of human environment (buildings, etc.)							
5. Neatness							
6. Traffic noise							
7. Traffic danger							
8. Traffic smell							
9. Ease of people movement							
10. Ease of parking							

There are three types of field studies:

1. **Field teaching.** This involves teaching students at a site other than the classroom (e.g., teaching a lesson on salmon at a salmon hatchery).

2. **Field inquiry.** Here students find out answers to questions on the field site. These questions could be posed by the teacher and/or by the students—e.g., at a museum: How many different types of materials were used in the construction of a pit house?; or at a shopping centre: How many stores cater to females exclusively?

3. **Field discovery.** In this type of study, students go to a site with no preconceived ideas of what to do when they get there. Rather, students and teachers use the site to generate interest in particular topics and in the answering of student-posed questions.

Field studies of any type can be carried out in different ways:

1. On a site with clearly defined boundaries (an industry, store, farm, village).

2. Traversing areas that differ from one another (going from a valley to a hilltop; from a residential to an industrial area; from a rural to an urban area; from a low-cost housing area to a high-cost one).

3. From a vantage point (a tall building or a hill).

In all these forms of field work, students can write answers to questions, draw, collect specimens, map, make graphs, take photographs, tape-record sounds, interview people, make charts, do scientific experiments, measure things, count things, and so on.

Field trips need not require extended bus travel; the school environs provide a rich source of possibilities for studying the local community. Even the school provides a "field trip" site. In the following example, questions are raised about the geography, economics, sociology, anthropology, politics, history, aesthetics, and philosophy of a school. You are encouraged to question many of the taken-for-granted assumptions of school and schooling.

Questions	Suggested Activities
Where is the school in relation to the community? In what surroundings? Why was it built there? What does this suggest about the relationship between the school and community?	**Mapping.** Interviewing school board members. Collecting information from the school board.
What are the architectural features of the school? What activities might it encourage? What attitudes does it communicate?	**Sketching.** Photographing. Surveying students, teachers, community on their attitudes.
How is space in the school used? Are there spaces in which students are not allowed? Are there spaces for various student activities that are determined by students (e.g., a space for skipping, for talking, for playing soccer on the playground; a space in the corridor that is only used by Grade Y)? Why?	**Mapping**—location of various activities. Demographic mapping. Interviewing students on their perceptions of school spaces.
What kinds of special facilities does the school have? Are there rooms for specific purposes? If so, what are these purposes? What can you infer from this about the kind of activities the school and community value most? How much space does each department have? Is the size of the classroom space a factor of grade level or subject matter taught? What kind of equipment is provided? Do some sub-	**Mapping.** Graphing. Collecting and classifying information.

jects/interests get more equipment than others? Why? What does all this tell you about what is important for school and community?

What is the interior decoration of the school? Is it aesthetically pleasing? Is it comfortable? What assumptions about school and learning does all this reveal?

Sketching. Collecting and classifying information. Interpreting information.

What are the classrooms like? What furniture is provided? Do students and teachers have the same or different furniture? Why? How is seating arranged? What does this suggest about how teaching and learning is carried out, and how teachers and students communicate with one another? What behaviours does the classroom seem to encourage? What does all this assume about teaching/learning?

Mapping. Observing. Interpreting information.

In the actual construction of the classroom, what materials were used? Where did these materials come from? Were any imported? What raw materials were used? How many different kinds of occupations were necessary to build the classroom? Where does the heating come from? Where does the electricity come from? What does all this tell one about the economics and geography of the wider community? What does it tell one about interdependence?

Observing. Inquiring. Making flow-charts. Webbing diagrams.

What kinds of pictures, posters, objects decorate the walls? What do they say? What messages do they convey? Who put them there? Why? What kinds of ideas, people, activities does the school seem to honour? Why?

Observing. Collecting, classifying, and interpreting information.

What rituals are performed at regular intervals? Why? What are their purposes? What values do they reflect? What kinds of symbols do they involve? What roles do people play? What cultural beliefs do they transmit?

Observing. Graphing. Classifying. Interviewing. Interpreting information.

What activities do students undertake most? Do males and females perform the same or different activities? Why? What do students study? For how long? What does all this tell one about what the culture expects students to do when they're adults?

Surveying. Observing. Graphing. Interpreting information.

How do people dress? Do teachers and students dress differently? What influences the way people dress? What materials go into the making of the dress? Where do these materials come from?

Observing. Graphing. Making flow-charts. Interviewing. Surveying.

What cultural values can be inferred from the way in which the school is governed? Who has authority? Why? Who can be involved in the decision-making processes?

ACTIVITY 12-B

Using your own faculty, college, or school, take one or more of the above questions and use the following inquiry procedure:

1. Ask question(s).
2. Generate hypothesis(es).
3. Decide what data are needed.
4. Decide on method(s) of collecting data.
5. Analyze, interpret, and evaluate data.
6. Confirm or deny hypothesis(es).
7. Conclude.

When a field trip is over and students return to the classroom, further work should be carried out. First, letters of thanks should be written to those who helped (guides, parent volunteers, etc.). Second, the work done on the field trip should be written up in the form of reports, charts, and so on. The information collected should be discussed and interpreted so that generalizations can be formulated. If the field trip was a significant one, then work should be displayed and parents invited to view it. The trip should be evaluated, both by the teacher in terms of student achievement, and by the students in terms of what they learned from it and whether they were interested or not. Teachers also should reflect on the whole trip and consider the following questions:

1. Was it well organized?
2. Could it be improved?
3. Was it the best way of getting the desired information?
4. Were there too many or too few activities for students to perform?
5. Did the trip try to cover too much or too little?
6. Did anything go wrong (if so, how could this be avoided next time)?
7. Were the objectives of the trip realized?

OTHER ACTIVITIES

1. Choose a location that would be worthwhile for students to study. Design three activities that students could carry out at this location.
2. Design a question sheet for students to answer when visiting a museum, art gallery, or industry with which you are familiar.

NOTE

1. P. Bailey, *Teaching Geography* (Newton Abbot, England: David and Charles, 1974).

CHAPTER 13

Maps, mapping & the teaching of geography

Maps are not only useful in finding a route from one place to another, they can also provide an enormous amount of information about a particular location. By using a variety of maps of one place, we can discover information about the climate, landforms, geology, demographics, economics, flora, fauna, history, and so on. Students need to understand these things if they are to begin to understand how humans relate to their environments and how particular environments can influence how people relate to one another. Thus, the teaching of geography and map skills plays a crucial role in the Social Studies.

Before students can use maps to obtain information, they have to experience and grasp basic topographical concepts such as open and closed curves, direction, continuity and discontinuity, boundaries and regions, points of reference, size, and area.[1] Young children understand these at a basic level and can build on their understanding as they learn from three-dimensional models and maps.

THE GLOBE

This is one of the first geographic models to introduce to students. Young children, through direct teaching and incidental learning, should learn that the world is a sphere and that there are continents and oceans. They should be shown that the world rotates, which is why we have night and day, and that the world revolves around the sun. In later grades, they should realize that the world is tilted on its axis, and that the tropics of Cancer and Capricorn are the limits on which the noonday sun is directly overhead at the solstices. Without knowing this, they will not be able to explain the seasons.

How the seasons occur can be demonstrated using a globe and a source of light in a darkened classroom.

Set up a projector in the middle of the room. Place a globe near the middle of one classroom wall. On the globe, stick mapping pins into plasticine on the equator, Cancer, Capricorn, and the Arctic Circle. Ensure that these are all on the same line of longitude and are on one edge of the globe.

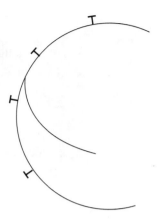

Place a sheet of white paper behind the globe or set up the globe against a white wall. Switch on the projector and note the length of the shadows cast by the mapping pins. Now move the globe (carefully) to the wall on the left, rotate the projector light so that the pins cast a shadow on the wall, and again note the shadow lengths. Continue as shown in the diagram below. As the globe is moved to the four walls, the length of the shadows cast by the pins changes. For example, at the winter solstice (December 22/23) when the noonday sun is directly over the Tropic of Capricorn, no shadow will be cast by the pin on the Arctic Circle, thus showing that there is no direct sunlight north of this location.

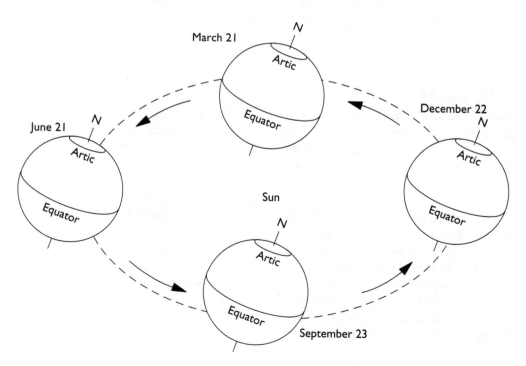

Here are some other activities to help students learn about the world as depicted on a globe.

1. Have students choose a place in the world to which they would really like to go.

(a) Calculate the distance to this place. At the upper elementary grades, students can be shown that a great circle route is the shortest distance between two distant locations.

(b) Determine what, if any, bodies of water will have to be crossed.

(c) Determine what countries will have to be travelled through.

(d) Find the easiest route to get to the location, and decide on the form(s) of transport to be used.

(e) Have students determine whether it is daytime or nighttime at their destination when it is daytime where they live in Canada. Also, have them ascertain what season it will be at the new location.

2. Have students make their own globes by blowing up a balloon and making the continents out of papier-mâché.

3. Give students cutouts of the continents. Have students label the cutouts and locate them on the globe.

4. Play a game in which teams are formed. Ask each team in turn to locate a place on the globe. If the team answers correctly, award a point.

5. Have students determine whether there is more land or water in the world. One way of determining this is to place cutouts of the continents in the oceans of the world as shown on the globe and then see how much space remains. This, of course, ignores the area taken up by lakes, rivers, etc., but it does provide an "eyeball" answer. The scientific way is to calculate the landmass area and the area taken up by bodies of water, and subtract one from the other. Most atlases provide the sort of information necessary to make these calculations.

6. Have students determine which is the largest continent and which the smallest one. Again, cutouts of the continents or information from an atlas could be used.

7. Whenever places are mentioned in stories or in current events, have students locate these places on the globe.

This last activity is a useful way of informally teaching students where places are in the world. There is no need for formal lessons, as familiarity with the globe over time will help students learn where places are located. These informal methods need to be pursued, as students don't learn location by osmosis. This was borne out in a recent assessment in British Columbia,[2] where it was clear that Grade 4 students had not been formally taught—and had not learned through informal means—where the Prairie provinces are in Canada. Only 58 percent of the students tested could correctly locate them on a map of Canada.

In the intermediate grades, maps should be related to the globe, because a flat map cannot give an accurate representation of shapes on a sphere. Students can discover this by drawing on an orange and seeing what happens to their drawing when the orange is peeled and the peel is flattened out.

MAPS

Students will probably be more familiar with maps than with the globe and, as a result, will have distorted views of the world. For example, maps that use the Mercator projection show Europe and South America to be relatively equal in size, even though South America has twice Europe's landmass. Africa appears smaller than North America, yet Africa is 50 percent larger. Further, Eurocentric views are fostered because two-thirds of the Mercator map is taken up with the northern hemisphere, and Europe is shown in the middle. All maps distort, but some are

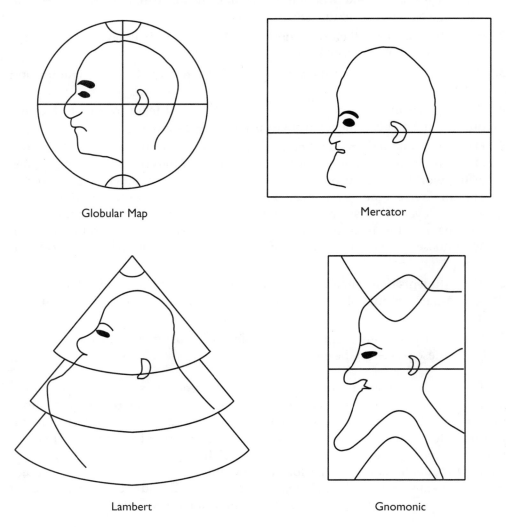

Globular Map

Mercator

Lambert

Gnomonic

worse than others.[3] Students need to be exposed to a variety of map projections and see the world from different perspectives. Have your students look down on the world from the north pole and from the south pole; have them view maps where Asia is in the centre.

The diagram on the previous page can be used to show students how maps distort shapes on a sphere.

ACTIVITY 13-A

In order for students to draw and read maps, certain concepts and skills will have to be taught. To discover what these are, take any topographical map and:

1. Choose a place on the map and determine its grid location (e.g., determine its latitude and longitude).
2. Choose two places and determine the distance between them.
3. See if you can locate any of the following: a river, a road, a building, a forest, a mountain, a hill.
4. Identify the highest land shown on the map.
5. Choose two places and state what the compass direction is between them.
6. Choose any place on the map. Pretend that you are actually standing on the ground. Facing in a chosen direction, draw what you would see.

The concepts of grid location, scale, symbol, elevation, direction, and perspective develop with age. The following chart indicates what map skills and concepts students should develop at different ages. It is based on a compilation of evidence from several sources.[4]

Perspective	By age 7	Ages 7–9	Ages 9–11
Direction	Follows directions of left, right, etc.	Uses pilot's-eye view. Uses compass to find NSEW.	States compass bearings in degrees. Aligns maps by means of a compass.
Location	Describes location in terms of in front, behind, etc. Uses globe to locate continents/ countries.	Uses simple grids. Locates objects on ground in approximate positions on a map.	Uses latitude and longitude.
Symbols	Uses symbols and colour on picture maps.	Draws and recognizes some conventional map symbols. Understands need for a KEY.	Uses KEY to locate objects on a map.

(Chart continues on next page.)

(Continued from previous page.)

Perspective	By age 7	Ages 7–9	Ages 9–11
Scale	Sorts objects by size and shape. Measures distances using hands and feet.	Draws and uses large-scale maps. Measures large objects accurately.	Measures accurately. Realizes that as scale decreases, generalizations on map increase.
Elevation		Uses colours to indicate elevation.	Reads simple contour maps.
Other	Draws routes between objects.	Draws route to school, plan of classroom. Finds countries in atlas. Understands purposes of different sorts of maps. Uses aerial photos of known areas. Compares map to globe.	Relates maps to aerial photos. Aware of limitations of maps. Compares map scales. Uses landsat maps. Infers climate from latitude, and economic activity, etc., from location in the world. Uses time zone map of North America.

Below are two maps. They show how students develop in their ability to draw maps. One is drawn by a Grade 1 student, the other by a Grade 3 student.

ACTIVITY 13-B

Compare these two maps. What are the differences? Why might these differences exist?

Grade 1 student's map

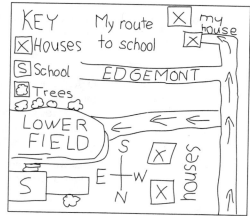

Grade 3 student's map

PERSPECTIVE

Young children find it difficult or impossible to imagine what something would look like if they were viewing it from a pilot's-eye view. They cannot put themselves in the place of the pilot. If asked to draw a map, young children will draw it as they see it—i.e., from ground level. They also have trouble orienting objects on the ground. The following maps show the sorts of problems young children have.

The bottom map shows how a young child draws a straight road that goes up and down hills.

The ability to see things from the pilot's-eye view develops with age. By about 8 years of age, most children will have this ability. To develop it further, try the following sorts of activities.

1. Have students look down on their shoes and draw them.

2. Put objects on a desk and have students draw them while looking down.

3. Ask students to draw a person while looking down on his or her head.

4. Have students pretend to be helicopter pilots hovering over the school; ask them to draw what they think they would see.

5. Have students pick an object on a map or aerial photo and draw it as if they were standing on the ground.

6. Obtain an aerial photo of the area in which your school is located. Have students draw a map of the area by tracing roads, buildings, etc.

Aerial photographs and stereograms can be used to enhance the ability to visualize from a map what a landscape actually looks like. This entails comparing what is seen in these photographs with the map. Whenever possible, maps that show where the students are situated should be used. Students can then practise orienting the map to the direction in which they're facing, comparing the map with the landscape, and noting what is not depicted on the map, or what is on the map but is no longer on the landscape.

We all visualize space in idiosyncratic ways. When students draw their route to school, they will include objects that are of import to them, and they will perceive scale in terms of what they think are long or short distances. Even adults do this. To find out how good your spatial perception is, try the next activity.

ACTIVITY 13-C

Draw a map of Canada without reference to an atlas, globe, or wall map. When your map is complete, compare it to a cartographic representation.

1. If you live in the West, did you have problems mapping eastern Canada? Why?

2. If you live in the East, did you have problems mapping western Canada? Why?

3. Did you include provincial boundaries, capital cities, major rivers, mountain systems, major lakes, and islands such as Baffin and Victoria? Why or why not?

4. Was your scale correct? Why or why not?

DIRECTION

Once students can use such terms as "left," "right," "in front of," "behind," and so on, and can locate objects using these terms, simple compass directions can be used. To illustrate the relationship between the above-mentioned terms and N, E, W, S, quickly answer this question: "If you are facing north, is west on your right or left?"

One of the most useful introductions to directions is the ME diagram. In this activity, students draw objects that are closest to them in each direction.

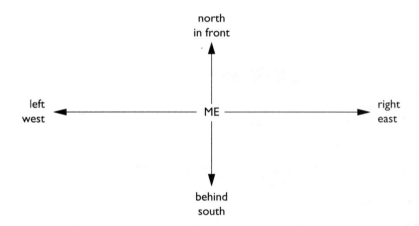

This activity can be modified to introduce other directions (NE, SW, etc.), and the concept of scale can be introduced by having students draw objects that are nearer or farther away from them.

Here are some other useful activities for practising direction:

1. Locate direction using means other than the compass (the sun, stars).

2. Divide the class into pairs and have one student give directions to the other. The other student has to correctly follow the directions. ("Go three paces north. Stop. Go two places east. Stop.")

3. Label the classroom walls with the correct compass bearings and give students directions. ("Face the north wall. Go to the west door.")

4. Hide an object in the classroom or playground and give students directions on how to find it.

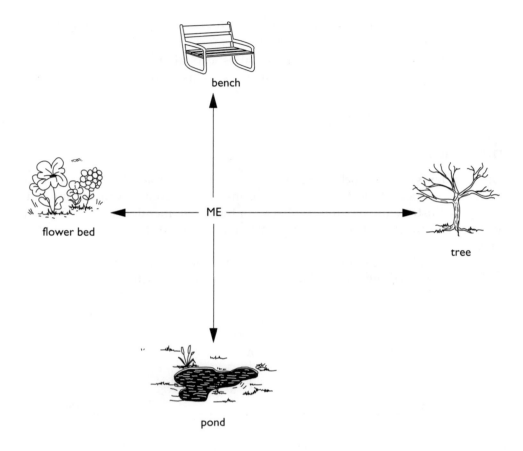

5. Give each student an imaginary map, read a story, and have students draw the route taken by a character. ("John walked north to the big tree. He turned west toward the river, etc.")

6. Have students observe a slow-moving object (person, insect) and map the moves it makes.

7. Use maps to determine directions from one place to another.

8. Ask students to plan routes between two locations on a map using various forms of transport.

9. Do simple orienteering. Give students a trundle and a map marked with a number of locations where students have to go. The playground could be used as the orienteering course. For example:

(a) Start at A. Walk north for 80 m. Pick up a stone.

(b) Walk west for 70 m. What is located there?

(c) In what direction would you walk to arrive at the corner of the school?

(d) Walk south along the side of the school for 60 m. What is located there?

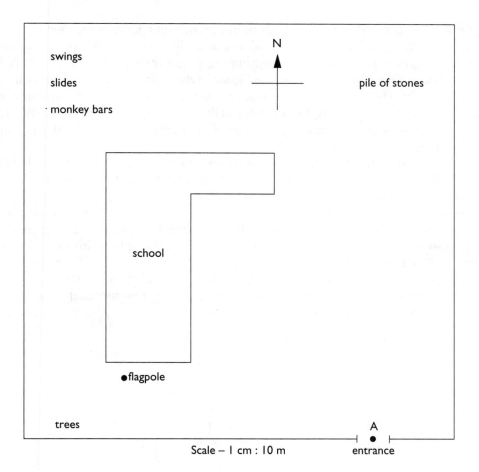

Scale – 1 cm : 10 m

GRID LOCATION

If you wish to get from point A to point B, it is not enough to know the direction; you have to know where points A and B are located. You have to have some reference points. You couldn't do a crossword puzzle unless there were numbers across and down. You couldn't play "Battleships" without letters and numbers to refer to each space. It is with these kinds of grids that you begin locating places.

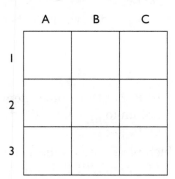

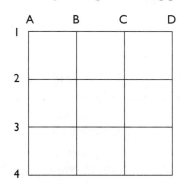

Students must realize the importance of having some kind of location system. Some ways to do this are: (1) Ask students how they would tell a parent where they were if they were lost and were phoning to get their parent's help. (2) Ask students how they would tell the coast guard where they were if the boat they were in had broken down. (3) Have students make a map of their classroom and ask them how they are going to locate correctly the positions of desks, chairs, etc. (Try using floor or ceiling tiles as guides, or place a grid system on the floor using chalk or tape lines.)

The conventional way of locating places on a map is to use latitude and longitude. These are quite complex concepts to fully understand and are not usually introduced until the intermediate grades.

Before latitude and longitude are taught, students must know something about the world. They must understand that the world is spherical, that there is a north and south pole and that the equator divides the sphere into two hemispheres. This latter point is easy to perceive, as globes are manufactured in two hemispheres that join at the equator. Longitude is more difficult, as the two hemispheres of a globe are not joined at the Greenwich, or prime meridian, and it is a historical "accident" that Greenwich is 0° longitude.

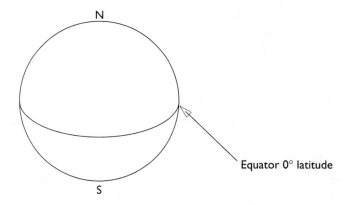

Once students have grasped these basic ideas and can point out lines of latitude and longitude on a globe and map, use some of the following ideas:

1. Hand out a map like the one shown on the next page and have students carry out these activities.

(a) Locate a town at latitude 10° S and longitude 10° W.

(b) Locate a lake at latitude 0° and longitude 10° E.

(c) Locate a boat at latitude 20° N and longitude 20° E. Put three other items on the map, give the map to a partner, and ask her or him to give the latitude and longitude of your three items.

2. Locate places using latitude and longitude. Which places are on the same latitude or longitude as Vancouver, Ottawa, or Tuktoyaktuk? If they are on the

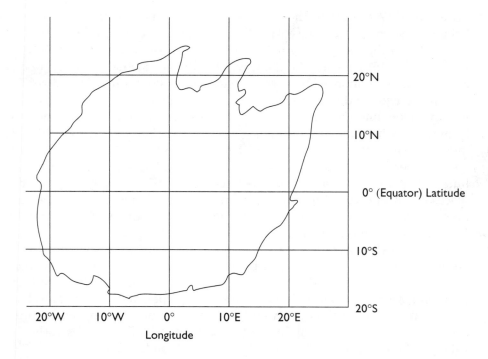

same latitude, will the climate be about the same? Find out what the climate is like, and if there are differences try to ascertain why (prevailing winds, closeness to bodies of water or particular land formations). Are there climatic similarities if places are on the same line of longitude?

3. Play a game in which students, in turn, call out the location of a place using latitude and longitude. The first member of the class to identify the location receives a point. This could be modified to make it a team game.

TIME ZONES AND THE INTERNATIONAL DATE LINE

If you landed in Fiji on the morning of your birthday, stayed overnight, and then flew to Samoa on the following day, you would arrive in time to celebrate your birthday. This fact baffles elementary school students and some adults. To teach about time zones and the International Date Line (IDL), you have to *show* how they "work." Students in the early grades can understand that if it is daytime where they are it will be night on the other side of the world. If they have travelled far enough east or west, they may have experienced changing the time on their watches, or may have wondered how they arrived by air in Vancouver from Toronto only an hour later than they left Toronto. And anyone who watches sporting events on television will know about the effects of time zones.

To demonstrate time zones in the classroom, use a flashlight and a globe. Assume that it is noon when the sun is directly overhead any place in the world (location A). As lands to the east are ahead in time and lands to the west are behind, it is afternoon to the east and morning to the west. To show this, shine the flashlight on the globe and rotate the globe 15° to the east (360° divided by 24 hours equals 15° for every hour). It will be noon at the new location (location B) and 1 p.m. at location A. If you were standing at location A, you would see the sun to the west and eventually watch it "disappear." Actual time zones do not exactly follow lines of longitude, so students will have to refer to a time zone map to find out where they are located. Places that are located midway between 15° intervals often set their times at a difference of half an hour from places east and west of them. (One example is Newfoundland.) Help students understand why time zones are not always located between each 15° of longitude and why some places choose to have half-hour differences. Once students have understood the necessity for time zones and their relative location in the world, you can demonstrate what happens at the IDL.

For this demonstration you have to pretend that the sun and time move around the globe. Make a strip of paper that will encircle a globe one-and-a-half times at the equator. Mark off the strip for every 15° of longitude and label the beginning *Monday, 12 noon*. Roll up the strip of paper, and starting at 0° longitude (the prime meridian at Greenwich), unroll the paper moving west around the equator. Call out the time at Greenwich as Monday noon reaches each 15° interval—e.g., "It is Monday, noon at 120° west, it is Monday, 8 p.m. at Greenwich." As the strip of paper gets longer, have a student help you hold it. When you get to the IDL tell students that days have to "begin" and "end" somewhere: that place is the IDL. When noon on Monday "crosses" the IDL, it "becomes" noon on Tuesday. Change *Monday, 12 noon* to *Tuesday, 12 noon* on the strip of paper. Students can see that Tuesday is to the west of the IDL (at Greenwich it is also Tuesday), and Monday to the east. Keep unwinding the strip (this is where you really need a student to help hold the paper), remembering that the day west of the IDL is now Tuesday. When Monday, midnight "crosses" the IDL it "becomes" Tuesday, midnight. As this is followed by 12.01 a.m. on Wednesday, Monday "becomes" Wednesday and a day is lost. Relabel your strip of paper to show this. (Don't worry, you "regain" it when you travel east across the IDL!) Looking at the strip of paper you can see that you would go from Wednesday to Monday when travelling east. Remember, as soon as midnight Monday "moved" off the prime meridian, it was 12.01 a.m. Tuesday at this same location, so the whole world doesn't miss all or any of Tuesday. You only lose one whole day if you cross the IDL at *midnight*. If you cross at other times you lose 24 hours, but not a whole day. For example, you still have 12 hours of Monday if you crossed the IDL east to west at noon, and have 12 hours of Tuesday on the other side.

Once students can identify the time at various locations in the world, they can figure out time zones and travel time. If you left Vancouver at midnight on Monday to fly to London, England, the time there would be 8 a.m. on Tuesday. (There is an 8-hour time difference.) If the flight took 10 hours, at what time would you arrive in London? To calculate this you have to know what time it is at your destination when you leave and add on the travel time. Thus, 8 a.m. Tuesday plus 10 hours gives an arrival time in London of 6 p.m. on Tuesday.

SYMBOLS

On the imaginary island map on page 153, students will have used symbols to show a town, a lake, and a boat. Although young children may use their own symbolic representations on their maps, you should introduce conventional map symbols in the primary grades. Here are some ideas to help students understand map symbols.

1.

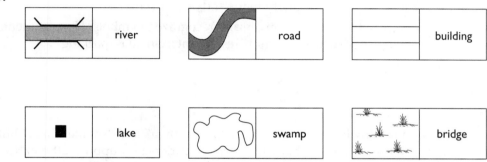

(a) Make cards like these.

(b) Fold a card in half and glue the halves together.

(c) Divide the class into four equal groups, and seat each group around a table.

(d) Place a set of cards in the middle of each table. Shuffle the cards.

(e) The first person in each group finds the symbol for a bridge and hands the card to the next person in the group. This person has to read the label on the back of this card, put the card back in the pile, and locate the card showing the correct symbol. This card is handed to the next person, and so on.

(f) With groups competing, play until one group arrives back at the symbol with which the game began.

(g) To extend what is taught through this game, add more symbol/label cards.

2. Make a set of cards like the ones below. For two students to play this game, you'll need about twenty cards with different labels. If you want the whole class to play, you'll have to have ten to twenty sets of cards.

(a) A pair of students is given a map (any topographical map, real or imaginary, will do) and a pile of cards.

(b) Each student in turn picks up a card, reads the label, and, if the symbol for that label appears on the map, puts it on the map. If there is no symbol for the label, the student keeps the card. The student with the least number of cards kept wins the game.

3. Compare a photograph of an area with a map of the area. Note the map symbols and compare them with what the photograph shows.

4. Give out a blank map of the playground or part of the local community. Have students walk in the area and use symbols on the map to show what is there.

5. Give students a map and true-false statements (either in written form or stated orally). For example: "There is a river on the map." "There is a marsh." Have students identify which statements are true and which are false.

6. Have students make up imaginary maps and invent symbols.

7. For many objects, there are no universally recognized symbols. Have students make up symbols for such as things as restaurants, cinemas, parking lots, etc.

SCALE

Young children usually have the concepts of "larger than" and "smaller than." But the concept of "exact scale" is hard to grasp, as it depends upon mathematical skills that aren't taught/learned until the intermediate grades. Young children can practise using scale by doing the following types of activities.

1. Use different scales to represent actual lengths. For example:
    one arm's length : one paper clip
    one pace : one eraser.

2. Use a length of string to measure distances from where students are on a map or globe to other places. When a number of distances have been calculated, students can be questioned as to which is nearest to them and which is farthest away.

To help students understand that when a shape is scaled up or down, it is the *area* which is made larger or smaller, you could do the following.

ACTIVITY 13-D

Work with a partner. Get a large sheet of paper and draw a simple grid on it. Have your partner lie down on the sheet of paper and draw around him or her. Get another sheet of paper that is half (or less) the size of the other one, copy the same grid onto it, and then copy your partner's outline onto it. Young children find it quite fascinating to see themselves a tenth of their real size, and even more so to see themselves twice their own size when the original drawing is doubled.

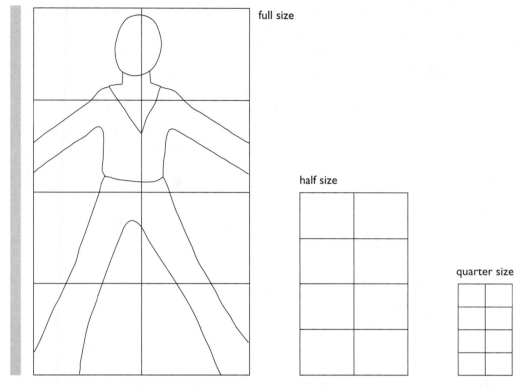

Older students can learn about scale by carrying out the following sorts of activities:

1. Find distances from their present location to places mentioned in the news, in stories, etc.
2. Make maps of the same area using different scales (1 cm : 1 m; 1 cm : 1 km).
3. Compare maps that use different scales.
4. Work out the shortest route between two places.

Students should first learn to use large-scale maps (1:2500). These show a great deal of detail, because they cover a small area. Small-scale maps like the ones found in atlases cannot show much detail, for they cover large areas. To remember the difference between the two, think of *large*-scale maps as showing *large* detail and *small*-scale maps showing *little* detail.

ELEVATION

So far, we've looked at maps as though everything were flatland. Maps also show elevation. Topographical maps use contour lines, but understanding these is an upper intermediate ability. The concept of elevation can be introduced by providing three-dimensional models so that children can *feel* as well as see the raised areas. Later they can use the atlas and the colour key (green for lowlands, white for the top of very high mountains) to locate various elevations. Where in the world (or in the country, or province) are there flatlands? Where are there mountains? To introduce contour lines, have students do the following:

1. Have students make a cone.

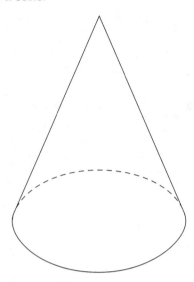

2. Have them place the cone, base down, on a piece of paper and draw around the base of the cone.

3. Have students measure halfway up the cone and draw around the halfway mark on the cone. Ask students where this line would appear on their piece of paper.

4. Have students indicate where the top of the cone would be drawn on the piece of paper.

5. Students should then label the heights indicated by the lines on the piece of paper, counting the base line as sea level. They should colour in the area between the base line and the halfway mark, and then use a different colour for the area between the halfway mark and the summit.

6. Have students use the elevation map to answer these questions:

(a) How high is the cone?

(b) If you were going to climb the cone, would it make any difference from which point on the base line you started? Why or why not?

ACTIVITY 13-E

Draw a contour map for the following shape, using the same procedure as outlined above.

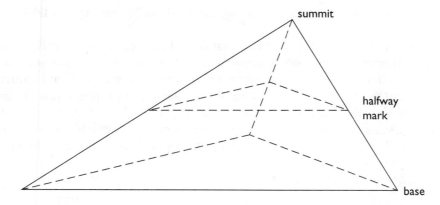

If you wished to climb this pyramid, which route would be easiest? Which the steepest? How can you tell?

ACTIVITY 13-F

On this map, draw contour lines linking benchmarks of the same height.

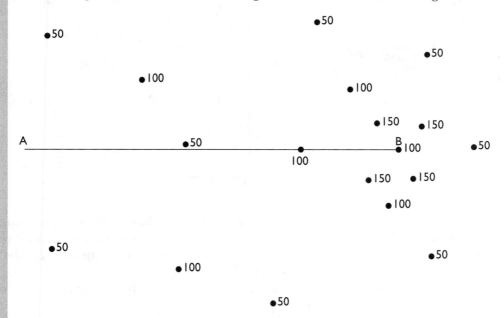

Cut out a piece of thick cardboard that would cover the area 50 m high or higher. Cut out a piece of cardboard to cover the area that is more than 100 m high. Cut out a piece of cardboard to cover the area that is more than 150 m high. Now, build your hill.

1. In order to climb this hill, what would be the least steep routes? What would be the steepest route?

2. What might you expect to find along the A/B line? How can you tell?

Elevation, however, is not a very meaningful concept unless students can relate it to something. Prairie-town students will tend to think of grain elevators as being very tall, whereas urban students will relate to skyscrapers, and students living in mountainous regions will compare the elevation of mountains. To give students a sense of the heights of various objects, give each student a copy of the large protractor, as shown below. Have them mount the protractor on stiff card, attach a piece of wood (a ruler will do) along the top, and drop a plumb line from the centre of the protractor.

They have now constructed a clinometer.

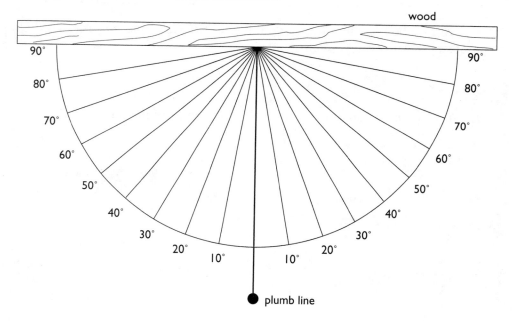

Students can find the height of an object (tree, telephone pole, etc.) by using the clinometer. Have them move away from the object and sight the clinometer to the top of the object, so that the plumb line is at a 45° angle. Then measure the distance from the base of the object to where the sighting was taken.

The height of the building is 30 m. How do you know this? Because you have an equilateral right-angled triangle.

If it is not possible to get in a position where the clinometer indicates a 45° angle, then use the following procedure.

Take a clinometer sighting and note the angle. Measure the distance from where the sighting was taken to the base of the object. On a sheet of paper, draw a large right angle, and, using an appropriate scale, measure the distance that you used from the base of the object to where you took your sighting. Now, using an ordinary protractor, draw the angle that was indicated by your clinometer reading.

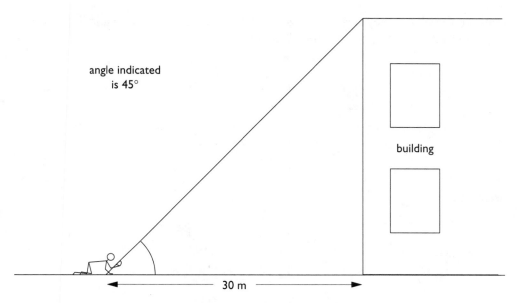

Measure from the base of the object to the top. By using the scale, students will find out the approximate height of the object. In this case, the building is approximately 70 m high.

The clinometer can also be used when students are making their own maps. Have students determine the boundaries of the area they wish to map and locate a sight line from which to measure angles. Replace the plumb line on the clinometer with a solid pointer. At a given location, students will hold the clinometer in front of them at eye level and sight the pointer at an object. They should determine the

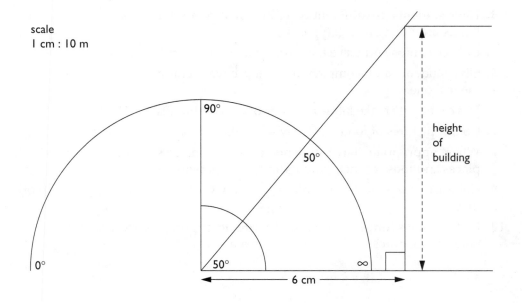

angle of the object they wish to place on the map, measure the distance from their location to the object, and plot the object on their map.

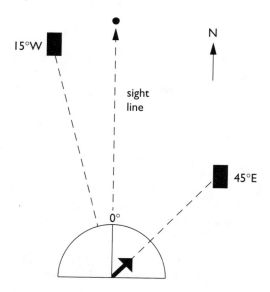

There are several other activities for students to carry out in order to learn about maps and mapping. Try the following ones.

1. Give students an outline map of an area in the community, take them for a walk in the area, and have them map what they see.

2. Have students decide upon the best route to take to certain places using different forms of transport.

3. Have students use different types of maps and find out what kind of information is provided on each type.

4. Collect stamps and place them on a map of their country of origin.

5. Give students an incomplete map, and have them finish it and compare it to the real one.

6. Have students make land-use maps of the community.

7. Collect pictures of foods eaten by students and locate their origins on a map.

8. Where appropriate, have students make class maps showing their own birthplaces and those of their parents and grandparents.

9. Collect pictures of various places in the world and locate them on a world map.

10. Make models, draw pictures, and write descriptions or stories about various landform features, and locate them on a map.

THE TEACHING OF GEOGRAPHY

Although maps are a vital tool in the teaching of geography, there are other means of teaching this discipline. One is to use pictures of an area, either to teach about the physical and cultural aspects shown or to have students make inferences and hypotheses and test these through recourse to information they can locate. Students could also read accounts of the physical and cultural landscape of a place, and, along with pictorial information, attempt to get a "feel" for the location. Children gain a sense of place through experience and by relating their experiences to new circumstances. If a student has experienced Africa only as a place where dark-skinned people live in semi-desert environments, then this knowledge can be used as a starting point for teaching about Africa. A useful strategy in beginning the study of a place is to ask students to write down, or say aloud, the first thing that comes into their minds when the place name is mentioned. What they know can be built upon as they are taught more about the place.

In the intermediate grades, it is best to start any study of a place with its latitudinal position. Latitude indirectly expresses the intensity of solar radiation, and this shapes the climate. This, in turn, affects soil conditions, vegetation, and fauna. All these influence human actions at that location.

As students develop geographic understanding, they should begin to learn about some general geographic patterns such as where deserts and volcanoes are located in the world, what general weather patterns affect various areas, and what the main ocean currents are. For example, have students locate deserts and then note the parallels of latitude between which they lie. Then, correlate this information with information derived from graphs that show the climatic conditions at locations where there are deserts. An effective way of teaching about ocean currents and climatic patterns is to trace the voyages of early explorers and correlate these to prevailing winds and ocean currents. When students understand some of these general patterns, they can use this knowledge to predict conditions in locations around the world and gain some appreciation for the myriad ways humans interact with their environments. Most of the information students will need can be found in an atlas. You will have to help students use atlases by showing them what these books contain and by giving them practice in locating particular information. Many school atlases contain information on how they can be used and activities for students to apply what they have learned.

In all these activities, the type of chart that appears on the following page can help students see the relationships between data and develop generalizations (see Chapter 14). To complete this chart, students use weather graphs for locations lying between the parallels of latitude and information from atlases. In this way, students can ascertain the relationships between latitude, proximity to oceans, and altitude on climatic and other conditions.

TROPICAL CLIMATE

Latitude	Countries	January temperature and precipitation	July temperature and precipitation	Vegetation
10°N–10°S (10°–20°N in Asia)				

OTHER ACTIVITIES

1. Use a Canadian school atlas and list the geographical information about Canada that could be learned from it.

2. Identify the mistakes this Grade 4 student has made in drawing the map shown here. See the ANSWERS section for a list of the mistakes. How would you help the student rectify the mistakes?

MY BEDROOM

KEY
⊢ chair
H bed
△ picture
\ door
▬ window

Scale   1 cm = 1 km

3. Have elementary school students of different ages draw a map of their route from home to school. Compare the results. What problems do the students have? How might these be corrected?

NOTES

1. C. Sunal and D. Sunal, "Mapping the child's world," *Social Education* 42:5 (1978), 381–83.

2. C. Bognar and W. Cassidy, *Social Studies in British Columbia: Technical Report of the 1989 Social Studies Assessment* (Victoria, B.C.: Assessment, Examinations and Reporting Branch of the Ministry of Education, 1991).

3. G. Rice, "Teaching students to become discriminating map users," *Social Education* 54:6 (1990), 393–97.

4. T. Burley and G. Atkinson, "Geographic skills: A research based sequence for grades one to nine," *History and Social Science Teacher* 22:2 (1986/87), 101–5.

S. Muir and H. Cheek, "Assessing spatial development: Implications for map skill instruction," *Social Education* 55:5 (1991), 316–19.

J. Bale, *Geography in the Primary School* (London: Routledge and Kegan Paul, 1987).

S. Catling, "Environmental perception and maps," in D. Mills, ed., *Geography Work in Primary and Middle Schools* (Sheffield, England: The Geographical Association, 1988).

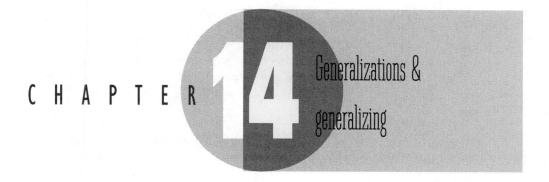

CHAPTER 14
Generalizations & generalizing

The instructional procedure outlined in this book begins with the identification of concepts necessary for the study of a particular topic or question. Students then acquire information about how these concepts apply, through expository and/or inquiry methods. The final step in this procedure is the development of generalizations. This instructional procedure is not the only one that teachers can use, but it does provide an effective structure for unit planning (see Chapter 16).

Generalizations are statements about relationships between and among concepts. They summarize large bodies of information. Generalizations are useful because, once they have been verified, they make it unnecessary to carry out research in each new case that is covered by the generalization.

There are several kinds of generalizations.[1] **Universal** generalizations cover every case to which they refer. They contain words such as "all," "never," and "every," and are true for all times and places. Here is an example: "Urban growth increases in relationship to industrial development." **Prevalence** generalizations contain terms such as "most, "the majority of," and "usually." "The majority of cities in the world suffer from air pollution" is an example. **Probabilistic** generalizations are identified by the use of the word "probable," with a number attached. Gallup and other polls often state their findings as probabilistic generalizations (e.g., this poll is accurate within 2 percent, 19 times out of 20). Finally, there are **enumerative** generalizations, which summarize data that have actually been counted. Statements about all the students in a particular classroom are enumerative generalizations.

ACTIVITY 14-A

Read the following excerpt from a Grade 5 Social Studies textbook,[2] and note which sentences are generalizations and what sort of generalization each is. Turn to the ANSWERS section when you are done.

How Do People Govern Themselves?

Every country in the world has a system of government. People living together in a group must choose a way of making decisions about their lives. If the group is small, the system of government can be simple. The larger the group, the more complex the system becomes. The type of government a country has is determined both by the beliefs of its people and the country's history.

In all countries of the world, governments provide services to the people. Governments build roads and hospitals, collect garbage, and supply other similar services to help people. Can you think of other services that governments in Canada provide?

Now that you have some understanding of what generalizations are, find out what generalizations are considered to be important for students to learn.

ACTIVITY 14-B

Locate, in the Social Studies curriculum guide in your province, the generalizations that students are supposed to learn. What sorts of generalizations are they?

We formulate generalizations through inductive reasoning; for example, "This A is a B, that A is a B—therefore, all As are Bs," or, "therefore, the next A will be a B." Enumerative generalizations can be verified by seeing if, in fact, all As are Bs. With other generalizations, it is usually impossible to see if every A is a B. This is why it is often said that, in inductive reasoning, we "leap" from what is known to a conclusion that we cannot be *certain* is true. In our everyday lives we make a few observations about something and generalize quite reliably to all future observations. When we generalize about complex, irregular phenomena such as human behaviour, however, our generalizations have to be more tentative.

In all cases of generalization, the following criteria should be applied:

1. There are enough instances to justify the generalization.

2. The generalization fits into a larger structure of knowledge.

Here are some ways in which students can develop generalizations and begin to apply the above criteria.

In primary classrooms, we can start by collecting information about students and creating generalizations about them: we all have unique characteristics; we all share certain needs. As students become more capable of dealing with bodies of information, data-retrieval charts can be used to formulate generalizations.

Data-Retrieval Chart

Nigeria

Climate	Agriculture	Transportation	Landforms	etc.
Data	Data	Data	Data	

To encourage the formulation of generalizations, pose the following sorts of questions:

1. What is similar about all the items under the _____ label? Can you formulate a generalization about _____?
2. How is agriculture related to the climate?
3. How is the transport related to the landform?
4. What has the transport system to do with agriculture?
5. Why is the southern area of Nigeria best for growing crops?

You can modify this chart to include other phenomena for comparative purposes. Other questions can then be asked to encourage students to make more substantial generalizations by summarizing larger bodies of information.

	Climate	Landforms	Industry	Agriculture	etc.
Nigeria	Data	Data	Data	Data	Data
Ontario	Data	Data	Data	Data	Data

1. How is the climate similar/different? What generalizations can you make about the climate in Nigeria and in Ontario?
2. What accounts for the differences between the industry in Nigeria and Ontario?

ACTIVITY 14-C

Below is a data-retrieval chart about an isolated Atlantic fishing community. The students who produced it have created maps, graphs, and pictures, and have learned how fish are caught and processed. They have written a story about life as a boy or girl in the community, and have discussed the advantages and disadvantages of living in a fishing community.

Location
- Atlantic coast
- Sheltered harbour
- Nearest town is 50 km distant

Building Materials
- Wood
- Stone

Population
- 750, increases to 1000 in summer

Climate
- Hot summer
- Cold winter with heavy rain and storms
- Frequent fog

Natural Environment
- Ocean
- Rocky cliffs
- Beach
- Arable land
- Trees

Jobs
- In-shore fishers
- Fish plant workers
- Marine outfitters
- Farmers—dairy
- Retailers
- Schoolteacher

Fishing season
- April–Oct. for cod and halibut
- Shrimp all year

Buildings
- Houses
- Post office
- Fish processing plant
- General store
- Marine store
- Church

- Elementary school
- Hotel with coffee shop
- Summer cottages

Unemployment
- 15 percent in winter
- 2 percent in summer

Transport
- Fishing boats
- Pleasure boats
- Rowboats
- Trucks
- Cars

Using the information above, answer the following questions.

1. How are jobs in the community related to the natural environment?

2. How are jobs related to the climate and unemployment rate?

3. How is the relative isolation of the community related to community services?
   Now pose two more questions that ask, "What has _____ got to do with _____?" Answer these questions.

Answering these questions will lead to the creation of enumerative generalizations about the community. For example:

Relationships	Enumerative Generalizations
The trees and rocks provide building materials.	Buildings in the community are built from materials found in the locality.
Location on the ocean provides such jobs as fishing, marine outfitting, and tourist services.	Many jobs in the community are dependent upon the natural environment.

If the enumerative generalizations based on this village are true of other isolated fishing communities, then we could formulate a prevalence generalization. For example: "In isolated fishing communities in Canada, there will likely be high unemployment (15 percent) during the off-season because of the seasonal nature of job opportunities." To arrive at this prevalence generalization, students would have to identify other isolated fishing communities in Canada. From these they could draw a random selection and find out if the generalizations made about the Atlantic Coast community were also true of other communities.

Students can be helped to understand how to formulate reliable generalizations from a sample of cases by carrying out the following sort of activity. Give students a statement about all students in the school: for example, "All students in the school like watching cartoons on TV" or "No students use non-biogradable drink containers at lunch." Tell them that it would take far too long to ask every student about watching cartoons or to observe all students to see if they use biodegradable drink containers. What has to be done is to observe or ask a *representative* sample. This means that the sample must reflect all the different types of students in the school, using characteristics such as age, sex, ethnic group, etc. If each class in the school is fairly representative of the entire school population, then a random sample of students from each class could be observed at lunch time or asked about their cartoon-watching habits. If individual students each drew a different sample, the results would be more reliable: the larger the sample, the more representative it is likely to be.

Students can also formulate generalizations by diagramming relationships between phenomena. Returning to our fishing village example, a particular phenomenon can be identified and students asked, "What does this need?" or "What is related to this?" By noting relationships, we can formulate generalizations—for example, "The success of the fishing industry is dependent upon the available technology, fish stocks and markets, people's skills, and climatic conditions."

ACTIVITY 14-D

Following is an incomplete diagram showing relationships among various aspects of the fishing industry. Diagram further relationships and then formulate generalizations. Is there enough evidence to support your generalizations? Do your generalizations fit into a wider body of knowledge about resource-based industries? To verify your generalizations, ask what would happen if a particular aspect of the generalization were modified in some way. For example, "If the government placed a ban on all fishing, what might happen?" or "If the cost of (oil, wood, etc.) went up, what might occur?" If the answers to these questions support your generalization, then the generalization is probably warranted.

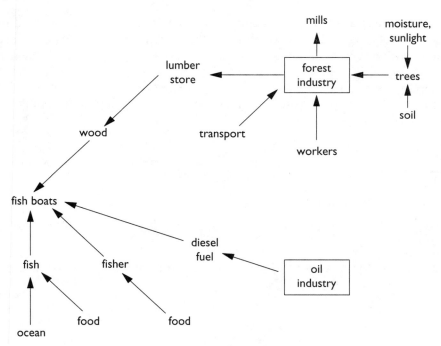

Most students appear to enjoy this activity and come to realize how complex and interconnected the world really is. For instance, a pictorial diagram showing the purchase of a chocolate bar by a student can demonstrate how this apparently simple act is related to the wider economic system.

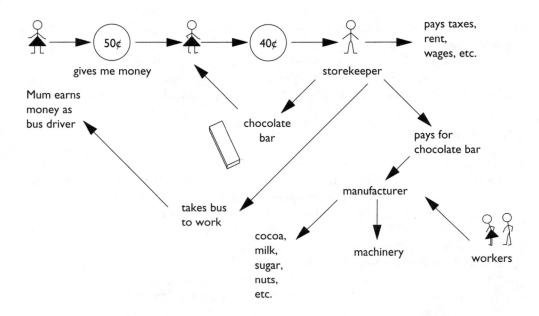

By extending this diagram, we could formulate the generalization: "All members of a society are interdependent; individual producers of goods and services exchange with others to get the goods and services they need to satisfy their basic wants."

As an alternative to having students formulate their own generalizations, present students with generalizations and help them determine if there is evidence to support the generalizations.

ACTIVITY 14-E

Here is a universal generalization:

Interaction between people and their environment influences the ways in which people meet their needs.

How would you discover if this was true in your own community? If this generalization is true, then:

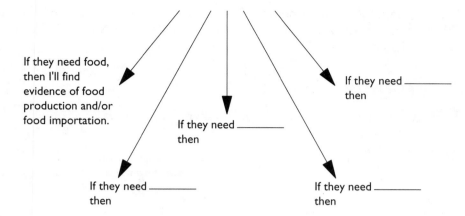

It has already been pointed out in Chapter 8 that one of the most common mistakes in reasoning is overgeneralizing. We have to teach students that, although we cannot possibly check the truth of all the generalizations we employ in our everyday lives, we have to be on our guard when we generalize. This is especially important in the recognition and avoidance of stereotypes.

ACTIVITY 14-F

What generalizations are being assumed in the following? Which ones are warranted? Answers are in the ANSWERS section.

1. I'm going to hire recent immigrants. They'll be good workers.
2. He's a boy so he won't cry.
3. The country will change culturally and economically with the arrival of so many immigrants.
4. As she has working-class parents, I expect she'll have problems in school.
5. I'm not going to Vancouver again in the summer. Last time I went it rained all the time.
6. He's wearing a turban so he must be from India.
7. She's a girl so she won't be good at baseball.

Helping students recognize the generalizations they use is important especially when these are not warranted. For instance, in (4) above, it is assumed that daughters of working-class parents have trouble in school. This is not necessarily true. These sorts of stereotypes can lead to prejudicial attitudes and possibly discriminatory actions. This is why it is extremely important to teach students the dangers of overgeneralization. Presenting students with examples of how overgeneralizations have created harm (e.g., the belief held at the beginning of World War II by members of the B.C. and Canadian governments that many of the Japanese living on the B.C. coast were real or potential enemies—a belief that led to their evacuation from their homes; or the belief that women could not perform certain roles in society, which resulted in their exclusion from these roles) can help students understand this point.

OTHER ACTIVITIES

1. Develop a generalization from the following information.

The Bedouin

February	A little rain	Move herds to spring pastures.
March		Make cheese and butter for the year.
April		Shear sheep.
May	No rain	Harvest.
June		Thresh.
July		Winnow.
August		Store grain.
September		Move herds often to new pastures.
		Water animals daily.
October	A little rain	Plant crops.
November	Some rain	Move to central camp.
December		New animals born.
January		

2. How would you test the generalization "As the size of the community changes, the services within the community change"?

NOTES

1. R. Ennis, *Logic in Teaching* (Englewood Cliffs, N.J.: Prentice-Hall, 1969), pp. 423–35.

2. R. Neering, S. Usakuwa, and W. Wood, *Exploring Our World: Other People, Other Lands* (Vancouver: Douglas and McIntyre Educational/Nelson, 1986).

CHAPTER 15 Student evaluation

Although it is possible to measure and describe what students know and can do without judging their efforts, teachers are required to make evaluations. Teachers need to know whether students are realizing curriculum objectives. Information on students' strengths and weaknesses is needed for completing report cards, giving feedback to students, and making curriculum decisions. Evaluation, then, is an ongoing process in the classroom. Teachers frequently use diagnostic evaluation as a means of establishing a baseline for teaching. We often observe students while they are engaged in an activity to ascertain how well they are performing. We use pre-tests to determine how much students already know, or can do, so that we can design our curriculum, and post-tests to discover how successfully students have performed. We also want students to evaluate their own progress. Thus, evaluation is a key aspect in any teaching situation.

There are a number of ways in which evidence can be collected for evaluative purposes. One of the most common is the test, with the score obtained by each student being the basis for evaluating that student. There are four basic ways of using test scores:

1. A student's score can be compared with a previous score.
2. Individual scores can be ranked ordered from high to low.
3. A student's score can be compared to a *criterion reference* (e.g., a standard such as "Students should be able to correctly identify the latitude and longitude of places on the globe").
4. A student's score can be compared against a *norm reference*, such as an average score derived from administration of the same test to other students. Standardized tests are an example of this type. Norms can be derived from various sizes of samples. Standardized tests may have provincial, national, or international norms.

Some situations allow you to choose what kind of evaluation procedures you want to use; in other situations, the choice is dictated by others. If your school, district, or provincial ministry of education requires that you administer a particular test to your students, then you are contractually bound to do so.

When information has been collected, evaluations about the students' progress can be made. Suppose that A scores 30 percent on the Social Studies test. Notice that this does not tell us a great deal about how well A is progressing. If the test was extremely difficult, for instance, this score might be exceptionally high. However, there is little doubt that the person who received such a score, and/or others who knew about the score, would conclude that this was not a good test result.

Suppose that A's score on the test is actually the lowest in the class and is below average in comparison to the provincial norm. Each of these comparisons of A's score implies an evaluation of A's progress. A's score is below the evaluative standard for each comparison group; therefore, A could be judged as not progressing well. However, it could be the case that A is working extremely hard and that the score is a vast improvement over A's previous test result. In this case, a positive evaluation might be made, despite the low score on the test. What is important to note here is that an evaluation is, by definition, a judgment. This judgment is based on evidence that is itself based on value judgments about what information should be collected and how it should be collected. Thus, as a teacher you will decide on what bases a student is to be evaluated and what criteria to use to evaluate students.

Before planning any evaluation, you have to answer several questions:

1. On what should the student be evaluated: knowledge, skills, attitudes, dispositions, behaviour? (See Chapter 21 for a discussion of the evaluation of attitudes.)

2. Why is it necessary to evaluate the student on X?

3. Should all students be evaluated on X?

4. What is the best way of collecting information about X? Should the same information be collected from all students?

5. How will results be recorded?

6. How will the results be used?

7. What criterion/criteria will be used to determine success?

Answers to these questions depend upon your conception of Social Studies. As was pointed out in Chapter 2, those who favour the Citizenship Transmission conception of Social Studies are likely to test for the acquisition of empirical information, using "objective" tests and ranking students on the basis of their performance. Those who hold the Reflective Inquiry conception are likely to evaluate student progress vis-à-vis previous performances and to test for more than the recall of specific information.

ACTIVITY 15-A

What is your position on evaluation? Do you agree or disagree with the following statements? Why?

1. Students should be compared with each other on any given performance. A *norm referenced*

2. Students should be tested only on "objective" criteria. *– yes*

3. Students should be evaluated on knowledge, skills, and attitudes. *– yes*

4. Students should be evaluated on the basis of results from tests that have Canadian norms. ✓

5. Students should be evaluated on an individual basis—improvement vis-à-vis previous performances.

6. Students should never be tested, because tests cause anxiety, and because tests examine only for low-level knowledge and are not objective. *D*

7. Because parents want to know how well their child is doing in relation to other children, students should be ranked. *A*

8. Students should be evaluated on the basis of informal observations and interviews. *A*

9. Students should be evaluated on *how* they tackle a problem, not on whether they get a correct answer. *A*

10. Test results should be used only to diagnose a student's strengths or weaknesses. *D*

11. Test results should be used only to improve instruction and the curriculum. *D*

Once decisions have been made about the purposes and nature of evaluation, decisions concerning the methods of evaluation are required. As pointed out previously, one of the most common is the test or quiz. These activities can take a variety of forms, each of which needs careful planning.

ACTIVITY 15-B

There is at least one thing wrong in the construction of each test item. Note what is wrong in each. Also, identify the type of test item used—i.e., multiple choice, true-false, etc. When you are done, turn to the ANSWERS section.

1. Jacques _____ sailed up the _____ river and _____ the Native people.

2. Brian Mulroney

(a) Was prime minister of Canada.

(b) Wears glasses.

(c) Was a good politician.

(d) Conservative.

3. Discuss pioneers.

4. The early explorers of Canada had to contend with disease, transport problems, lack of maps, hostile native people, and difficult terrain. TRUE or FALSE.

5. Before contact with Europeans, the native people ate

(a) Spaghetti

(b) Buffalo meat

(c) Wild rice

(d) Curry

(e) None of these

(f) All of these

6. Van Horne was born in _____.

7. _____ St. Lawrence River   **(a)** A river in Canada
       _____ Ottawa   **(b)** Capital city of Canada
       _____ Yurt   **(c)** A Mongolian house

The items in Activity 15-B all test for the recall of information. To evaluate students' acquisition of concepts requires you to pose questions that ask students to define terms, give examples of a term, and differentiate between a given term and other closely related ones. Here are some examples:

1. Give a definition of _____.

2. Use the term _____ correctly in a sentence.

3. From a list of definitions, select the one that correctly defines the term _____.

4. From the following list, select those that are examples of _____.

5. From the following pictures, identify the one that is an example of _____. For instance, which one of these is an island?

6. From a number of examples, identify the concept.

7. Given a list of word pairs, identify the similarities and differences between the two terms in each pair—e.g., car/truck, nurse/doctor, farm/ranch, need/want.

8. Given a concept, identify examples and state what all the examples have in common—e.g., food, plant, continent, role.

9. Given a list of attributes, identify which ones are relevant to a given concept. For example:

Law

(a) Something you have to obey.

(b) Punishment occurs if you break it.

(c) Created by adults.

(d) Designed to protect people.

(e) Tells someone what should be done in a particular situation.

(f) Enforced by the police.

10. Make up a sentence in which the concept _____ is used.

ACTIVITY 15-C

Design a test for students at three different grade or age levels to determine their ability to define and use one of the following concepts: power; independence; sexism; prejudice. In your view, what would qualify as an adequate understanding of your chosen concept at each of the chosen grade/age levels?

To test for knowledge of generalizations and the ability to generalize, the following sorts of items can be used.

1. Give students the following directions: Carefully study the generalization shown below. If any of the evidence below the generalization could be used to support it, indicate this by placing the letter Y (for "yes") opposite the statement. If the evidence does not support it, indicate this by placing the letter N (for "No") opposite the statement.

Cultures change in varying degrees when they come into contact with another culture.

(a) The native peoples of Canada were influenced by French and English fur traders.

(b) Some Australian aborigines still maintain the same lifestyle that aborigines practised a thousand years ago, despite the influx of many Europeans.

(c) Many Inuit have replaced their dog sleds with snowmobiles.

(d) The first English settlers in Canada lived in ways to which they were accustomed.

2. Give students a number of similar cases or events, and ask them to formulate a generalization:

In place A, which relies solely on fishing, there is high unemployment during the non-fishing season.

In place B, the mine is the major source of employment. In July, the mine was closed and heavy unemployment resulted.

Place C is a lumber town. When lumber prices decreased, many workers were laid off.
What generalization can be made about these three events?

ACTIVITY 15-D

Design a test item to test student understanding of one of the following generalizations:

All families have rules.

Conflicts develop between individuals and groups when goals and expectations differ.

Contact between cultures brings changes in the social institutions within them.

Multiple choice, fill-in-the-blank, true-false, matching, short answer, and essay items can be used in a variety of testing contexts. For example, to test for the ability to draw inferences and think critically about information, you can use the following sorts of items.[1]

Archeologists are excavating the site of an ancient Haida community on the Queen Charlotte Islands.

1. The archeologists find a stone axe. One of them says, "The Haida knew how to make stone axes." Is the archeologist correct? Why or why not?
2. The archeologists know that the Haida made clothing out of cedar bark. They examine the trees in the area and find that only small strips of bark were taken from the trees. Why might this be done?

(a) Because cedar bark is not useful.

(b) Because taking too much would damage the tree.

(c) Because taking a lot would be too much to carry.

These kinds of items can also be used to evaluate students in other areas. For example, the following question is designed to find out whether or not students know where to locate information:

In which source would you look if you wanted weather information for Montreal today?

1. An encyclopedia
2. Today's newspaper
3. A magazine about Montreal
4. An atlas

There are several things to remember in test construction.

1. The purpose must be clear. What exactly is it you wish to test for?
2. The test items must match the purpose of the test. If you want to find out how well students can use inquiry procedures, one of the best means would be to

give them an inquiry task and evaluate their performance. This sort of performance, or "authentic" assessment, evaluates the way(s) in which students tackle a particular problem, not just the results of the performance.

3. You must choose the most appropriate form (essay, multiple choice, etc.) of test.

4. The questions should be clear and unambiguous.

5. If you wish to rank students, the test should contain questions that will differentiate between students at the high and low ends of the scale.

6. The test should be reliable. That is, if the test were given again, students should get about the same score as they obtained the first time.

7. You must have justifiable criteria for evaluating student answers.

Paper and pencil tests are one way of collecting information about students' performances. Another way is to observe students both in and out of the classroom. As a teacher, you will constantly be observing children and making decisions on the basis of your observations. By collecting observational data in a formalized way, you will obtain more reliable data.

As with all evaluations, decisions have to be made about the purposes of the observation, the method, and the timing. Observations can be carried out by time sampling, in which a sequence of behaviours is recorded (e.g., how a student acts in a given period of time), or by observing a particular event, such as the behaviour of a student in a discussion group. To record these data, you will need to keep checklists. These can require a *yes* or *no* for the behaviour being recorded, or they can contain a rating scale, or a space for anecdotal comments. Checklists can be quantitative or qualitative. Here is an example:

Use of the Library

	Uses card catalogue	Uses table of contents	Uses index	Uses picture file
Names of students				

When a student is observed using the card catalogue, a check mark is put against his or her name (Quantitative). You could also evaluate students' use of the card catalogue by rating their performances as *Excellent, Good, Fair,* or *Needs Improvement* (Qualitative).

The following sort of checklist could be used if group work is to be evaluated:

Name of Students

Express support for others				
Asks for information				
Gives help to others when needed				
Encourages others to contribute				

When a rating scale is necessary, a checklist could be constructed as in the examples below:

GROUP WORK

Name of student _____

Enthusiastic	____	____	____	____	____	Unenthusiastic
Confident	____	____	____	____	____	Apprehensive
Responsive	____	____	____	____	____	Reticent
On task	____	____	____	____	____	Not on task
Cooperative	____	____	____	____	____	Uncooperative
Respectful	____	____	____	____	____	Disrespectful

PICTURE STUDIES

Rating Scale

1 = can do this only with prompts
2 = can do this with few prompts
3 = can do this independently

	Describes what is in a picture	Generates inferences from a picture
Names of students		

INQUIRY CHECKLIST

Student name _____

	Good	**Adequate**	**Causes concern: remedial action needed**
Understanding the question	Knows what the question means. Can paraphrase the question.	Has adequate grasp of the concepts contained in the question.	Has insufficient understanding to make sense of the question.
Generating hypotheses	Can generate several plausible hypotheses.	Can generate one or two plausible hypotheses.	Generates no hypotheses or implausible ones.

ACTIVITY 15-E

Design a checklist for a particular behaviour. Identify the specific behaviours you would observe, and state why you think these are the crucial ones. State what your criteria would be for excellent performance.

These sorts of checklists, along with other techniques such as student–teacher interviews, can be used in "authentic" assessment, in which students are evaluated on the way(s) in which they perform a task. They can perform these tasks either on their own or in a group situation. Through careful observation—listening to student discussion (when the task is a group one), having students talk about what they are doing and why—and through teacher questioning, students can display what they are capable of doing in a "real" situation. In a formal testing situation, students may not perform as well as they are capable of, and thus their results may not accurately reflect their competence. An "authentic" assessment tries to avoid these problems. One drawback is that authentic assessment is time consuming. Teachers in England who use it as part of the National Testing Program complain about the amount of time it takes and the amount of paperwork it entails.[2]

Students should be encouraged to judge their own performance. If we want students to take responsibility for their own learning, then we have to provide them with opportunities to evaluate their own performance. When given the chance to assess their own strengths and weaknesses, students can begin to make their own decisions about what and how they should study. They can use a self-evaluation checklist like the following:

	All the time	Most of the time	Occasionally	Never
I listened to others				
I shared ideas				
I worked hard				

A great deal of information is needed to evaluate students thoroughly. Information can be collected from test results, observations, and interviews with the student. Especially useful in this regard is a comprehensive collection of the student's work, including written work, photographs of projects, audio or video recordings of presentations given, and self-evaluations. All these items should be collected throughout the school year. Seek the student's own input on these items: What does the student think is exemplary work? What would the student like to show to his/her parent(s) or guardian(s)? For teachers, the portfolio provides a great deal of data on which to base evaluations. In parent–teacher interviews, the portfolio provides a picture of the kind of work the child has done over time.

Using data to evaluate student progress is but one of the reasons for collecting data. Another reason is to help you improve your instruction. If on the basis of test results you find that students are unable to answer certain questions, then you should ask yourself why this is so. Was the content or skill beyond the students' capabilities? In this case the curriculum needs to be changed. Was your instruction inadequate? If so, it needs to be improved. Was the test item ambiguous or badly worded? In this case you need to write better test items. Whenever test results do not measure up to your expectations, you need to question them, and to question the accuracy of your own expectations.

Evaluating students is a complex task. What is evaluated, how information is collected, what criteria are applied, for what purposes evaluations are carried out, and how results are used are questions that need careful consideration.

OTHER ACTIVITIES

1. Design ways of evaluating student performance on the following objectives:

   (a) The student should know the names of four continents. *Checklist*

   (b) The student should understand the concept "interdependence." *test*

   (c) The student should use a map of Canada to locate Toronto. *checklist*

   (d) The student should work cooperatively in a group activity. *checklist*

(handwritten margin notes) journal / checklist / test / test

(e) The student should state what is unique about herself/himself and what characteristics she/he shares with others.

(f) The student should give an example of a case that would support the generalization "Technological development contributes to the nature and extent of cultural change."

(g) Given a picture and a number of statements about the picture, the student should identify which are observation statements and which are inferences.

2. How would you find out whether students knew:

(a) How to critically assess an advertisement in a newspaper?

(b) The events leading to the election of a provincial premier?

(c) How an Egyptian pyramid was built?

(d) How to use a video camera?

(e) How to conduct oneself on a field trip?

(f) How to behave in a discussion group?

(handwritten margin notes) checklist / checklist

NOTES

1. Adapted from C. Bognar and W. Cassidy, *Social Studies in British Columbia: Technical Report of the 1989 Social Studies Assessment* (Victoria, B.C.: Assessment, Examinations and Reporting Branch of the Ministry of Education, 1991).

2. J. Clanchy, "Tests: The final straw," *The Observer: Schools Report* (May 16, 1993), 3–6.

16 A synthesis & unit framework

In this chapter we look at a framework for an entire unit plan, focusing on major concepts, specific empirical information, and generalizations. As a teacher, you need to have a unit framework so that you and your students know approximately what the result of your teaching is supposed to be. A unit framework gives you a map of where you want to go and how you intend to get there. By careful planning you can ensure that you have covered the important aspects of the chosen topic, that it is organized in a logical way, and that you have considered all the major curriculum and instructional variables.

The framework described in this chapter contains some of the key variables that have to be considered, but it does not contain them all. This is a practice run. The provision of resource material, evaluation procedures, integration with other subject areas, and individual lessons to teach needed skills are omitted or mentioned briefly.

For a more thorough review of unit planning, see Chapter 22. However, *this* chapter's framework does provide one logically and pedagogically sound format, which can be adapted to suit particular topics of study and particular school, classroom, and student characteristics. It is sequenced in the following way:

1. Concepts appropriate for the study of the topic are developed.

2. Inquiry is carried out into how these concepts apply to the topic.

3. Generalizations are developed.

Suppose you want to develop a unit on a particular culture. Using the framework above, broad objectives might be stated as follows:

1. Students will be able to define concepts useful for the study of a culture (e.g., food, shelter, clothing, recreation, religion, education, language, rights, responsibilities).

2. Students will be able to state how the above concepts apply to the culture being studied (e.g., details of how food is gathered, prepared, and eaten).

3. Students will understand the following generalizations:
   All people adapt their environment, and are adapted by the environment.

All cultures share certain characteristics—for example, all have a form of government.

4. Students will develop competency in such areas as carrying out research, using a map, etc.

These objectives can be phrased in more specific terms when the culture to be studied is chosen and when a grade level is specified. Activities could then be sequenced as follows:

Topic: Culture X

1. Show a picture of some aspect of Culture X. Make it as puzzling as possible in order to motivate student interest. Ask students where they think this picture was taken and who are the people portrayed.

2. Using maps and the globe, locate the area of the world where the people live. Have students find out how far away it is. How could they get there—what countries, seas, etc., would they have to cross? Guess what climate, landforms, economic activities, etc., they might find there.

3. Show the students a *representative* set of pictures (showing as many aspects of the culture as possible). Show about five pictures and carry out the *Taba concept development procedure* (Chapter 5).

(a) Have students list in writing or draw items that they see in the pictures. If students notice only major features, point out the small details.

(b) Have students tell you what they have noticed. List about twenty of the items on the blackboard. If the students have drawn the items, collect the pictures and display them on a bulletin board.

(c) Take the first item noted on the blackboard and ask whether anyone can see any item that would go with it.

(d) Once a group of items have been identified, ask students to label the group. When a concept label has been chosen, make sure that all the items are examples of the concept.

4. When the blackboard list has been classified, either have students copy the classification chart into their notebooks or make a large classroom display chart.

DATA-RETRIEVAL CHART

Landform	Transport	Climate	Dress	Daily life	etc.
Desert	Camels	Sandstorms	Long white	Children care	
Oases	Walking	Very hot in day	robes	for goats	
Rolling	Jeeps	Cold at night	Sandals	Worship	
sand dunes	Trucks	No rain		each day	
etc.	etc.	etc.	etc.	etc.	

5. If students have collected other information derived from the initial presentation, have them fit it under the appropriate concept labels. Create new categories if an item does not fit the existing concepts.

6. Each student should now have a chart identifying the major concepts that are useful for the study of the culture. From this point, a number of different approaches may be taken. You could take each concept in turn and teach about it, or students could carry out inquiry procedures (Chapter 8). The students themselves could choose a concept and questions for study.

   If cooperative learning (Chapter 9) is the approach taken, the questions and activities chosen by the students could be these:

Group One Food

- What do these people eat?
- How is food collected?
- How is food prepared?
- Are there traditions or customs that are related to the eating or preparation of food?

Write a hypothesis for each question and find out if your hypothesis is correct.

Group One Activities

- Make a menu
- Prepare a meal
- Draw pictures of the food
   etc.

Group Two Shelter

- What forms of shelter do they have?
- What is used to make the shelters?
- How are shelters constructed?
- Is the shelter suited to the environment?

Write a hypothesis for each question and find out if your hypothesis is correct.

Group Two Activities

- Make a model of a house
- Draw a chart showing how houses are built
   etc.

7. When students have completed their inquiries, collect their work, display it, and fill in the data-retrieval chart.

8. Ask questions that relate the various concepts to each other. ("What has climate got to do with dress?" "How is the transportation adapted to the environment?" "What part do religious beliefs play in education, daily life, etc.?") Through this procedure generalizations can be formulated (see Chapter 14). For instance, by noting how members of the culture have adapted to the environment and, in turn, have adapted the environment, the generalization "People adapt to their environment and adapt the environment to realize their needs" can be formulated.

9. Throughout the unit, compare the culture being studied to the students' own culture.

	Food	Shelter	Clothing
Culture X			
My culture			

10. Generalizations developed about the culture being studied can be applied to new situations by asking hypothetical questions such as "What would happen if a new need/want arose in the culture?" or "How would this affect how people adapted to, and adapted, their environment?"

11. Throughout the unit you will need to think about how to evaluate student learning and whether students have met your objectives (Chapter 15). Groups of students might evaluate other groups (see the example of the culture fair in the next paragraph) by asking question about the cultures studied, and then commenting on the answers given and on the displays shown and presentations made.

12. As a grand finale, a culture fair could be held in which all student work is displayed. Below are some photos of the culminating activity of a unit on World cultures, past and present. Various self-chosen groups of intermediate-grade students worked on projects of their choice. They created their own data-retrieval charts and formulated generalizations about the culture they were studying. Each group then visited other groups to find out if their generalizations applied to other cultures—e.g., did all the cultures have systems of government? If generalizations differed, they tried to ascertain why.

At the cultural fair, parents, other students in the school, and school board officials viewed displays, listened to songs, watched dances, and ate foods from the cultures studied. Students made every effort to present the cultures in an acceptable way: not as "objects" but as living and changing dynamic entities in which differences and similarities could be understood and respected.

ACTIVITY 16-A

Create your own unit plan. Try applying the framework outlined in this chapter in Part A. In Part B, a concept or generalization is required as the focus for the unit; you can also use Egan's story-telling approach (see Chapter 6).

PART A

Topic: What was life like on a fur trading post in the eighteenth century?

Grade Level: 4 or 5

1. How would you motivate student interest in this question?
2. From the pictures below, list the categories (concepts) that would be useful for organizing information. How would you get students to identify these concepts? (See Chapters 4 and 5.)

3. What questions need to be asked so that more information is collected about each category? (See Chapter 7.)
4. How would students obtain answers to these questions? (See Chapters 6, 8, and 9.)
5. What resource materials would be needed? (See Chapter 10.)
6. How could students record their answers? (See Chapter 10.)

7. How would the data be organized so that generalizations are formulated and the topic question answered? (See Chapter 14.)

8. How would you assess student learning? (See Chapter 15.)

What you have just done is to incorporate concept development with inquiry methods and generalization development in order to write a broad outline for a unit plan. Your plan might take several weeks to implement, and involve a variety of teaching/learning techniques and resource materials. It may well include more than is outlined above, but you do have a valuable general framework in this outline.

PART B

Topic: Firefighting

Grade Level: 2

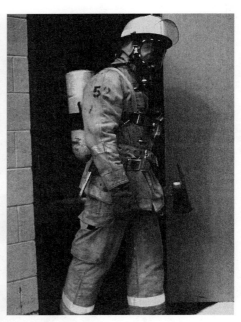

1. Given this topic, what concepts or generalizations would act as a focus for this unit, or, using Egan's story-telling approach, what bipolar concepts would be appropriate?

Examples might include:
- How does the concept "technology" apply to firefighting?
- Does the generalization "Community needs are met by groups of people engaged in many related activities" apply to firefighting?
- What does this topic have to say about *survival* and *destruction?*

2. Analyze your chosen focus, breaking it down into appropriate organizing concepts and/or questions.

3. State how you would motivate student interest.

4. Indicate how you would sequence your unit.

5. List what information students would need, how they would obtain the information, and how they would be organized to learn it.

6. State how students would present their conclusions.

7. Describe how you would have students synthesize the information so that your focus is addressed.

8. State how you would assess student learning.

OTHER ACTIVITIES

Obtain a unit plan. You can find these in journals; as well, your instructor or education library may have some unit plans on hand. Answer (at least) the following questions:

1. Are the objectives, content, instruction, and evaluation procedures congruent? Is each objective addressed in the teaching plan? Are students evaluated on each objective?

2. Is the sequence logical?

3. Do lessons focus specifically on the major concepts, or is it taken for granted that students will know what they mean?

4. Is there a variety of activities for students to carry out? Do these actively engage students?

5. Are there opportunities for students to work in groups? Is it assumed that students will know how to work in a group, or are there specific activities to help them do this?

6. What skills are students supposed to be able to display? Is it assumed that students will have these skills, or are there specific lessons to teach them?

7. What resource materials are required? Are these provided? If not, are they easily available?

8. Do you think the unit is worth teaching? Give your reasons.

PART 3

Decision-Making, Value Claims & Questions

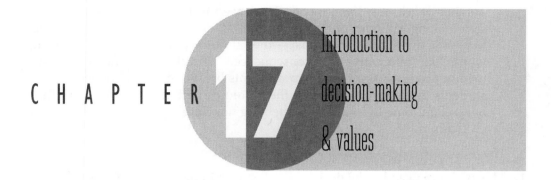

CHAPTER 17

Introduction to decision-making & values

In Part 2, we were concerned with teaching concepts and information. Throughout this discussion, decisions were made about what to teach, how to teach, and what resource materials to use. Teaching requires that decisions be made about these matters, as well as about what rules of behaviour students should observe and how students ought to be evaluated. In Part 3, we focus on decision-making and the values on which we base our decisions. As you will see in the activity below, value judgments cannot be avoided in decision-making.

ACTIVITY 17-A

Read the following vignettes and decide whether the decision-maker has made a good decision or a bad one. On the basis of your evaluations, identify the criteria that should be used to judge (and make) decisions.

1. I decided to buy this car. I can afford it. I need a car to get to work; the bus service where I live is terrible. According to the motoring column in the local newspaper, it has the lowest gas consumption of all cars of its type on the market. It has all the accessories I want. It's a safe car to drive. It's my favourite colour. It has the latest pollution-control devices. Servicing will not be a problem, as there's a service centre three blocks away that specializes in repairing this type of car. And, being a sports car, it'll suit my lifestyle.

2. I've been offered a one-year teaching position in Nigeria. I've decided to accept it, as an immediate reply was required. I would love to go to Africa; here's my golden opportunity. I haven't discussed this with my wife, who is pregnant and hates hot weather, but I'm sure there'll be good medical facilities in Nigeria and she'll get used to the heat. Anyway, I'm sure she won't want to stay in Canada on her own for a year, and when I explain to her why I've accepted the position I'm certain she'll understand.

3. I've decided not to introduce decision-making to my Grade 2 students for a

number of reasons. First, my students need to learn the basics, and decision-making isn't part of the basics. Second, decision-making is far too difficult for my students to grasp—they'll be incapable of understanding words like "alternative" or "consequence." Third, decision-making always involves controversy. I don't want parents breathing down my neck or my students getting upset because there are no right answers. And fourth, I haven't got time to introduce something new into an already overcrowded curriculum.

The following criteria should be used for evaluating decisions:

1. The evidence used by the decision-maker should be true or well confirmed.

In Vignette 3, for example, there is ample evidence to suggest that children in Grade 2 can understand the term "consequence." Thus, the contrary argument is not a reason that would support the decision. If the evidence used is suspect or false, then the decision may not be a good one. This is why we emphasized the evaluation of empirical claims in Chapter 8.

2. The decison-maker should consider all the relevant evidence.

The decision-maker in Vignette 2 has not considered other relevant evidence such as housing in Nigeria, the cost of living, the salary he would receive, and, especially, the effects on his wife.

3. The decision-maker should consider all reasonable alternatives.

In Vignette 1, the decision-maker might be faulted for not considering the use of a bicycle to get to work. By not considering all reasonable alternatives, the decision-maker might ignore the best choice.

4. The decision-maker should use concepts accurately.

In Vignette 3, it could be argued that the "basics," by definition, do include decision-making. If the concepts used in the decision are not used in an accurate way, then the decision may not be justifiable.

5. The decision-maker should base his or her decisions on values that are justifiable.

In Vignette 1, the decision-maker appears to have satisfied his/her personal values, having considered his/her own self-interest. In Vignette 2, the teacher's lack of concern for his wife is not justifiable; he has not considered the well-being of another person.

In the above vignettes, the decision-makers have made their decisions on the basis of certain values and preferences. While certain decisions can be based on preferences alone, in decision-making contexts where there are serious consequences for the decision-maker and/or others, the consideration and justification of all relevant values is required.

All values share some common characteristics. They are all "things" that are deemed to be of significant worth in a person's life. They guide and influence behaviour. For example, if wealth is valued, then actions are taken to obtain it. If people value political freedom, they may try to overthrow oppressive regimes. It is often the case that when people are strongly committed to a value, they will make efforts to persuade others to accept it. Preferences, on the other hand, are expressions of taste. Unlike values, they need not be based on firm convictions, nor need they necessarily be justified. Usually, if I said that I preferred vanilla to chocolate ice cream, no justification would be necessary (can you think of a situation in which you would want someone to justify this preference?). On the other hand, if I said that I preferred you to act in a certain way, than it would be legitimate to ask for justification. Smoking is a clear case of where personal taste has became a social value issue. In this and the following chapters, the focus is on values, because it is these that are significant in human affairs.

The values people hold can be expressed in three ways:

1. Simple value statements: X is good/ugly/efficient, etc.
2. Comparative value statements: X is better/worse/more beautiful, etc., than Y.
3. Prescriptive value statements: X ought to be done. People should do Y.

In justifying values, people formulate arguments in which some empirical claim about the value is linked to a value conclusion. For example, if you believe that students should learn about significant events in the history of Canada, then you may decide they should learn about Louis Riel and the 1885 resistance. Your decision, written in argument form, will look like this:

Value Premise (standard): Students should learn about events in Canadian history that historians consider significant.

Empirical Premise: The 1885 resistance is an event in Canadian history that historians consider significant.

Value Conclusion: Therefore, students should learn about the 1885 resistance.

If you were asked why students should learn about events in Canadian history that historians consider significant, you might formulate another argument and appeal to another value. For example:

Value Premise (standard): Students should learn whatever is required to foster good citizenship.

Empirical Premise: Learning about events in Canadian history that historians consider significant is required to foster good citizenship.

Value Conclusion: Therefore, students should learn about events in Canadian history that historians consider significant.

This type of argument—two premises that lead logically to a conclusion—is called a syllogism. It has the same form as the well-known argument below. Notice, however, that in the arguments above the conclusion and the major premise are value judgments, whereas in the one below the conclusion is an empirical claim.

Major Premise:	All persons are mortal.
Minor Premise:	Socrates is a person.
Conclusion:	Therefore, Socrates is mortal.

ACTIVITY 17-B

Fill in the conclusions for the following syllogisms. When you are through, refer to the ANSWERS section.

1. **Value Premise (standard):** Students should engage in activities that help them respect one another.

   Empirical Premise: Having students work in cooperative groups will help students respect one an other.

   Value Conclusion: _____

2. **Value Premise (standard):** Students at age 9 should learn whatever mapping skills they are capable of learning.

   Empirical Premise: Students at age 9 are capable of learning conventional map symbols.

   Value Conclusion: _____

3. **Value Premise (standard):** Students should come to understand whatever is necessary to become good citizens.

   Empirical Premise: Students have to understand the Canadian Charter of Rights and Freedoms in order to be good citizens.

   Value Conclusion: _____

Good arguments are those in which conclusions follow logically from the premises, and the premises are believable or defensible. This is why the first part of this book is devoted to empirical and conceptual matters—value judgments are based on these matters. If the empirical claims are not supported, or if concepts are used inappropriately, then the value conclusions may not be justifiable.

Often, our value premises are not explicitly stated when we argue for something. We might argue that students should be engaged in group learning activities because this will encourage mutual respect, and simply take for granted that mutual respect is desirable. Or we might claim that students shouldn't damage school property because it's against the school rules, and merely assume that school rules should be obeyed. To justify the conclusion of a value argument, we must also be able to justify the value standard in the major premise. We have been concerned until now with the *form* of an argument, to point out the importance of making the value standard explicit. Value standards are discussed in the next chapter.

People can be committed to a plethora of different values. They can value justice, wealth, pleasure, beauty, equality, physical health, salvation, antiques, and so on. Some of these will be "ultimate" values and some will be "instrumental" ones. If one's "ultimate" value is personal pleasure, then collecting antiques may be instrumental in realizing this value. What is important to note is that different values demand different justifications.

In the decision-making vignettes at the beginning of this chapter, the teacher in Vignette 2 clearly valued his own interests over and above the needs and feelings of his wife. In this case, *moral* values (having to do with how people ought to be treated) were overridden by *prudential* values (having to do with self-interest). Simply put, moral values are *other*-regarding, whereas prudential ones are *self*-regarding. Young children (and some older ones and adults) tend to confuse these two categories, using prudential arguments to justify a moral decision. In such cases decision-makers use a prudential point of view when a moral one is clearly required.

We use the term "point of view" here to refer to the *kind* of value judgment being made, or the *kind* of reasons and value standards needed to justify them. Although the number of different points of view is a matter of debate, most experts in this area recognize the following points of view: *prudential, moral, religious, aesthetic, environmental*, and *intellectual* (having to do with logic, reliabilty, and validity). The decision-maker in Vignette 1 has used the aesthetic, environmental, and prudential points of view. Notice that something can be judged negatively from one point of view and positively from another. As pointed out above, an action can be both prudentially acceptable and morally unacceptable.

Both in and out of school, students make value judgments and act on them. They make judgments about environmental concerns; they judge actions according to their conceptions of fairness; they make consumer choices; and they have conceptions of honesty, promise-keeping, justice, and so on. As they mature, they will begin to make decisions and take actions within the political arena. Students should learn how to make defensible value judgments and intelligent decisions about both personal and social matters. Because the content of Social Studies is centred on people, moral values cannot be avoided in the classroom. How people are treated, and how they relate to their physical and social environments, are fundamentally moral concerns.

The fact that students make value judgments, however, does not mean that these will be well considered. Just as we help students deal with empirical and conceptual matters, so we must help them grapple with the myriad value questions that impinge on their lives.

OTHER ACTIVITIES

Identify the value standard in each of the following arguments. Answers are in the ANSWERS section.

1. Because children are people, they should be treated with respect.
2. Hitting a child is morally wrong, as it's a form of child abuse.

3. Students who wear glasses in my classroom should not be given special consideration. They're not handicapped.

4. Watching TV for five hours a day is harmful to children, so they should not be allowed to do it.

18 Approaches to teaching values

In the last chapter, we saw that value judgments cannot be avoided in the teaching of Social Studies. All teachers attempt to instil values in students. This is especially the case with young children. Two justifications can be advanced for this. The first is that there are some values to which children must be committed in order to ensure their continued well-being and that of others in society. The second justification is that young children cannot understand the often complex reasons why certain values ought to be acted upon. Reasoning may not persuade children to act in particular manner; they have to be convinced in other ways.

Children obtain their values in two basic ways. One is through reinforcement. A child is praised for virtuous behaviour and punished for behaviour that is contrary to what is desired. Reinforcement can take the form of exhortations, lectures, the giving of rewards, the removal of privileges, or the use of facial expressions to show approval or disapproval.

The second way children obtain their values is through modelling. Children "pick up" the values of their families, their peer groups, and the society in which they live through interaction with them. In the classroom, teachers either consciously or unconsciously exemplify acceptable values; the literature and textbooks studied also exemplify them.

You may remember that when you were at school, certain people were regarded as heroes and heroines, whereas others were viewed as villains. You may also recall the fables, parables, and stories read to you that were designed to teach you particular moral lessons. Today, children's exemplars are often media stars, and their moral lessons derive from television.

As children mature, they will develop reasoning abilities and will use arguments to defend their value positions. How they argue will depend, in the main, upon their developmental level, how they are taught, and what models they have of good reasoning.

ACTIVITY 18-A

In a group, divide up a Social Studies curriculum guide so that each group member analyzes approximately the same number of pages. Then identify the values that are emphasized. Classify these, where possible, into moral, prudential, aesthetic, and intellectual categories. Share your list with your peers. What values are given most emphasis?

This chapter examines the various approaches to the explicit teaching of values. The brief summaries provided here cannot do justice to all the complexities involved in values education—there are no "quick fixes." Readers should consult the references listed at the end of this book for further guidance.

THE INCULCATION APPROACH

ACTIVITY 18-B

What values do you think your students ought to act upon in the classroom? Make a list of these and share your list with your peers. Do you agree or disagree? Why? What implications do your agreements or disagreements have for your conduct as a teacher? What points of view (moral, prudential, aesthetic, etc.) did you use to justify your decisions?

The purpose of the *inculcation* approach (often labelled "character education" in the United States) is to instil in students certain values that are considered desirable. These often include virtues such as tact, honesty, perseverance, obedience, and courtesy. Proponents of these and other values often defend their teaching on the basis of the rise in juvenile crime, drug use, vandalism, and gang wars. It is assumed that if children are taught the "right" values, then these phenomena will decrease. Such values may be those deemed to be universally acceptable, or they may be those shared by a society or particular group within a society. The values could be moral, prudential, religious, or aesthetic. In many cases they will be enshrined in law or in a religious code.

Proponents of this approach regard the individual as a reactor rather than as an initiator. The individual is to be taught the values thought desirable, in much the same way as the three Rs were traditionally taught. Proponents may also believe that children should be indoctrinated (the initiation into doctrine-like beliefs that are fixed and not held on the basis of evidence or the consideration of alternative positions) with desired values.

This approach uses several teaching/learning strategies. All are based on behaviourism and social learning theory. One strategy is to use literature in which characters exemplify desired values. A story is presented that illustrates the adherence or non-adherence to a particular virtue (modelling); then students are led through questioning and discussion to arrive at the "correct" answers (reinforcement). The same intent is present when stories of heroes and heroines and villains drawn from history are presented. In these cases, students are rarely told why they should admire the heroes and heroines, or that had many of them had less-than-desirable traits. This avoidance of presenting all sides of an issue is used in this approach when controversial issues are taught. Students receive only evidence and arguments that support the "right" answer; questions posed about the issue are designed to lead students to this answer. Often, where the intent is to have students avoid certain actions, such as smoking or taking drugs, scare tactics are used. The student is denied any opportunity to question the evidence or the arguments presented. Or children are taught to "just say no," without consideration of why they should say this.

Superka[1] has formulated a procedure for inculcating values in a systematic manner:

1. Determine the value to be inculcated.
2. Determine the level of internalization desired (e.g., awareness of the value, commitment to it).
3. Specify the behavioural goal.
4. Choose an appropriate method.
5. Implement the method.
6. Assess the results.

To use the *inculcation* approach requires that we first consider several questions: (1) Who is to decide what values to inculcate? (2) What should be done when two acceptable values are in conflict? For example, should a person refrain from stealing food when that is the only way of saving somebody's life? (3) In a multicultural classroom, how does a teacher deal with values that may conflict with those of the dominant society, or with school values that conflict with parental ones? A further consideration is the efficacy of this approach. If the right values are instilled in children, will they act upon them?

VALUES CLARIFICATION

Rather than inculcating values in students, this approach aims to help students identify their own values and act on them.

ACTIVITY 18-C

Below are a variety of *value clarification* activities. They are all adaptations of activities proposed by Simon et al.[2] Try several of these and then answer the questions at the end.

1. Rank the following behaviours from the most reprehensible to the least.

(a) Hitting a child who is misbehaving _____

(b) Being sarcastic to a child _____

(c) Ignoring a child who needs help _____

2. On your retirement from teaching, your students present you with a scroll. If you were to write this scroll, what would you like it to include? For what would you like to be remembered?

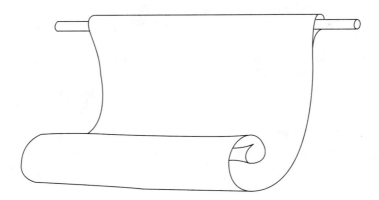

3. What is your attitude toward the use of snowmobiles in national/provincial parks?

allow   ban
unlimited use   completely

4. I wish the federal government would _____
_____
_____

5. In order to become a better teacher, you could carry out the following activities. Which would you try or consider?

	Try	Consider
Read textbooks		
Read professional journals		
Attend counselling seminars		
Observe "master" teachers		
Attend "in-service" sessions		
Attend conferences		
Take extra university or college courses		

6. Reflect on what you have done so far this week. What made you happy? What made you upset? What are you proud of having done? Could your week have been better? How?

7. You expect students to work very hard for you and to attain very high standards. Your students always do well on tests. Your principal decides to give you a class of intellectually immature students, but you like working only with better-than-average students. Your principal, however, is adamant.

(a) How could this be resolved?

(b) What might happen as a result of each solution?

(c) Which solution do you think would be best?

8. A friend of yours in a university course has copied an assignment from a student who did a similar course at another university. He/she obtained a very high mark, whereas you obtained a very low mark, despite the fact that you spent a great deal of time and effort on the assignment. Would you tell your instructor? What would be the advantages and disadvantages of telling?

9. Choose any value issue and discuss it with a group of your peers. When statements are made that positively or negatively evaluate the issue, use these questions, where appropriate, to further clarify the statement(s).

(a) Are you glad about that?

(b) What do you mean by _____ ?

(c) What would be the consequences of that?

(d) Have you thought of any other possibilities?

(e) Are you going to act on that idea?

Having considered these activities, answer the following questions:

1. What do you think the aim(s) is/are for each of the above activities?

2. Do the activities help you clarify your own values?

3. What procedures did you follow to arrive at answers in the above activities?

4. What types of values are to be found in the above activities?

5. Rank the activities in terms of the importance of the value issue. Which contains the most important value(s)? Which contains the least important?

6. If you disagreed with a peer regarding the solution to one of the above activities, would it matter? Why or why not?

7. What would be the advantages of having a clear set of values? Would there be any disadvantages?

According to *values clarification* theory, in order to have a value one must:[3]

1. Choose – freely
        – from alternatives
        – after thoughtful consideration of the consequences of each alternative

2. Prize – cherishing, being happy with the choice
   – willing to affirm the choice publicly

3. Act – doing something with the choice
   – repeatedly, in some pattern of life

The approach relies on the individual as the initiator of valuing. It is she who has to decide which values are positive and, in order to demonstrate that she has chosen a particular value, she must act upon it.

This approach can be used to clarify all types of values (moral, prudential, aesthetic, etc.), as well as tastes and preferences. As preferences are a matter of personal opinion, *values clarification* can become relativistic—i.e., "Your preference is as good as my preference." Extreme proponents of *values clarification* take the view that all values are relative, but most agree with the statement made by Louis Raths:

> If, for any reason, we do not want a child to choose a particular alternative, like setting fire to a house, we should let him/her know that this is not within the realm of choice.[4]

Using *values clarification* raises questions about whether values and preferences ought to be justified in the same way; whether values are, or ought to be, relative to the individual; and whether the result of using the seven steps of the valuing procedure realizes values that are morally defensible.

THE COGNITIVE-DEVELOPMENTAL APPROACH

In the approaches outlined above, any type of value can be inculcated or clarified. The *cognitive-developmental* approach focuses only on moral values. Whereas the *inculcation* approach relies on *instilling* value content, and the *values clarification* approach focuses on the *processes* of valuing, the *cognitive-developmental* approach stresses *reasoning* about moral questions.

ACTIVITY 18-D

Read the following dilemma.

> Chris wanted to go to camp. Her father promised that she could go if she saved up the money. Chris worked hard on a paper route and saved the $75 it cost to go to camp. But just before camp was going to start, her father changed his mind. Some of his friends decided to travel to Toronto to see a hockey game, and he didn't have enough money to go. He asked Chris to lend him the money she had saved. Chris didn't want to give up going to camp, so she thought of refusing to give her father the money.

Decide whether Chris should give the money to her father.

If your decision is that she should give the money to her father, look at the sentences in the YES column below. Choose the one you think is the best reason for saying *yes* and put a 1 (one) in the box provided. Then choose the second-best reason and so on until all sentences have been ranked.

If your answer is *no*, look at the sentences in the NO column. Choose the one you think is the best reason for saying *no*, and put a 1 (one) in the box provided. Then choose the second-best reason and so on until all the sentences have been ranked.

YES

1. Because if Chris did refuse, her father might not treat her well in the future.

2. The father has responsibility for her welfare. If he decides that it is best for her not to go to camp, then he is acting responsibly.

3. Chris's father may not always keep his word, but he is trying to help Chris in the best way he knows. Chris should respect him for trying to be a good father.

4. Because he's her father, she should listen to what he says.

NO

1. Chris has had the experience of working hard and saving money. This will foster industry, initiative, and responsibility, all of which are necessary for the well-being of society.

2. It's her money, so she should be able to do whatever she wants with it.

3. The father should recognize Chris as a person who is different but equal to himself; Chris has a right to make personal decisions.

4. Chris's father made a promise. He is behaving selfishly by breaking that promise.

According to *cognitive-developmental* theory, especially as conceptualized and researched by L. Kohlberg,[5] these reasons fit into a developmental pattern.

Stage 1 This stage focuses on the avoidance of punishment, and doing what authority figures say is right.

Stage 2 The concern here is with serving one's own needs and interests while realizing that other people have their own interests. What's right is an equal exchange— "I'll keep my promise to you if you keep your promise to me."

Stage 3 At this stage, a person wants to be viewed as good according to conventional standards—what is expected of you by others and by your own standards of "goodness"—e.g., showing concern for others, being loyal, maintaining mutually satisfying relationships.

Stage 4 The concern at this stage is with maintaining society—obeying the law, contributing to society—so that the system doesn't break down. This stage is often referred to as the "law and order" stage.

Stage 5 At this stage, individuals feel an obligation to obey society's laws because of a social contract that protects people's rights and welfare. These rules should be impartial. Some values like "life" and "liberty" must be upheld in any society.

Stage 6 Universal moral principles are used to justify actions. If such principles as justice, equality, and respect for people conflict with laws in a particular society, then the *principle* must be acted upon.

Kohlberg argues that these stages are successive—an individual cannot skip stages—and hierarchical, as each stage is based upon the preceding stage and each is "better" than its predecessors. The reasoning displayed at each stage is not completely a product of external sources, as in the *inculcation* approach, nor is it solely a product of internal ones, as in the *values clarification* approach. Reasoning is a product of the interaction of both environmental and genetic stimulants. Development through the stages, therefore, depends on a person's maturity and on the social milieu, with such variables as "intelligence" and role-taking ability being especially relevant.

Kohlberg's theory has been criticized by feminist scholars for being male-oriented. (Kohlberg did base his theory initially on research involving only male subjects.) These scholars claim that females tend to use an ethic of caring and are concerned with mutually satisfying relationships rather than with justice.[6] Feminism is an important area of scholarship; these arguments need to be carefully considered in implementing a values education program based on Kohlberg's theory.

The basic instructional procedure in this approach is to present students with hypothetical or real-life dilemmas, which are discussed in small-group situations. Solutions are generated and reasons for the solutions are presented. It is assumed that if students at a given stage are exposed to arguments at the next-highest stage, they will be stimulated to begin to think at this higher level.

Here is an example.[7] Students are given a story in which a young girl promises her father not to climb trees. Her friend's kitten is caught in a tree and she is the only one who can rescue it. Should she climb the tree to save the kitten? If she climbs, she breaks a promise; if she doesn't, the owner of the kitten will be heartbroken, as his mother has told him that if the kitten gets into trouble once more, the kitten will be given away.

Once the dilemma has been posed, the class is divided into groups of students. To ensure that there is initial conflict in the groups, each one should contain students who either reason at different stages of moral reasoning or disagree on whether the girl should climb the tree. The groups discuss their response to the dilemma, and then state their conclusions and the reasons for their decisions. The following questions are posed:

1. Would it make any difference if the girl's father didn't know whether she climbed the tree?

2. Would the girl's father understand if she did climb the tree?

3. Should all promises be kept?

4. How will the kitten's owner feel if the kitten is (is not) rescued?

5. Suppose the girl doesn't like the kitten's owner. Should that make any difference to her decision?

6. How would you feel if you were the girl? the owner of the kitten?

The *cognitive-developmental* approach also raises questions. First, it is primarily based on dilemma discussions, yet not all value questions are dilemmas. It is not always the case that whatever action is taken will disadvantage someone. Second, what approach does one take if a student gives "good" Stage 1 or 2 reasons for deciding do something immoral? Third, in the dilemmas used by Kohlberg, all the facts of the case are presented, whereas in real life one may need to discover the facts and evaluate them prior to reaching a decision.

THE VALUES ANALYSIS APPROACH

This approach is based on the assumption that there are rational ways to resolve value issues. The focus is on the logic of arguments, the truth of empirical claims, the clarification of concepts, and the justifications for the value principles, rules, or standards that are used to arrive at a decision.

Here is an example. Students have been asked to collect money for UNICEF when they are trick-or-treating at Halloween. They debate whether to do this; the question is raised about the need to give aid to other countries. The teacher poses the question "Should we (members of the class) give aid to other countries?" She decides to use a case study of a village in Somalia. The students read about the problems the villagers face and list the sorts of aid they receive. They clarify the concept of "aid" by giving examples, and eventually arrive at a list of what would qualify as aid (see Chapter 5 for ideas). In inquiry groups (see Chapter 9), students then carry out research about other countries that receive aid. They draw up a list of reasons for its provision and create a chart.

Should we give aid to other countries?	
We should give aid.	We should not give aid.
Giving aid will prevent starvation.	Giving aid will mean poor people in Canada won't be helped.
It'll help people who are ill and can't get medicine.	It'll result in people not helping themselves—they'll rely on aid all the time.
It'll provide schools for children.	Some children in class can't afford to give money, and they'll feel bad if everyone else does.

The students evaluate the reasons for and against giving aid. Would students who could not afford to give money feel badly when other children did so? Does aid prevent starvation? Here, you can use the standards for assessing the reliabilty of empirical claims outlined in Chapter 8. "Truth" may well be difficult or impossible to establish in some cases, and teachers must use their judgment about the level of reliability required. For example, there is no way that students can *check* how many people are actually starving. Students will have to rely on figures from UNICEF and other relief agencies. These figures are likely to be reliable: if relief agencies were found to be untruthful, it is unlikely that people would continue to give money to them.

The next step consists of identifying the value standards to which students have appealed. The standards behind the reasons above for giving aid are these: We should prevent starvation; we should help people who are ill; and we should provide schools for children. On what value standards are the reasons for not giving aid based?

The final step is to "test" the value standard. This is where the *values analysis* approach differs fundamentally from the other approaches. In the *inculcation* approach, the standard is taken for granted if it is socially acceptable. According to the *values clarification* approach, so long as the seven steps of the valuing process have been carried out, the standard is acceptable. According to the *cognitive-development* approach, the value standard is based on the stage of reasoning attained.

In the *values analysis* approach, the justification for the value standard or principle is judged by applying four principle tests:[8]

1. **The Role Exchange Test.** You may remember being asked as a child, "How would you like that done to you?" if you had done something wrong to someone else. The point of this question is that if you would not want the action to be performed on you, then you should not do it to someone else. This is the basis for the Role Exchange Test. The question, however, should be posed as, "Would it be *right* for you in the role of the other person to do X?" It is not just a question of liking. A child may not *like* to go to the dentist, but it would be *right* for a parent to insist that the child go. The steps to follow are these: (1) imagine what it would be like in the other person's situation and experience the consequences the action would have on that person; (2) consider whether it would be right for the other person to take the action if *you* were the one experiencing the consequences; and (3) decide whether to accept or reject performing the action because of the consquences to the other person. This test is best applied when the consequences to the other person are undesirable.

2. **The Universal Consequences Test.** You may also remember from your childhood being asked, "What if everybody did that?" when you had done something wrong. This question's point is that if the consequences would be disastrous if everybody performed a particular act, then *you* should not do it. In this test, the decision-maker has to imagine the consequences if everyone who was likely to perform the same action for the same reasons were to do so. For example, can a motorist justify speeding with the argument that he was

late for an extremely important meeting? We can imagine a number of motorists wanting to use this as a reason, and we can imagine the consequences if they were all to speed. Thus, this reason does not justify speeding— although the justification offered by an ambulance driver carrying a critically ill patient might be acceptable for every ambulance driver in a similar situation. The steps in this test are as follows: (1) imagine the consequences if everyone who was likely to perform the same action for the same reason were to do so; (2) consider whether the imagined consequences would be acceptable; (3) conclude that the action is right if the consequences are acceptable, and then subject the decision to the other principle tests, or conclude that it is wrong if the consequences are unacceptable.

3. **The New Cases Test.** A third question that you may have been asked when you were engaged in some bad behaviour is "Would you do the same thing in (another similar) situation?" This question focuses on the presumption that people ought to be consistent in their judgments. In this test, a standard that has been accepted is applied to new, logically relevant cases. The power of the test depends on applying *difficult* cases. If a child has said that stealing from someone in the class is wrong, it is probably ineffective to ask whether the child would steal from friends, relatives, other children in the school, etc. Rather, pose a problem where stealing would lead to desirable consequences, such as saving a life. Then the student must determine whether she thinks the principle "in no circumstances whatsoever should people steal" is justifiable or whether another principle such as "people should not steal except in circumstances where a life is at stake" is more acceptable. The latter principle would need to be tested with new cases in order to determine if the reasoner was willing to hold to it consistently. The steps are as follows: (1) choose a case that logically falls under the value standard being appealed to; (2) consider whether to judge this case in the same way as the original decision was judged; (3) if the case is judged in the same way and it is the hardest case that can be imagined, then accept the decision.

4. **The Subsumption Test.** This last test is different from the other three. It is designed to determine if the value standard in question falls under and is consistent with a more general, higher principle that the decision-maker accepts. It is useful in discerning the general value principles on both sides of a conflict. For example, in the foreign aid case, the more general principle may be that we should help *all* people who are worse off then we are. The decision-maker then has to decide whether or not this general principle is acceptable by applying the other three tests.

It may appear that all this is far too complex for elementary school students. But we do ask young children, "How would you like that done to you?", "What if everybody did that?", and "If you would do that in this situation, would you do it in X situation?" These questions are the bases for the Role Exchange, Universal Consequences, and New Cases tests. Of course, elementary students cannot apply these tests in a sophisticated way, but they can be asked to consider the consequences of their actions for other people. Even though primary grade children will have difficulty applying the Role Exchange test—as they will believe that their perspective is shared by other people—this does not mean that they should not consider the effects of their actions on others. By about age 7, children do realize that others can have different perspectives, and that these have to be taken into account when interpersonal decisions are made.

Here is an activity that asks to apply the principle tests.

ACTIVITY 18-E

Read the following vignette and answer the questions that follow.

> The Fraser family—mother, father, a 3-year-old, and a 5-year-old—are looking for a place they can afford to rent. They are getting quite desperate, so when they see an advertisement for an affordable duplex, the parents hurry over to look at it. The parents decide that it is just what they are looking for, and tell the owner, who gets out a rental contract and starts to fill it in. He asks them if they have children. They reply that they have two. The owner tells them that they cannot rent the duplex, for he does not rent to families with children. He claims that children make too much noise and are likely to damage his property.

Should the owner have the right to refuse to rent the duplex to the Fraser family?

Suppose you argue that the owner should have the right to refuse to rent the duplex, because it's his property and he has the right to do what he likes with it. The value standard is "Property owners ought to be able to do whatever they like with their own property." How would you answer the following questions?

1. Imagine you are a member of the Fraser family. Would the owner's decision be right if you were the one experiencing the consequences?

2. What would be the consequences if every property owner in the city refused to rent to couples with children because children create noise and might damage property? Are these consequences acceptable?

3. Suppose a man comes to the owner and is told that the duplex is available for rent. The owner asks for his name and is told that it is Levin. The owner asks if he is Jewish. The answer is "Yes." The owner says he does not rent his duplex to Jews. Should the owner have the right to refuse to rent the duplex to Jews? Suppose a person in a wheelchair wanted to rent the duplex but is told by the owner that he does not rent to people who are physically challenged. Should the owner have the right to do this?

4. If you were asked to justify the principle that property owners could do whatever they pleased with their property, what higher principle would you use?

Suppose you argue that the owner should not have the right to refuse to rent to the Fraser family, because that would be discriminatory. The value standard would then be "People should not have the right to discriminate." How would you answer the following questions?

1. Suppose you were the owner. Would it be right for you to experience the consequences of having renters who you believe will be noisy and will damage your property?

2. Would the consequences be desirable or undesirable if no property owners were allowed to choose to whom they rent?

3. Suppose two young males who have a reputation in the community for drug dealing and gang warfare wish to rent the duplex. Should the owner have the right to refuse to rent to them?

4. If you were asked to justify the non-discrimination principle, to what higher principle might you appeal?

The *values analysis* approach demands that critical thought be applied to value questions. Difficult as it may be, it it is not beyond the capabilities of students to begin to grasp some of the complexities of value reasoning. As Beck says:

> While value questions are indeed complex and subtle, they are not beyond the capacity of ordinary adults and children. In fact, we all solve hundreds, perhaps thousands of value problems quite successfully every day.[9]

Several questions can be raised about this approach: What role should emotions play in reasoning about value issues? What does one do in situations where, after applying the principle tests, there is still disagreement about the right thing to do? Is this approach appropriate in a multicultural society where there are different conceptions of what is morally correct?

ACTIVITY 18-F

Identify a value issue in a Social Studies curriculum guide or text. Do you think students will find it to be significant? Is it relevant to their lives? Ought it to be relevant? Do you think students are mature enough to make decisions about the issue? If there are activities for students to carry out or questions for them to answer that are meant to help them examine or resolve the issue, evaluate these. What approach do they seem to take? What assumptions are being made about the nature of values, how students learn them, and how value questions ought to be resolved? If there are no activities or questions, design some so that students can be helped to examine the issue and arrive at their own conclusions.

Despite the fact that all teachers are value educators, values education is a contentious issue in Canada. Few provinces have a well thought out policy or program. This is because, as with all curriculum decisions, politics is involved. Whatever stance a governing body takes seems to raise the ire of at least some people. Some parents do not want their children to be exposed to any form of values education, believing that it is the task of parents or the church to do this. Others want the schools to take a particular approach to values education. Teachers are caught in the middle. Yet values cannot be ignored, especially in Social Studies, where one of the major foci is on how people interact with one another. It is not enough to merely identify the values people hold and the things that influence people's interactions—we must also help students make rational decisions about actions that affect their lives and the lives of others. Issues of violence, environmental degradation, genetic engineering, sexism, and racism confront us all; we need to learn how to deal with them. This requires us to develop particular areas of knowledge, abilities, and dispositions. Coombs[10] has described the attainments of the morally educated person.

1. Knowledge of what one's society regards as morally right and wrong.

    Thinking about moral questions takes place in a society that has a moral code. Making moral judgments is more a matter of rethinking that moral code than it is of devising a completely new one. Thus, students need to know what the moral rules of the society are and why a system of public morality is necessary. Such knowledge is gained through teaching children that there are some values, such as not killing, deceiving, or lying,[11] which, *in the main*, are morally justifiable. Through activities that focus on the consequences of not having moral rules, children can realize that they are better off in a society that upholds such rules than one that does not. A further justification for this attainment is that we cannot stop every minute to consider the moral acceptability of our actions. Some value judgments have to be habitual.

2. Knowledge of moral concepts such as stealing, cheating, lying, prejudice, discrimination, equality, and so on.

    Concepts determine how we see a situation. If shoplifting isn't viewed as "stealing," then it is unlikely to be viewed as wrong. If a situation in which a person is denied something on the basis of race, gender, or religion is not perceived as "discrimination," then it is unlikely to be regarded as immoral.

3. Ability and inclination to apply principle tests to the rules and standards used in making moral judgments.

    This includes the ability to role-take (and this requires the disposition to empathize with others), to imagine the consequences if everyone who was likely to perform a particular action actually did so, and to have knowledge of what harms people, both physically and emotionally.

4. Ability and inclination to seek out all information relevant to a value question.

    Too often we make judgments based on either incomplete or false information. For example, in a discussion I held with a Grade 6 class, it was widely believed that shoplifting didn't harm anyone (the store owner had insurance, or wouldn't miss the item). These students did not realize that shoplifting created additional costs for the store owner, and ultimately to consumers. Thus, in tackling any value question, we need to collect information about the facts of the case, and about alternative solutions and the consequences of acting on them.

5. Resolution to do what one has decided is a right action, and to refrain from doing what one has decided is wrong.

   It is all very well to make decisions about what is right and wrong—we also have to act. Thus, we have to encourage students to participate in social action projects (see Chapter 20), and as teachers we have to create a classroom and school environment in which right actions are encouraged.

6. Ability to clarify personal values using appropriate *values clarification* activities.

   Many of the *values clarification* techniques encourage reflection on the values that are important to a person.[12] For example, the "Twenty Things You Love to Do" activity asks students to list things they love to do, and then separate them into those costing money, those done alone, those done five years ago, those done daily, weekly, monthly, or yearly, and so on. Reflecting on their list can give students insights into what they think is of value.

This list of attainments raises many questions about both theory and practice. You are advised to consult the bibliography for further guidance. All these attainments, however, are crucial when we focus on how to help students make decisions, the topic of the next chapter.

OTHER ACTIVITIES

I. State how you would apply one of the approaches to values education (*inculcation, values clarification, cognitive-developmental,* or *values analysis*) in the following situation.

   Jack is the star player on the school baseball team. It is mainly due to his pitching and batting that the team is in the league finals. The day before the championship game, Jack is showing off to his friends by swinging his bat around. He has been warned on two previous occasions not to do this, and he's been told he'll be punished if he's caught. Other members of Jack's class have also warned him about his bat swinging. But Jack is on top of the world because he's in the championship game. In swinging his bat around, he hits Bill on the head. Bill isn't too badly hurt, but he'll have a large bruise on his temple. The teacher sees the incident and immediately suspends Jack from the championship game. The team members circulate a petition asking the school principal to cancel Jack's suspension, allow him to play in the game, and give him some other punishment. Should Bill sign the petition?

NOTES

1. P. Superka, C. Ahrens, J. Hedstron, with L. Ford and P. Johnson, *Values Education Sourcebook* (Boulder, Colo.: Social Science Education Consortium, 1976).

2. S. Simon, L. Howe, and H. Kirschenbaum, *Values Clarification: A Handbook of Practical Strategies for Teachers and Students* (New York: Hart).

3. L. Raths, M. Harmin, and S. Simon, *Values and Teaching*, 2nd ed. (Columbus, Ohio: Charles E. Merrill, 1978).

4. Raths et al. *Values and Teaching*, p. 32.

5. L. Kohlberg, *The Psychology of Moral Development: The Nature and Validity of Moral Stages* (San Francisco: Harper and Row, 1984).

6. C. Gilligan, *In a Different Voice: Psychological Theory and Women's Development* (Cambridge, Mass.: Harvard University Press, 1977).

7. One of a series of dilemmas posed in *First Things: Values* (New York: Guidance Associates, 1979).

8. A rationale for these tests is developed in Association for Values Education and Research, *Value Reasoning Series* (Toronto: Ontario Institute for Studies in Education Press, 1979–1990).

9. C. Beck, *Better Schools: A Values Perspective* (New York: Falmer, 1990), p. 2.

10. Adapted from J. Coombs, "Attainments of the morally educated person," in D. Cochrane and M. Manley-Casimir, eds., *Development of Moral Reasoning: Practical Approaches* (New York: Praeger, 1980).

11. See B. Gert, *The Moral Rules* (New York: Harper and Row, 1966).

12. S. Simon et al., *Values Clarification*, pp. 30–34.

CHAPTER 19 Simulation games & decision-making

Students can begin to explore value questions involving decision-making in a variety of ways. One highly motivating technique is to use a simulation game in which significant value questions arise.

ACTIVITY 19-A

THE INCINERATOR SIMULATION

Play this in your class. On the map on the following page, designate a town lot for each member of the class. If there are fewer than thirty-six students, spread ownership over the entire map.

Background. The town of Actum, a small tourist resort, has a garbage problem. All the landfill sites outside the town limits are full, and garbage must now be disposed of within the town limits. The town has been granted federal money to build a garbage incinerator. The incinerator will have a 20 m chimney and will take up space equivalent to one house lot. The problem is where, within the town limits, to locate the incinerator. As there is no alternative to garbage disposal, the incinerator *must* be built.

Each individual should choose a site for the incinerator. Then hold a town meeting and decide where to locate the incinerator.

The following questions should be asked on completion of this simulation:

1. What influenced your choice for the site of the incinerator (wind direction, aesthetics, transport routes, proximity to houses, stores, parks, farmland)? What values did you appeal to? What point(s) of view did you adopt? Did prudential concerns outweigh concerns for the well-being of the community? What values are likely to be in conflict in this situation? Should what is best for the entire community override an individual's prudential interests?

2. How did the town decide (voting, compromise, total agreement of all concerned, being "ordered" by someone)? Would you want all similar decisions to be made in the same way?

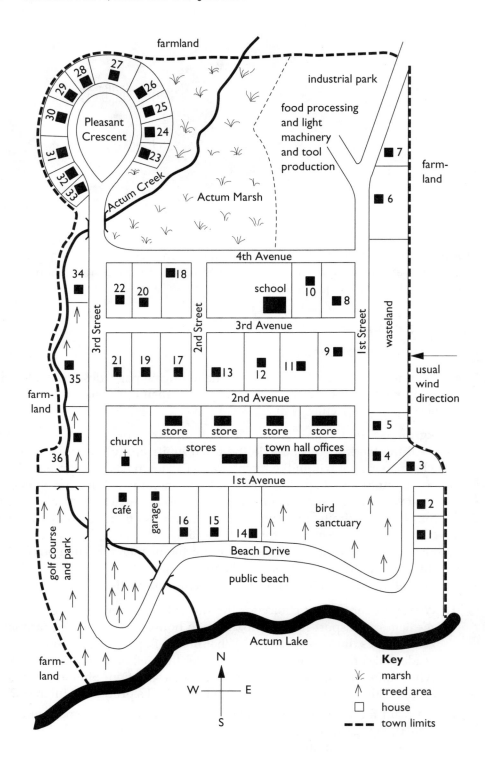

3. What is the best way to make such decisions? Is there any way such decisions can be made without disadvantaging someone? If we accept a democratic form of government, do we then have to accept the fact that we will not always have our wishes acted on?

4. If your choice was not accepted and the incinerator location is disadvantageous to you, how do you feel? As a member of a minority, could you do anything? Should you do something?

5. Should people get involved in planning their communities, or should they leave it to elected (or unelected) officials?

6. Do situations like this really occur? Where? How are they resolved?

Primary grade children can also play this game, but instead of a map, use a model of the community. The children can actually *see* the incinerator and, by moving it to different sites, *see* the consequences of their decisions. The game can be adapted for different situations: where to locate a new swimming pool, industry, park, store, firehall, community centre, ice rink, etc.

Most simulation games designed for elementary school students are found in journals. This means that it is unlikely that you will find them in publisher's catalogues, local resource centres, or the school library.

Before you have students engage in any simulation, consider the following:

What is the game problem?
What are the objectives?
What are the rules?
What roles do players have?
What procedures are used in the game?
What is the sequence of the game?
What moves are possible?
What are the consequences of the moves?
How many people can play?
How is an outcome reached?
What could be learned through playing this game?
How will this game realize curriculum-related knowledge, skills, and attitudes?
How could the game be modified to suit my students or make it appropriate for a
    different context?
What problems might be experienced in implementing the game in the classroom?
    How can it be organized so that possible discipline problems are avoided?

DESIGNING A SIMULATION GAME

1. Specify the objectives (e.g., knowledge of particular information, development of particular skills or attitudes).

2. Select a situation that fits into the topic you are teaching and involves a person or persons making a decision—e.g., a community group that has to

decide how a park ought to be developed, or a town that has to deal with high unemployment.

3. Analyze the situation into its constituent parts.

(a) What goals do the players have?

(b) What resources will be available to the players?

(c) What alternatives will be available to the players?

(d) What will be the consequences to the players of acting on particular alternatives?

(e) How will players decide what alternatives to act on?

(f) How will the players be informed of the consequence of acting on a particular alternative?

(g) If there is a group decision, what will be the interactions among the players? How will one person's actions affect other players?

4. What will the sequence be? How will the simulation conclude?

5. What external factors will be considered (i.e., factors outside the players' control that will affect the outcome)? Can chance factors be represented by throwing dice?

6. What materials will the simulation game require (role cards, a game board, paper money, worksheets, etc.)?

7. What will the rules of the game be?

8. How will you "debrief" the players? What sort of questions should be asked? How will connections be made between the game and real-life situations? Will emotions generated during the game have to be diffused? If so, how?

9. How will students be evaluated?

10. Does it "work?" When the simulation has been devised, test it. Then, if necessary, revise it. Try to ensure that it is easy to play and is as realistic as possible.

There are some possible pitfalls in the use of simulation games. If competition will win the game, then discussion should ensue on the justification for this. If the game is oversimplified, then students might get the impression that solutions are easy. If students can win by doing something immoral (such as taking resources away from another player), this should also be discussed. In simulations that involve role-playing, students may not take their roles seriously. And, as alluded to above, there may be discipline problems or occasions when there is a great deal of emotion involved; this will need diffusing. However, with careful planning and with adequate "debriefing" these pitfalls can be avoided. Simulations are a powerful way to teach particular content and skills, and foster certain positive attitudes. They are extremely motivating for most students.

In the preceding simulation game, you had to make a decision. You did this on the basis of the alternative sites available and an evaluation of the consequences of locating the incinerator at any particular site. These are the steps that you followed:

1. Definition of the problem.
2. Identification of alternatives.
3. Identification and evaluation of the consequences of acting on each alternative.
4. Making a decision.

In the first step, the decision-making situation is presented. This could be in print or pictorial form. It could arise from a current event or it could be an actual classroom or school situation—for example, What should the class do to celebrate Christmas/Hanukkah? How can fighting be stopped on the school playground? The situation has to be clarified so that students understand what the problem is. Terms may have to be defined and research may have to be carried out in order to comprehend the background to the problem.

To ensure that it is a *decision-making* situation, rather than one where a mere choice would suffice, the problem has to be significant to the decision-maker. Although the terms "choose" and "decide" are often used interchangeably, the term "decision-making" will refer in this book only to significant contexts where substantial thought is required. The distinction between "choose" and "decide" can be noted in the following sentences: The judge *chose* to sentence the accused to life imprisonment. The judge *decided* to sentence the accused to life imprisonment. In the latter, it is implied that the judge thought seriously before he or she acted, whereas the former could imply mere whim.

The second step involves the generation of alternative solutions. Sometimes there may only be two alternatives. This would be the case if someone were deciding whether to tear down or renovate a historical building, or deciding to do something rather than nothing. In other situations, there may be several alternatives, as is the case in the incinerator game.

Sometimes the alternatives will have to be generated by the decision-makers. For example, if you decide to have students make a decision about how to make the community a better place in which to live, it will be up to them to generate the alternatives.

In the third step, the consequences of each alternative are identified and evaluated. This will entail asking "What might happen if A is done?" and tracing possible consequences for both the short and long term. For instance, if one possible solution for making the community a better place in which to live is the building of a swimming pool, the short-term consequence may be that people will be happier, but, in the long term, taxes may be increased. In this case, a choice has to be made between personal pleasure and increased taxation. In the incinerator game, a student may have put prudential values (e.g., NIMBY—not in my backyard) ahead of consideration for the well-being of the entire community. Students have to be aware that the values they hold affect their decisions. They have to identify their own and others' values in order to begin to understand the roles values play in life.

The decision-making procedure is an extremely useful one in the study of current events. Students can identify the issues and conflicts that are germane to the event, find out what alternative courses of action are proposed, generate their own alternatives, determine what they think the consequences of acting on the various alternatives will be, and arrive at their own decisions. For example, students in schools in Vancouver are involved in making decisions about environmental issues and are taking practical actions to alleviate pollution and garbage problems. Some are taking direct political action by protesting the logging of British Columbia's old growth forests. In fact, this is one situation in which a simulation game can help students understand the issues.[1]

IDENTIFYING VALUES

How can we help students identify the values that they or others hold? One way is to use the following sort of activity.

ACTIVITY 19-B

1. What do you think is happening here?

If there is more than one interpretation, pose the following questions for each interpretation:

(a) How do you think the person feels?

(b) Would you feel this way if you were in this situation?

(c) Do you think the person likes feeling this way?

(d) What do you think is important to the person?

2. Create a chart to show responses. For example:

Feelings	Values
satisfaction	wealth
happy	happiness

3. If you hold a particular value, do you feel positive about it?

4. If you have a feeling, do you value it?

Feelings and values are linked. If you hold a value, then you have a positive feeling, but the reverse isn't necessarily true. You might have a feeling of anger, act on it, and then regret it because you really didn't think that anger was the appropriate reaction in this situation. Your immediate feelings overrode your usual judgments about the justification for being angry and what constitutes defensible behaviour in such situations.

Other ways can be used to help students identify values. For example, you could ask students to analyze their classroom situation and identify what is important in it (e.g., respect, safety, learning, kindness, competition, etc.). Or you could ask explicitly what students value, and compile a list of their values. If you decide to carry out this activity, be careful not to invade the students' right to privacy.

You could also use stories and have students identify the values that characters hold.

When studying cultural groups, students can note what values people hold by inferring them from what people do. Here, the focus should be on similarities, not differences. Rather than emphasizing the different ways people practise religious beliefs, we can focus on the way all cultures value some form of spirituality.

In using Social Studies textbooks, we can help students identify the values people hold or held: What motivated Canadian fur traders? Why did the English invade Quebec? Why did the French oppose the British?

When students have identified some of the values they hold and are aware of the values that should be considered in a particular decision-making situation, you should have them weigh the advantages and disadvantages of acting on any particular alternative. Pose problems where the class will have to decide whether prudential values should override social/moral values, and where they resolve conflicts in situations when acting on one alternative benefits some people but not others.

Here is a decision-making situation presented in a lesson plan format.

Tayreez has found a stray kitten. She takes it home and her parents tell her she can look after it while attempts to find the kitten's owner are made. After two weeks, the owner has not been located despite the fact that Tayreez has talked to the neighbours, placed advertisements in the local paper, and has put up signs around the neighbourhood. Now the family has to decide what to do with the kitten. Tayreez wishes to keep the kitten but her parents aren't sure. It'll cost money to keep, and when the family is away someone will have to look after it. Also, the kitten is always getting into trouble and has already damaged drapes in two rooms and made messes on the floor.

Objectives

1. The students should arrive at a decision using the following procedure: (a) define the problem, (b) generate alternatives, (c) identify the consequences of each alternative, (d) evaluate the consequences.

2. Students should consider the interests and feelings of the parents and of Tayreez.

3. Students should give defensible reasons for their decisions.

Tell students that they are going to help someone make a decision. Read the story and:

1. Identify the decision to be made by asking, "What has to be decided?" "Why?" Students might relate their own experiences with stray cats and tell the class what happened.

2. Ask, "What are some ways to solve this problem?" Students can list or draw alternatives, or a list can be put on the blackboard. This could be done individually, in groups, or as a whole class.

3. Ask, "What might happen if this (a particular alternative) were carried out?" "If that happened, what else might happen?"

It may be necessary to research answers to questions such as "What does the SPCA do with stray kittens?" or "How much does it cost to feed a kitten?" Focus here on how Tayreez would feel and how her parents might feel. Students could list or draw consequences of each alternative, or could make a chart:

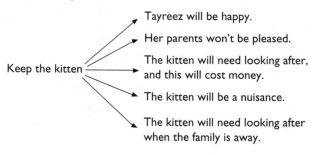

Keep the kitten
- Tayreez will be happy.
- Her parents won't be pleased.
- The kitten will need looking after, and this will cost money.
- The kitten will be a nuisance.
- The kitten will need looking after when the family is away.

Students should consider the consequences of each alternative and note how likely each is to occur—that is, if Tayreez cared for and trained the kitten, would her parents be less inclined to disapprove?

4. Ask which of the consequences are desirable, which are undesirable, and why. Students could place a check mark or "happy face" sign against those consequences deemed desirable. You may want them to rank order the consequences in order of desirability.

5. Ask, "What is the best thing to do?" Have students individually, or in groups, come to a decision and give the reasons for their choices.

Another effective technique for teaching decision-making is to engage students in role-playing, which allows students to explore alternative solutions. Here are the steps to follow:[2]

1. Present a decision-making situation and ask students how they would feel in this situation and what solutions are possible.

2. Select role-players who will play the participants in the situation. The rest of the class act as observers. They are given questions to focus their attention on the role-play (see below).

3. Have the role-players enact one possible solution. Ask the observers to evaluate the solution and generate other solutions.

4. Have the same role-players, or new ones, enact these other solutions.

5. Evaluate the activity. Did the role-players play their roles in realistic ways? Which is the best solution? Why?

Role-playing has several benefits. It helps students try out alternative behaviours in a safe context while avoiding "real-life" consequences. It gives them opportunities to express feelings that they might not otherwise express.

Great care has to be taken in role-playing, however. Decision situations should be carefully chosen. Unwilling children should not be forced to participate, and those who love "acting" should not be allowed to dominate. In role-play situations where negative behaviour is exhibited it is important to discuss with the class how they felt about it and the justification (if any) for it. But if role-playing is implemented in a pedagogically sound way, it can provide students with many insights into human behaviour and decision-making. Furthermore, students usually enjoy the activity.

Below is a simulation activity in which students take on the role of one of the people involved in a decision-making situation.

ACTIVITY 19-C

Grandma Smith lives by herself many miles away from her daughter's family home. Her daughter and son-in-law and their two children are unable to visit her very often. She is now incapable of looking after herself on a regular basis, and she cannot afford a private nurse or homemaker. Nor can her daughter's family afford to pay for such care. Grandma Smith could move into a senior citizens' home, but the family know that she will absolutely hate having to do this. The daughter suggests that the grandmother come to live with them. This will mean that one of the children will have to give up a private bedroom, as there are only three bedrooms in the house. There is no other space in the house where Grandma could stay. Grandma Smith does get a small pension, which is adequate to cover her immediate needs, but if her condition worsens, extra money will be required.

In groups of four, choose to play one of the following roles. Hold a family conference and arrive at a decision about whether or not Grandma Smith should move into the Smith home. The sex of the grandparent can be changed, as can that of the children.

In some cultural groups it is taken for granted that grandparents are looked after by their children and live with them. If the situation above is regarded as problematic, then change the situation to involve an elderly man who lives next door to the family. He is like a grandparent to the family. The house in which he lives has burnt down, and he will be forced to live in a senior citizens' home. He would absolutely hate to have to live there, so the family considers whether or not to invite him to live with them.

MR. JONES — He is opposed to the plan. He does not make much money and it is difficult for him to buy all the things he thinks the family needs. If Grandma Smith came to live with them and her condition worsened, he would not have enough money to pay for sporting equipment and music lessons for the children.

MS. SMITH — She wants to look after her mother. Her mother will be able to carry out some of the duties that Ms. Smith now performs, such as waiting at home for the children to return from school. She knows that it will not be easy to have an extra person in the house, but she thinks she has a duty to her mother in these circumstances.

MICHAEL JONES — He would have to give up his bedroom. He is not at all pleased about this: he likes his own space in which to keep his stuff and listen to the music he enjoys and which his brother dislikes. He thinks his grandmother should move into a senior citizens' home where she will be looked after. He is prepared to visit her frequently, as he gets on well with her.

DAVID JONES — He does not want to have to share his room with his brother, but he loves his grandmother a great deal and thinks the family ought to look after her. He thinks she will be able to help his mother and allow her more free time.

I. In your group, was there a majority position? If so, upon what was it based?

2. In your group, was there a minority position? Upon what was it based?

3. What "points of view" were used in your arguments? What "point of view" does each family member take? What values does each hold? In this case, should prudential values override moral ones? Do all children have a duty to look after their parents when they are old?

4. How did you arrive at a decision?

(a) By persuasion?

(b) By one member of the family giving orders to the rest of the family?

(c) By somebody acquiescing to the majority position?

(d) By voting?

What is the best way of reaching a decision in circumstances like these?

5. How did you feel when:

(a) your choice was the family choice?

(b) your choice was not the family choice?

6. If you disagree with the rest of the family about whether Grandma Smith should live with you, should you be forced to accept the decision? Why or why not?

7. Were there alternatives that could not be chosen because of the rules of the simulation? Would any of these alternatives be better than having Grandma Smith come to live with the family?

If you are teaching primary school students, you might want to engage them in the following decision-making situation. Read this story to them or, if possible, have students read it for themselves.

> Geraldine is Alice's best friend. One day Alice forgets to bring her lunch to school, and although Geraldine shares her lunch with Alice, Alice is still hungry. She asks Michelle, who has four chocolate bars, if she can have one of them. Michelle says, "No, I want them." When Michelle isn't looking, Alice takes two chocolate bars. She goes back to Geraldine and says, "I took Michelle's chocolate. She's greedy. She doesn't need four chocolate bars. Don't tell anyone." Michelle notices that her chocolate bars are missing, and tells the teacher. In class, the teacher says, "Someone has taken Michelle's chocolate bars. Does anyone know who took them?" Geraldine knows that Alice took them. Should she tell the teacher?

Now, ask the following questions:

1. "What is the problem?" – Students clarify the problem.

2. "In what ways could the problem be solved?" – Students list the alternatives.

3. "For any solution, who is worst off?" "What sort of harm could occur to this person?" – Students discuss the answers.

4. "If you were the worst off person, would it be right for you to take the proposed action?" – Students role-play the proposed solutions.

5. "What would be the consequences if everyone in a similar situation acted in this way?" – Students imagine the consequences and state what these are.

6. Students then write down their own solutions and justify them.

OTHER ACTIVITIES

1. Design a lesson plan using the decision-making procedure for a primary class. Choose an appropriate decision situation and outline how you would teach the lesson.

2. Critique the following lesson on decision-making and compare your critique to the one in the ANSWERS section.

TEACHER: Today, class, we're going to help someone make a decision. Please read the story and then we'll help Alice decide what to do. (*hands out the story to the class*)

Sharon is Alice's best friend. They walk to school together every day. They play together at recess; they roller-skate and go swimming together. Sometimes older kids tease Sharon, who wears a hearing aid because she can't hear very well. They make fun of her and whisper nasty things that she can't hear. This always upsets Sharon and that makes Alice angry. But Alice is not sure what to do when kids start teasing Sharon.

Alice's mother tells her to ignore the teasers and they'll soon stop.
Alice's father advises her to ask the teasers how they would feel if someone were teasing them.
Alice's sister tells her to go the school principal.
Alice's brother tells her he will beat up the kids who are teasing Sharon.

TEACHER: What's Alice's problem?

STUDENT: She has to decide whether to ignore the teasing or tell the principal about it.

TEACHER: Good. Now, let's consider what Alice could do. What are her alternatives? As I write them on the blackboard, I want you to copy them down in your notebooks.

STUDENT: She could get her brother to punch out the teasers.

STUDENT: She could ignore them.

TEACHER: O.K. Let's not have any more. Let's see what the consequences would be if she acted on either of these.

STUDENT: Her brother might get beaten up.

TEACHER: I don't think that will happen. Her brother is much bigger then the teasers. Anyway, it's not a good idea to beat up people.

STUDENT: Her teasers might stop if they knew her brother would beat them up.

TEACHER: Do you all agree?

CLASS: Yes.

TEACHER: Would that be a good consequence?

CLASS: Yes.

TEACHER: What if she ignored the problem?

STUDENT: The teasers would get fed up and stop.

STUDENT: No, they would just keep doing it.

TEACHER: Let's take a vote. Who thinks the teasers will stop teasing Sharon? (*ten hands go up*)

Who thinks they'll keep on teasing Sharon? (*fifteen hands are raised*)

So, we've decided that won't work. What should Alice do?

STUDENT: She should tell her teacher and get the teacher to stop it.

TEACHER: Yes, I think that would be a good idea. So, have we decided that Alice should talk to her teacher?

CLASS: Yes.

NOTES

1. For an example of a simulation concerning a logging issue, see V. Bowers and D. Swanson, *Exploring Canada: Learning from the Past, Looking to the Future* (Vancouver: Douglas and McIntyre Educational, 1985).

2. F. Shaftel and G. Shaftel, *Role Playing in the Curriculum*, 2nd ed. (Englewood Cliffs, N.J.: Prentice-Hall, 1982).

CHAPTER 20

Value issues in citizenship, multicultural, global, law-related, human rights & peace education

In this chapter, our concern is with various curriculum areas that are generally included in Social Studies: citizenship, multicultural, global, law-related, human rights, and peace education. All of these areas are fraught with significant value questions. Indeed, how each is conceptualized is a value question in itself. In the discussion on the nature and purposes of Social Studies (Chapters 1 and 2), the point was made that the way Social Studies is conceived depends, in large part, upon the judgments made about what students should learn. If we believe that students should memorize a multitude of facts about Canadian history, then what is done in Social Studies will be influenced by this belief. Similarly, if we think that a good citizen is someone who always obeys the law, then what is done in the name of citizenship education will be based on this belief.

Each of these curriculum areas rests on assumptions about how people ought to be treated. In multicultural education we are concerned with various ethnic or cultural groups in Canada; in global education our concern is with all of us on this planet. If the area is citizenship education, then we are concerned with how people should be governed, and how people ought to act either as citizens of Canada or as citizens of the world; and if our area is law, then our concern is the laws that should govern people's behaviour, who should create laws and enforce them, and what procedures should be used to resolve disputes. All of these are value questions. Although their resolution requires empirical information, information alone will not suffice .

This chapter introduces the various curriculum areas and outlines broad objectives for each. At the end of the chapter, you will find activities designed to meet these objectives. As you work through the chapter, you will notice that the boundaries between the curriculum areas under discussion are often quite flexible.

CITIZENSHIP EDUCATION

The primary focus in Canadian Social Studies is education for citizenship.[1] Citizenship consists not only of knowing how people are governed, or what the laws of the land are (the sorts of empirical questions dealt with in the first part of this book), it also involves decision-making. Citizenship confers a particular status on a person. It entitles that person to certain rights and privileges and, in turn, entails particular responsibilities.

Citizenship has to do with governance in the broad sense of the term. It is not just concerned with relationships between an individual and the federal, provincial, and municipal governments. Governance also is a matter of how people relate to one another in family, church, labour union, business, industry, recreational, and community organization settings.

It also has to do with classrooms. In all these settings, notions of rights, responsibilities, rules, authority, justice, and power arise. It is not enough to transmit knowledge about these concepts or to inform students about politics, government, law, and the norms of society. If we assume that people in a democracy have a right to make up their own minds, then students should be taught how to deal intelligently with a broad range of issues: whether money collected from a school fundraiser should be given to the Food Bank or spent on a class field trip; whether the government should give aid to other countries or to those in need in Canada; whom to vote for as class president; or whom to vote for in a municipal, provincial, or federal election.

ACTIVITY 20-A

Find out how your institution is governed. Who has decision-making power? Who is involved in decision-making? Who has ultimate power? Are you, as students/teachers, involved in any of the decision-making? Should you be? Is your institution governed according to democratic principles? Are you treated fairly?

In order to answer the above questions, you not only have to acquire and evaluate information, you also have to understand certain concepts—power and democracy, for example. You have to use decision-making procedures to arrive at conclusions about whether you should be involved in the governance of your institution and whether you are being treated fairly.

The following guidelines for citizenship education are suggested. Students should begin to:

1. Learn how to locate and use information about governance situations.
2. Acquire competency in decision-making.
3. Acquire competency in communicating effectively with decision-makers.
4. Know the main structures and functions of government.
5. Understand the function of laws.
6. Acquire competence in cooperating and working with formal and informal organizations involved in promoting one's personal interests and the interests of others.

Each of these goals has to be translated into appropriate objectives. For example, in a primary class, students can identify services provided by the government in their community. They can examine laws that directly impinge on their lives, such as traffic regulations, and they can become involved in decision-making situations in which their decisions are acted upon—choosing where to go on a field trip; deciding how to raise money for a particular school project; or deciding how to celebrate a special day (Canada Day, etc.).

Students might also be involved in "action" projects such as helping people in need, visiting people in hospitals, or collecting for charity.[2] They might even lobby for something—a crosswalk at a dangerous intersection near the school, or the better treatment of zoo animals (both actual cases in which elementary school students were involved). Note that there is sometimes controversy about whether or not students should be involved in social action projects like these. Student maturity, the level of student commitment to the action as a follow-up to their own decision, parental expectations, and institutional rules and regulations should all be carefully considered before embarking on such projects.

In the intermediate grades, students can begin to examine levels of government, how governments are formed, how representatives are elected, how government works, how the judicial system functions, and how laws are made and enforced. They can also come to understand concepts like justice, authority, rights, responsibilities, and freedom at a relatively sophisticated level.

Intermediate students should begin to study local, national, and world issues. Where feasible, they should become involved in events that are of import to them. If social action is not appropriate, students can at least be given the opportunity to make judgments about policy questions.

ACTIVITY 20-B

This activity could be used with elementary school students by changing the question to "What are the characteristics of a good elementary school citizen?" The activity, however, is for you, and the questions are: (1) What is a "good citizen"? (2) Is there a rule or law that covers the characteristics you identified in (1)? (For example, you may state that a good citizen should vote in elections, but there is no Canadian law that enforces voting.) (3) Whether there is a law/rule or not, should there be a law/rule? Why or why not? (4) If there is a law/rule, or you decide that there should be one, who should enforce it? (5) What should be the penalty for not upholding the law/rule? Why? (6) How do you intend to act on your beliefs about the characteristics of a good citizen? (7) Are these questions relevant to the other curriculum areas discussed in this chapter (e.g., multicultural, peace, or global education)?

MULTICULTURAL EDUCATION

Canada's population is ethnically and culturally diverse. In addition to the aboriginal peoples who were here when the French and English arrived, there have been large influxes of immigrants of European, Asian, and Indian origin. This diverse population has created both problems and opportunities for educational policymakers in Canada. Earlier in this century, the school's policy was to assimilate new immigrants into Canadian society. Immigrants were encouraged to cast off their cultural roots and live like "Canadians." The same Citizenship Transmission approach was used when aboriginal children were forced into residential schools. Fortunately, this extreme assimilation/citizenship approach is no longer viewed as justifiable. However, a certain degree of assimilation must take place if society is to operate; new immigrants have to accept the basic tenets of Canadian democracy and the ethical principles of the society.

All teachers must remember that multiculturalism is official government policy, and that discrimination on the basis of race or ethnicity is illegal. The aim in Canada is to

> recognize and promote the understanding that multiculturalism reflects the cultural and racial diversity of Canadian society and acknowledges the freedom of all members of Canadian society to preserve, enhance, and share their cultural heritage.[3]

And Section 15 of the Canadian Charter of Rights and Freedoms states:

> Every individual is equal before and under the law and has the right to equal protection and equal benefit of the law without discrimination and, in particular, without discrimination based on race, national or ethnic origin, colour, religion, sex, age, or mental or physical disability.[4]

With these policies in mind, educators have developed multicultural curricula (some of which include issues of sexism and/or are placed in a global education framework) and specific antiracist and antiprejudice programs for schools. Some educators differentiate between antiracist programs and multicultural education, with the latter focusing more on learning about cultures and celebrating cultural traditions, and the former aiming to help students understand the history and contemporary nature of discrimination, and the unequal social and power relations in institutions and in society in general; and to help students take personal or collective actions to redress inequitable practices. There is intense debate about which of the two approaches should be emphasized. In my view, there is no compelling evidence at present to favour one over the other. For purposes of this chapter, they are treated together.

In the Social Science approach to Social Studies, students look at multiculturalism through the lens of the disciplines. They learn about the various cultural groups that constitute Canada; about racism as a social phenomenon; about immigration and other government policies; and about how ethnic groups were treated in the past.

Another approach treats multiculturalism issues as topics for inquiry: students are taught how to tackle issues and how to reason about policy decisions.

Given that various approaches can be taken toward multicultural education, which approach(es) would you take?

Examine your answer by carrying out the following activity.

ACTIVITY 20-C

In the community in which you teach, there is an ethnic minority group. Members of the group have been living in the community for fifty years and have been attempting to maintain their ethnic identity. The majority of the population of the community is prejudiced against them, and there have been overt acts of discrimination and harassment. Your objective with your class is to attempt to reduce this prejudice. Which of the following would you emphasize? Why?

1. Teaching about the culture so that students realize that the group is very different from the majority.

2. Teaching about the culture to show that the group shares the same basic needs as all other people, but has different practices.

3. Teaching that many of the statements made about the group by members of the majority group are erroneous.

4. Teaching about the culture by going on a field trip to the area in which the group lives, so that students can have some actual experience of how the group lives.

5. Presenting cases in which the group was discriminated against.

6. Having students role-play members of the group—dressing up, eating their food, dancing, etc.

7. Having students read accounts of the life of the group, written by members of the group.

8. Teaching about the contribution the group has made to Canada.

9. Taking students to the museum to see artifacts used by the ethnic group in the past.

Notice that having information about this group is not enough to reduce the prejudice in the community. This is not to say that knowledge isn't necessary; it is to say that multicultural education must consist of more than teaching/learning information.

Although knowledge of cultures other than one's own can reduce prejudice,[5] it can also engender negative attitudes in students. If we take an outsider's perspective and compare our own culture to the culture being studied, we may emphasize differences rather than similarities, thereby creating an "us–them" mentality.

Even if an insider's perspective is taken in which an attempt to learn about the culture through the eyes of the participants, students may still judge the culture to be inferior. This perspective, however, does allow for a more realistic view. Members of the culture can recount their own version of their ideals and problems. Young children tend to judge negatively what is unfamiliar or what they find ambiguous, whereas information can help the unfamiliar become familiar and the ambiguous become clear. Children make mistakes when defining racial categories;[6] reliable information will help them create categories that are accurate and non-stereotypical. This explains why teaching about other ways of life and participating in the songs, dances, etc., of other cultures are worthwhile.

Another approach is to discuss cases of racism with students in an attempt to convey the message that racism is wrong. However, the message may not get through to students and, even if it does, students may be disinclined to accept it.

What then should be done? According to Aboud,[7] propositions about how children become prejudiced should guide the development of multicultural education programs. These are:

Propositions related to 4-to-7-year-olds.

1. Prejudice is based on a polarized and simple dichotomy of positive and negative emotions. Greater differentiation among emotions will reduce prejudice.

2. Prejudice is based on the egocentric judgment that only one way of experiencing the world is the right one. Learning that there are many ways of being right reduces prejudice.

Propositions related to 7-to-12-year-olds.

1. Judging people on the basis of internal rather then external criteria increases with age, and is inversely related to prejudice.

2. Attending to between-group similarities and within-group differences increases with age and is inversely related to prejudice.

3. Recognizing that one's own perspective may differ from another's, and that both perspectives can be valid, increases with age and facilitates the acceptance of ethnic differences.

Based on these propositions, you should encourage your young students to recognize a range of feelings and emotions. Show them that although feelings such as anger and happiness are universal, they affect different people in different ways. (For example, what makes one person happy can create feelings of dislike in another.) Children should be helped to realize that we can experience mixed emotions. One way to do this is to use examples from the students' lives, such as a best friend winning the race that you wanted to win, or being glad that you got a present from your aunt even though it was not exactly what you wanted. Make your students aware of other universal characteristics of people. All of us are vulnerable—we can all be injured or killed; all of us are fallible—we all can make mistakes; each of us has limited knowledge and skills; we each have conflicting desires and wants; and we all make choices. All students should be encouraged to look at people as individuals and judge on the basis of internal rather than external criteria. Let your students understand that there are as many differences within a group as there are between groups. (An example of how you might do this is described later in this chapter.) Encourage them to see that different ways of living can be perfectly acceptable.

All of Aboud's propositions have been applied in curriculum materials developed by Alternatives to Racism.[8]

Among the other guidelines proposed by the many educators working in the area of multicultural education are these:

1. Accentuate similarities rather than differences between people.

    The message to be conveyed here is not that we should all be treated the same in every respect and that any differences are aberrations. Rather, it is that we share fundamental characteristics, including certain rights, and that we all should be treated as "persons." A focus on the similarities between people can reduce children's tendency to negatively evaluate what is different.

2. Use cooperative learning groups in which there is an ethnic mix to foster positive attitudes toward members of those different ethnic groups.

    Research studies have indicated that cooperative learning can lead to the reduction of prejudice and the fostering of positive attitudes toward other cultures.[9]

3. Have students understand the nature of prejudice and discrimination.

    Students should understand that prejudice is a positive or negative attitude based on inadequate or erroneous evidence. Discrimination involves acting on prejudices so that individuals, or groups of people, are denied fair and equal treatment. These acts consist of physical attack, verbal hostility, avoidance, and unjust treatment. Ask students to identify examples of each of these types of behaviour and those against whom they are directed. Have students write a story about an act of discrimination, identifying the feelings experienced by the people involved. Use puppets to enact the story. (Using puppets encourages spontaneity. Children are more willing to express themselves freely with puppets because "the puppets" are doing the talking, not the students.)

4. Have students learn how to reason well about empirical, conceptual, and value matters.

    Value judgments made about other cultures are based on beliefs held about those cultures as well as the value standards held by students. Principle testing the value standards used by students (see Chapter 18) has been shown to reduce prejudicial attitudes.[10]

Avoiding mistakes in reasoning can help students avoid erroneous beliefs. In the next activity, state what fallacies are being committed. Check your responses in the ANSWERS section.

ACTIVITY 20-D

1. New immigrants are really hardworking. My next-door neighbour, who is a new immigrant, works from dawn to dusk seven days a week.

2. The unemployment rate is higher now than it was in 1960. As there are more immigrants now than there were in 1960, the high unemployment rate must be due to immigration.

3. In the past, the majority of immigrants came from Europe. Therefore, the majority of new immigrants should come from Europe.

4. In a recent poll, it was found that the majority of business executives thought that the secretary of state should cease giving money to ethnic groups for cultural activities. We must take these important people's views seriously and stop giving money to these groups.

5. Unless we stop all immigration, Canada's economy will crumble.

6. If we allow native peoples to govern themselves, then the Hutterites will want self-government, and soon every group will want self-government and Canada will cease to exist.

In classrooms where student self-esteem is fostered, where there is equality of opportunity, and where students are encouraged to judge others on the basis of internal rather than external characteristics, there is less likelihood of racism and prejudice. When an entire school is committed to the aims of multicultural education, and attempts are made to communicate effectively with minority parents and students, then those aims are more likely to be realized. This will entail teachers' and administrators' becoming knowledgeable about the beliefs, values, and sociolinguistic conventions of students in the school, and learning how best to communicate with them.[11] The school is a microcosm of the larger society. If students and teachers can bring about a "society" in which diversity is accepted within a unified and cohesive "nation," then many of the aims of Canadian multiculturalism will have been realized.

GLOBAL EDUCATION

ACTIVITY 20-E

In what ways are other nations involved in, or connected with, each of the following:

1. The room you are in now
2. The clothes you wear
3. The language you speak
4. The weather you are experiencing
5. The income tax you pay

6. The TV you watch

7. The requests you receive for charitable donations

8. The food you eat

As the world becomes increasingly interdependent, Social Studies educators have begun to aim for a global perspective in curricula. Although there is dispute about the definition of global education (some view it as a means to enhance people's ability to compete in a global economy, others perceive it as a stepping stone to world government, and some include human rights, multicultural, and environmental education under the global education umbrella[12]), most proponents emphasize the study of world history, world systems and institutions, world cultures, and world issues. Students are asked to consider themselves as world citizens. In order to bring this about, educators such as Kniep,[13] have proposed the following objectives:

1. Students should, through historical studies, understand the development of humankind, the rise and fall of civilizations and empires, and the causes of contemporary global problems.

At the elementary school level, students should be exposed to more than just the history of Canada or Western Europe—they should also study the history of other cultures, and look at events in one part of the world in the light of what was happening in other parts. For example, in studying the first European explorers of Canada, you should emphasize the events that led to these expeditions so that students begin to understand causation and interconnectedness. If students in Canada are constructing time lines of their own or other people's lives, they should also construct a time line showing what was occurring in other parts of the world.

2. Students should understand how Canada relates to the rest of the world, and how they themselves are a part of various global economic, political, technological, and ecological systems.

A start can be made by having students identify products they use that are of foreign origin, or a language they speak other than French or English, or a media or sports star they admire who is not Canadian. They can make a list of ten words that they use frequently and find out the derivation of the words. In the intermediate grades, they can begin to understand world geographical patterns (see Chapter 13), learn about international organizations such as the United Nations, and look at the provisions of the Universal Declaration of Human Rights and of the Declaration of the Rights of the Child.

3. Students should be aware of various world views—political, economic, spiritual, aesthetic, and moral.

Students in the primary grades can begin to understand that, although there are fundamental similarities among people, there are also some deep differences. Students in the intermediate grades can begin to look for world patterns by extending the topic they are studying to the rest of the world. For example, if students are studying a country that has a Muslim population, they should identify the key tenets of this faith and find out which other countries have Muslim populations.

4. Students should realize that their actions can contribute both to world problems and to their solutions.

There are several ways to show children how they contribute to world problems and to their solutions. One is to focus on development projects sponsored by Canada and supported by Canadians' charitable donations. Students could be given scenarios such as the following: You are _____ years old. You live in _____. You have no _____ (water supply close to where you live). How would you cope? What skills would you need to overcome the problem? Students could then suggest solutions. These need to be evaluated carefully; giving money to people or sending in foreign experts may not be the best course of action.

5. Students should avoid stereotyping other people and countries.

As we have seen, stereotyping can lead to prejudice and discrimination. To challenge student stereotypes, teachers have to first identify them. You can do this by asking students to write down what they think they know about a particular country or group of people. Where appropriate, students should then compare lists. Ask them where they acquired their information, and whether they think it is true. Then have students find evidence for their statements. If many students share the same beliefs, they could work together. When they have located evidence to support or reject their initial beliefs, they should present it to the rest of the class. Care should be exercised here. Teachers should first check that the students have not written racist or other derogatory stereotypes. If these are present, the teacher should question the student about the derivation of these stereotypes and attempt to persuade the students that they are not justifiable.

6. Students should understand "interdependence" as it relates to themselves and the physical and social world.

This requires teachers to draw relationships between the immediate world of the student and the rest of the planet. In the elementary grades, students can begin to compare their own families and communities with those in other countries, and begin to see that people share many common needs, goals, and problems. Students can also draw connections between themselves (the food they eat, and so on) and the rest of the world.

In the intermediate grades, you can discuss global issues and the role that Canada plays (and that students play) in international affairs. Through studies of other cultures, past and present, students can further develop such fundamental concepts as interdependence, change, conflict, scarcity, and culture.

One significant concept is "sustainable development." Although this has an accepted definition—it is usually explained as "development which meets the need of the present without compromising the ability of future generations to meet their own needs"[14]—what qualifies as sustainable development in any particular instance is often a matter of dispute. A basic introduction to the concept, however, is relatively straightforward. Students can be made aware that many of the world's ecosystems are in danger; that the world's population will probably double in fifty years' time; that 20 percent of the world's population consumes 80 percent of the world's goods; and that the gap between rich and poor nations is growing. This information can provide a background to the study of global issues and international development initiatives. In this regard, the Canadian International Development Agency (CIDA) has encouraged and funded a number of initiatives to implement global education in the schools. Eight provinces have their own programs, and two have Global Education Centres. Nearly all of them publish newsletters and curriculum materials. CIDA publishes *The Developing World Kit* and other materials free of charge. They are available from 200 Promenade du Portage, Hull, Quebec K8A 1G4. The Canadian Teacher's Federation (School Twinning Program, 110 Argyle Street, Ottawa K2P 1B5) has a program that matches classes in Canada with a partner class in a Third World country. In this way, students can have their own pen pals and perhaps gain insights into issues of development and interdependence.

The following sorts of activities will help realize the goals of global education.

1. Create webbing diagrams showing how students interact with one another and with other persons in the school. Do the same for the community in which students live, the country, and eventually the world. For an example, continue the chocolate bar diagram in Chapter 14, linking the various phenomena to the rest of the world.

2. Have students trace the origins of the food they eat, the clothes they wear, the toys they play with, etc. Show how all these are dependent on skilled workers, raw materials, transport, and so on (in effect, an economic system).

3. Have students trace the origins of the words they use. How many different languages are represented in the languages students speak in the school?

4. Examine social problems in Canada—e.g., pollution, poverty—and have students inquire into the roles various people, including themselves, will have to play if pollution or poverty is to be reduced.

5. Inquire into particular aspects of foreign aid and foreign development. How is Canada trying to help the less fortunate? Are these efforts worthwhile? Are they well designed? Are they working?

6. Inquire into particular situations in which Canadians are in need of help. Can students do anything to alleviate the suffering of their fellow citizens?

7. Examine a global problem—e.g., forest depletion—and have students inquire into the suggested causes and solutions. Can students be part of the solution? How? When choosing problems to study, remember that the objective is not to create the impression that students are powerless or that the problem is too complex to be resolved. Choose problems that provide a chance (if students

decide to take it) for some kind of action, even if it is only informing others about the problem.

In all of the above it is necessary to engender certain dispositions in students so that they move from a narrow, parochial viewpoint to a more global one. These dispositions include openmindedness, empathy, the inclination to look beyond simplistic accounts and solutions to complex problems, and the willingness to put aside (where appropriate) personal and national self-interest. These dispositions cannot be directly taught. They have to be modelled by teachers in the classroom and supported by the wider community.

LAW-RELATED EDUCATION

Given that Social Studies is concerned with the study of relationships among people and that many of these relationships are regulated by rules and laws, law-related education has an obvious part in the curriculum. The focus should extend beyond the *what* and *how* of specific laws, to include an understanding of *why* we have a particular system of law. In addition to specific content, such as statutes and regulations and how they are enacted, the court system, and the role of judges and the police, we need to study the very idea of law and the principles that lie behind it. This will entail understanding some basic legal/moral concepts such as authority, freedom, rights, and justice. How these concepts are defined and applied will help students see how a legal system is justified.

Understanding these issues will help students develop the ability to determine whether a particular action is an instance of the concept under consideration. Suppose we are concerned with the concept of justice. Suppose, further, that a student is accused of breaking a school rule. What would constitute justice in such a situation? Is the student given a fair hearing? Can the student call witnesses? Is the student deemed innocent and is it up to the "authorities" to prove guilt beyond a reasonable doubt, or is the student deemed guilty and the responsibility placed upon him or her to prove innocence? This type of reasoning is common to situations in which a decision has to be made about whether a particular action falls under a particular rule or concept. So, in baseball, was X a foul ball? In school, was Y a case of cheating?

The point of this type of activity is not to produce student lawyers. Rather, it is to help students understand our law-governed society and to reason about the complex conflicts and issues that face us all.

Law-related educational objectives can be realized not only through the direct teaching of law but also by applying a legal perspective to other Social Studies content. This can be carried out in numerous ways. Students can begin to:

1. Understand how rules and laws impinge on their lives in the classroom, the family, the community, in industry, in government, etc.

ACTIVITY 20-F

(a) What laws directly affect you as a pre-service teacher, or as a practising teacher?

(b) Are laws related to any of the following activities? If so, what laws are involved?

　　(i) Buying food at the supermarket

　　(ii) Mailing a letter

　　(iii) Having a meal at a restaurant

　　(iv) Walking a dog

　　(v) Buying clothing at a local store

　　(vi) Telephoning a friend

　　(vii) Driving a car or riding a bicycle

　　(viii) Watching TV

2. Understand how laws are made and what influence the public can have in making and changing laws.

3. Understand how the court system operates. Here, the use of mock trials is useful. Students can try Goldilocks for eating the bears' porridge; they will be assigned the different roles (the judge, jury, witnesses, defence lawyer, and so on) and act out the trial procedure.

4. Understand the role of the police, judiciary, legislators, and so on.

5. Understand what rights and freedoms Canadians have under the Canadian Charter of Rights and Freedoms.

6. Understand such concepts as human rights, authority, power, democracy, responsibility, freedom, justice, equality, and rules.

7. Realize that law is closely bound up with conceptions of morality, and that laws can be changed in response to changing public views of what is immoral.

You can help students realize these objectives through the following activities.

1. Play a game in which the rules are unclear or unfair or changed arbitrarily. Have the students sit in groups of five or six. Give one student in each group a ball. Tell the students that the first team to pass the ball around the group will win. Before any group completes this task, stop the game and tell the students that the ball must be passed with the left hand only. When group members complete this task, tell them that they are disqualified because they passed the ball clockwise (or anticlockwise). You can now add other rules that are unclear (pass the ball vigorously) or unfair (only students who are blue-eyed can play). By this time, the students will be thoroughly frustrated and a fruitful discussion about rules can be held.

2. Identify rules that directly impinge on students' lives. Identify the purpose of each rule. Ask what would happen if nobody obeyed the rule. Should there be any exceptions to the rule? Who should enforce the rule? Should there be some kind of penalty if the rule is broken? Who should decide the penalty?

ACTIVITY 20-G

Which of the following would be good classroom rules? Why? What purpose do they serve?

A. Nobody shall talk in class.

B. You should enjoy what you do in class.

C. Don't interrupt when someone is talking.

D. Keep your desk tidy.

(a) Could the purpose be better achieved by means other than a formal rule?

(b) What will be the effects of the rule?

(c) Identify the strengths and weaknesses of the rule:

   (i) Is it well designed?

   (ii) Is it understandable?

   (iii) Is it clear as to what is expected?

   (iv) Is it fair?

   (v) Is it designed to minimize infringement of important values?

3. Play a "desert island" game in which the class is marooned. You can decide what food and shelter are available, and what the landscape and climate are like. Have the class decide what they'll need to survive, how they will organize themselves, and what rules/laws they will need. Or give students a list of rules and have them decide which ones would be good rules—for example:

A. Females/males shall do all the cooking.

B. The strongest male/female will be the leader.

C. Everyone should be allowed to speak and vote on decisions that affect the whole society.

D. There shall be no stealing of other people's property.

E. The people who do the most work shall receive the most food.

Students could make up their own rules prior to any group discussion. Copies of the rules would be distributed to the class and these would form the basis for the decision-making activity. The rules could be compared to the rights listed in the Universal Declaration of Human Rights and in the Canadian Charter of Rights and Freedoms.

4. Give students situations in which a legal decision is required. In the following vignette, one student plays Nick, one student is Lorne, and the third is the

judge who has to make a decision. Nick and Lorne argue their cases to the judge. They use the following information:

- Nick lends ten comic books to Lorne.
- Lorne promises to return them in one week.
- Nick warns Lorne to take care of them.
- The comic books cost Nick $1 each.
- Lorne returns the comic books at the end of the week.
- Five comic books are torn and unreadable.
- Lorne says that his younger brother (age 3) took the comic books from his room and tore them up.
- Nick demands Lorne pay him $5 to replace the damaged comics.
- Lorne refuses to pay.

Based on this evidence the judge decides how this matter should be resolved.

5. When studying other nations/cultures, whether contemporary or in the past, have students find out about the legal system. For example, in studying ancient Babylon, Hammurabi's Code is a fascinating vehicle for discussion; it contains such laws as "If a man accuses a man, and charges him with murder but cannot convict him, the accuser shall be put to death."

6. Study laws that directly impinge on student's lives. Are they:

    (a) A means of social control over antisocial behaviour?

    (b) An effective means of resolving disputes?

    (c) A means of providing social benefits?

    (d) A means of providing guidance in daily social affairs?

7. It appears that quite young students differentiate between two kinds of rules: conventional mores (e.g., eating food with a knife and fork) and moral rules.[15] The former they view as conditional; the latter they view as absolute even if there is no law. To further develop this distinction, show pictures in which a social custom is displayed (e.g., shaking hands with someone), and ask, "Would it be all right to bow, to rub noses, to embrace when greeting someone?" Then show pictures of scenes in which a moral rule is violated (e.g., a child hitting another) and ask, "Would it be all right to do this even if there is no rule against it?"

HUMAN RIGHTS EDUCATION

The concept of human rights is involved implicitly or explicitly in all the curriculum areas discussed in this chapter. Citizenship is bound up with the rights accorded members of a nation state; multiculturalism with the rights of ethnic groups; law-related education with rights within a legal system; and global education with universal human rights.

While issues of human rights have been of concern for centuries, it was not until 1948 that the nations of the world, under the auspices of the United Nations, adopted a Universal Declaration of Human Rights. In this declaration, nations committed themselves to the advancement of such rights as equality, life, liberty, freedom of speech, education, and justice. Similarly, the UN Declaration of the Rights of the Child affirms that all children are entitled to such rights as "love and understanding and an atmosphere of affection and security, in the care and under the responsibility of their parents whenever possible," and "protection against all forms of neglect, cruelty and exploitation."

While these declarations have no legal force, the Universal Declaration of Human Rights has been influential. Its principles are evident in the Canadian Charter of Rights and Freedoms, which was entrenched in the Canadian constitution in 1982. However, knowing that the Universal Declaration of Human Rights exists and knowing that the Charter of Rights and Freedoms guarantees certain rights is not enough. Students need some understanding of why we have rights and what having certain rights entails. Thus, students should understand (1) the importance of human rights and the consequences of not having them; (2) the basic tenets of the Universal Declaration of Human Rights, the UN Declaration of the Rights of the Child, and the Canadian Charter of Rights and Freedoms; (3) the distinctions between types of rights—equality rights, language rights, religious rights; and (4) that having rights entails the responsibility to uphold the rights of others.

The study of children's rights is an ideal way to study contemporary issues. Because rights cross all realms of human experience and directly concern children as individuals and as members of a group, students can easily understand their importance.

In the primary classroom, activities that focus on basic human needs and goals, and the consequences of not being able to fulfil them, can help students begin to realize the import of human rights. (It is noteworthy that young children *do* think that there are rights to which all people are entitled.[16]) Cooperative learning activities can help students come to this realization and accept responsibility for upholding the rights of others. In the intermediate grades, students can begin a more formal examination of human rights documents and begin to consider the rights of minorities, the handicapped, and so on. They can begin to understand some of the complexities involved in resolving cases of discrimination. Students can also begin to consider foreign aid programs and how these are influenced by concerns for human rights. Further, they can begin to study problems within their own community and within Canada where human rights are at issue. In all cases, they should consider the ways in which people have acted to protect or gain human rights, and how people have organized programs to alleviate human suffering on a local, national, or international basis.

All this has to occur in a classroom where rights are respected. How teachers handle disagreements between students, discuss political issues, and react to students from backgrounds different from their own is crucial.

GENDER ISSUES

Sexism is a human rights issue. Issues of gender, therefore, have an important place in Social Studies. For too long females have been relegated to a minor role in Social Studies curricula. There has been some progress, but sexism still needs to be addressed. Elementary students can carry out a variety of activities on sex-role stereotyping and discrimination.

1. Have students state what they like and dislike about being a boy or girl. Compare their statements and have students identify which things, if any, could be changed. Are their likes and dislikes things that girls or boys are "supposed to" like? In the intermediate grades, have students pretend that they are parents and state what behaviours they would expect from their male and female children.

2. Give students the following sort of letter and have them answer it.

   Dear Abby,

   In my class, the girls get to set up the science experiments and supervise the use of the computers. We boys get to wipe tables and clean the sink. It should be the other way round. What should we do?

3. Provide students with pictures of various occupations and sports. Students should state whether males and females could be involved in these. If students say that only one sex can be involved, they usually make the claim that there is some difference between males and females that precludes the other sex from participating. Have students carry out some research and collect evidence about men and women engaged in non-traditional roles.

   Another idea is to ask students what they want to be when they are adults. Can both males and females occupy their chosen roles? Are there equal opportunities for both sexes to train for their chosen jobs? With primary school children, discuss who does what jobs in the home and whether both sexes can do the same jobs.

4. When discussing historical topics, ensure that the role of women is given equal consideration to that of men. Have students focus on the role of women in native cultures, in the first European settlements and all subsequent settlements, and in politics, the arts, and science. When there is a focus on famous women (see Kirman[17]), students could role-play an interview between the person and a student interviewer, or write a diary as if they were the person.

   An interesting historical topic is "costume." Have students find out what males and females wore at different times, the trends in fashion, how these were advertised, and what effects fashion had on how males and females portrayed themselves. For example, Victorian middle-class and upper-class women wore clothes that restricted their freedom of movement, but which demonstrated that they did not perform "menial" tasks. For further ideas, especially on how women have been treated in the curriculum, see Tetreault.[18]

When studying other cultures, look at clothing and relate it to how males and females view themselves, or are viewed by others. Why do men wear skirts in some cultures? Why do women wear trousers?

5. To help students understand the role played by the media in sex-role stereotyping, have students watch television programs and complete the following sort of chart.

ACTIVITY 20-H

Try this activity for yourself. Watch a couple of programs and complete the chart.

	Women	Men	Boys	Girls
1. Activities carried out • for fun				
• as work in the home				

(Table continues on next page.)

(Continued from previous page.)

	Women	Men	Boys	Girls
2. Occupations				
• Who was in charge?				
• Who needed help?				
3. What people worried about				
4. What decisions people made				

After watching the programs, what general statement can be made about how males and females are portrayed in television programs?

Ask your students to answer the following sorts of questions when they watch commercials:

(a) Whom was the product being sold to?

(b) Whom will the product help?

(c) Who was shown using it?

(d) Who was talking about the product?

(e) What activities were males and females shown doing?

(f) What message was conveyed about what males and females should be like?

(g) What values were seen to be important to males and females?

Students could also inquire into how cartoons portray males and females. Are women still viewed as being weaker and less intelligent then men? Do they have jobs? Do they make important decisions?

6. Primary students could discuss the portrayal of men and women in fairy stories and nursery rhymes. What do girls and boys do? Who is strong? Who is weak? Would the story be equally sensible if the roles were reversed—for example, a boy being scared by a spider? In the European version of Little Red Riding Hood, she has to be rescued from the wolf by the woodcutter. In the Chinese version, the female character, Lon Po Po, triumphs over the wolf. Teachers could read to students stories in which there are strong female characters, and ones in which girls perform roles once reserved for boys. Or students could make up a story in which traditional sex roles are reversed.

Sex roles are learned early in childhood and are reinforced by society. Telling children stories in which there is no sex-role stereotyping results in less sex stereotyping by children.[19]

Students need models. Therefore, the school must be conscious of its role and be careful not to perpetuate sex-role stereotyping. Teachers especially must be aware of the vital role they play in modelling non-sexist behaviour and fostering it in students. Teachers should ask themselves:

1. Whether or not they seat and group students by sex.

2. Whether they have different expectations for boys and girls.

3. Whether girls and boys are allowed to participate equally in all classroom and school activities.

4. Whether the roles of women in the curriculum are given equal consideration to those of men.

5. Whether there is a focus on non-traditional sex roles.

PEACE EDUCATION

Peace education takes on various guises. For some it concerns disarmament and the avoidance of war; for others it relates to conflict resolution in general. Peace may be seen as an ultimate goal or as a means to achieve human rights. Whatever conception is adopted, peace education should at least introduce students to the following sorts of questions:

1. What is (the student's) conception of peace?

2. How do other people conceive of peace?

3. What would be the benefits of peace?

4. Is preserving peace more important than fighting for liberty or security?

5. Is the use of force ever justified?

6. Can the use of force (in a particular situation) be avoided? How? Does playing with war toys or watching violent TV programs lead to aggression?

7. What causes wars? What are the effects of war?

8. Is a peaceful life possible without having basic human rights?

Students should not be required to give firm answers to all these questions, but rather encouraged to think about peace. The purpose of peace education is to produce students who are disposed to reflect upon this significant human concern. It is noteworthy that the most interest in war is demonstrated by boys in Grades 5 and 6. It is also this age group that shows the most tolerance of other people. This seeming paradox has yet to be explained, but it does suggest that boys at this age may be more disposed to reflect on issues of war and peace and how people ought to be treated.[20]

Classroom environment is as key a factor in peace education as it is in all education concerned with how people ought to be treated. If students work together cooperatively and are treated with respect, if conflicts are dealt with in appropriate ways, and if students are encouraged to discuss and to have input into classroom decisions, then it is much more likely that the objectives of peace education will begin to be realized.

ACTIVITIES

In the introduction to this chapter, it was pointed out that the boundaries between the curriculum areas discussed here are flexible. What is common to each is the question of how human beings ought to be treated. Whatever the specific objectives of citizenship, multicultural, global, law-related, human rights, and peace education, they are (or should be) concerned overall with helping students understand themselves and others in many different types of relationships. Students should, in particular, begin to learn how to reason well about value issues. Thus, the guidelines presented in the previous chapter are relevant to the activities proposed in the following sections.

A. Activities to help develop an understanding of self and others

1. Have students list their needs. What could they do without in order to survive? Extend the basic needs of food, shelter, water, and air to include basic human goals—freedom, security, wealth, self-respect, and pleasure. What would life be without these? Inquire into whether people in Canada and in other parts of the world can fulfil their needs and goals. What happens when they can't? To what degree do all people require freedom, and so on? To what extent do individual students require these human goals? Have students list what they are free to do and whether or not they want to pursue these freedoms. Have students list what they are not free to do and the reasons why. Ask students to identify constraints in their lives and discuss whether these constraints are justifiable. Can or should we do anything when people's needs and goals are not being met?

2. Have students identify what they share with all other people and what makes each individual unique.

ACTIVITY 20-1

Individually, prepare a list of such things as likes and dislikes, what you're good at, and what hobbies or interests you have. Identify your country of origin or the ethnic group(s) to which you belong. Share your list with someone from another country of origin/ethnic group, and with someone who is from your country of origin/ethnic group. Do you share anything with either person? Do you think that, if you're a member of some identifiable group, you will necessarily share the same characteristics? What characteristics are you likely to share? What characteristics might differ? Do you think that you and a member of a group to which you don't belong will necessarily share no common characteristics?

Children of about 3 years of age begin to be aware of racial and ethnic characteristics. The above type of activity can demonstrate that there are both within-group and between-group similarities and differences.

3. Young children believe (a) that in a particular situation, their emotions or feelings will be shared by others in the same situation; (b) that a particular facial expression can mean only one specific feeling; and (c) that mixed emotions cannot exist. To help students see that a particular situation can invoke different feelings in different people, show pictures of scenes, or have students discuss events in their own lives, and have students infer people's feelings—e.g., a birthday party where someone is crying (because of happiness or sadness?) or where parents are trying to show that they're not upset at the mess and noise the children are creating.

4. Students often tend to stereotype others. The realization that there are both within-group and between-group similarities and differences can help students avoid stereotyping, as can the following activities.

(a) Categorize people under a variety of labels to show that a member of a particular group can be classified in a number of ways.

(b) Where a stereotype does exist, show exceptions to that stereotype.

(c) As young children tend to sex-role stereotype at an early age, show students the options that are open to both males and females and ask, "Could this person look after children, be a truck driver, etc.?" This activity could be extended by showing pictures of people from various ethnic groups and pictures of people who are handicapped.

(d) Read stories to students in which sex-role stereotypes are challenged.

5. To demonstrate that people share certain universal characteristics, read folk tales, sing songs, and play games from other countries in order to show that all share the same sorts of themes.

6. To help students develop a positive self-concept, we can encourage, praise, listen to, respect, and accept student contributions. We can also carry out activities such as "Pride Time," in which students write about something they're proud of.[21]

B. Activities to help develop an understanding of value concepts

1. Concepts such as justice, equality, democracy, honesty, and so on are value-laden. How they are applied in particular contexts requires value questions to be answered. The type of activities outlined in Chapter 5 can help students clarify concepts; activities like the following can aid students in thinking about the value aspects of particular concepts.

In this activity, you present students with a problem in which the application of a particular concept is fundamental to its resolution.

ACTIVITY 20-J

Which of the following would qualify as an act of cheating? In which would the action be wrong?

(a) A looked at B's quiz and copied down B's answers.

(b) A happened to see the quiz on the teacher's desk and looked at the answers. When A did the quiz, A remembered the answers he'd seen.

(c) B told A that he'd seen the answers on the teacher's desk and told A the answers. A used what he'd been told to answer the quiz.

(d) To answer the quiz, A needed to remember where various countries were located. The teacher had forgotten to take the world map off the classroom wall. A used the map to answer the questions.

(e) By mistake, the teacher gave A a quiz sheet on which the answers were pencilled. A copied the pencilled answers, then erased them.

(f) A had missed a lot of school because of illness, but his parents insisted he do the quiz and do well on it, so A wrote the information needed to answer the quiz on a piece of paper that he hid up his sleeve. A then used this information to answer the quiz.

Is there intent to deceive in the above vignettes? Are all cases of cheating? If not, what attribute of "cheating" is missing?

2. If a student states that a clear case of a moral concept is X, then pose other relevant examples to see whether the student accepts these as being cases of X.

3. If a student accepts that a particular attribute of a value concept should apply, then use the Role Exchange and Universal Consequences tests to see if the student would abide by the decision. For example, if the students say that it would be fair to hit someone who hit them (i.e., fairness is defined as "an eye for an eye"), then ask whether the consequences of holding this concept of fairness would be acceptable in all cases, and whether they would be willing to accept it if they were the initial hitters.

OTHER ACTIVITIES

1. Design an activity that would help students clarify a particular moral concept such as fairness. Create cases in which the concept might or might not apply, so that students are encouraged to discuss what constitutes fairness in any particular case.

2. Create activities to realize the following objectives:

(a) Students should recognize that a right entails a responsibility.

(b) Students should participate in a social action project to help alleviate human suffering.

(c) Students should understand that there can be conflicting points of view on any issue.

(d) Students should participate in the formulation of classroom rules.

(e) Students should be able to give an example of sex-role stereotyping and suggest ways of avoiding the stereotype.

NOTES

1. V. Masemann, "The current status of teaching about citizenship in Canadian elementary schools," in K. McLeod, ed., *Canada and Citizenship Education* (Toronto: Canadian Education Association, 1989).

2. C. Chamberlin, "Citizenship as the goal of social studies: Passive knower or active doer," *Canadian Social Studies* 26:1 (1991), 23–26.

3. From Bill C-93, An Act for the Preservation and Enhancement of Multiculturalism in Canada, House of Commons, July 12, 1988.

4. Canadian Charter of Rights and Freedoms, Constitution Act, 1982.

5. J. Banks, "Multicultural education: Its effects on students' racial and gender role attitudes," in J. Shaver, ed., *Handbook of Research on Social Studies Teaching and Learning* (New York: Macmillan, 1991).

6. N. Wyner and E. Farquhar, "Cognitive, emotional and social development. Early childhood social studies," in J. Shaver, ed., *Handbook of Research on Social Studies Teaching and Learning* (New York: Macmillan, 1991).

7. F. Aboud, *Children and Prejudice* (Oxford: Blackwell, 1988).

8. These include: *Alternatives to Racism, New Friends* (1984); V. Bowers and D. Swanson, *More Than Meets the Eye* (1989); V. Rogers, *All the Colours of the Rainbow: A Multicultural Storybook* (1990); and V. Rogers, *Apple's Not the Only Pie: A Multicultural Storybook* (1990). All have accompanying teachers' guides and all are available from Pacific Educational Press, University of British Columbia, Vancouver, B.C. V6T 1Z4.

9. J. Banks, "Multicultural education," p. 461.

10. J. Kehoe and F. Echols, "Educational approaches for combatting prejudice and racism," in S. Shapson and V. D'Oyley, eds., *Bilingual and Multicultural Education: Canadian Perspectives* (Avon, England: Multilingual Matters, 1984).

11. J. Kehoe, A *Handbook for Enhancing the Multicultural Climate of the School* (Vancouver: Pacific Educational Press, 1983).

12. W. Werner, "Whither global education?" *Canadian Social Studies* 27:2 (1993).

13. W. Kniep, "Social Studies within a global education," *Social Education* 53:6 (1989), 399–403.

14. D. Roche, "The impact of sustainable development on development education," *Institute Newsletter,* Institute for the Humanities, Simon Fraser University, 5:1 (1992), 15-17.

15. L. Nucci, "Conceptual development in the moral and conventional domains: Implications for values education," *Review of Educational Research* 52 (1982), 93–122.

16. L. Stone, "Intercultural and multicultural education," in V. Atwood, ed., *Elementary Social Studies: Research as Guide to Practice* (Washington, D.C.: National Council for the Social Studies, 1986).

17. J. Kirman, "Women's rights in Canada: A sample unit using biographies and autobiographies in teaching history chronologically," *Social Education* 54:1 (1990), 39–42.

18. M. Tetreault, "Rethinking women, gender, and the Social Studies," *Social Education* 51:3 (1987), 170–79.

19. J. Banks, "Multicultural education," p. 465.

20. L. Stone, "Intercultural and cultural education," p. 36.

21. J. Canfield and H. Wells, *100 Ways to Enhance Self Concept in the Classroom* (Englewood Cliffs, N.J.: Prentice-Hall, 1976).

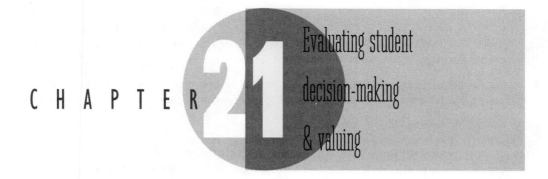

CHAPTER 21

Evaluating student decision-making & valuing

In Chapter 15, several different evaluation procedures were discussed. All of them can be used to evaluate students in the areas of decision-making and valuing. For example, you can test steps in the decision-making procedure using a variety of methods ·with which you are already familiar.

I. The first step—clarification of the problem—could be evaluated using the following sort of item:

On Saturday, Judy has been invited to (1) attend a birthday party, (2) go swimming, and (3) go to a movie. She doesn't have time to do all three, and doesn't like swimming. What is Judy's problem?

Another item could consist of a vignette in which students have to identify the decision that has to be made.

Your class has decided to have a bake sale next Thursday. Everyone has offered to do something to help with the sale. Which of the following is the most important decision that has to be made next?

_____ when to have the bake sale

_____ who will buy the food at the sale

_____ whether you want to have a bake sale

_____ who will bring what food to sell

ACTIVITY 21-A

Create at least one test item that would test students' ability to clarify the potential problems of "latchkey" children (children whose parent[s] are not at home when they leave for school and/or are not at home when they return from school).

2. To test for student competency in generating alternatives, students can be presented with a particular event and asked to list as many alternatives as possible. Alternatives can be judged on the basis of quantity and plausibility. Here is an example:

Your baseball team needs new uniforms, but the team has no money. List as many ways as you can think of to get the money to buy new uniforms.

ACTIVITY 21-B

Create at least one test item to determine how well students can generate alternatives for solving one of the following problems: (a) too much traffic in the downtown area; (b) fighting on the school playground; (c) girls not being involved in after-school baseball because the boys make fun of them; (d) homelessness in the community.

3. The following sorts of items might be used to evaluate student ability in identifying consequences.

(a) You have a decide what to do in the summer. On the left is a list of choices. On the right is a list of things you might gain from each choice. Match each choice with its *most likely* gain.

Choices	Gains
Taking swimming lessons	Rest
Getting a baby-sitting job	A healthier body
Taking art classes	Money
Relaxing at home	New skills

(b) List as many consequences as you can of the following event:

If the Great Lakes dried up _____.

ACTIVITY 21-C

Create at least one test item to determine if students can identify the consequences of acting on the proposed courses of action in the following situation:

In order to make it safer for students to cross a busy intersection, the following proposals have been made: (1) to hire a crossing guard; (2) to build an overpass or underpass; (3) to put in traffic lights; (4) to put up warning signs for motorists; (5) to give all students instructions on how to cross the road safely.

4. These sorts of items are fairly straightforward, and good answers are not too difficult to determine. However, the criteria for determining good answers to value questions are sometimes more difficult. This does not mean that students' reasoning, or the products of their reasoning, cannot or should not be

evaluated. The following sort of "test" can be administered and the teacher can use the criteria outlined below to evaluate student responses.

A vignette is presented in which someone has to make a decision that concerns other people. The following questions are then posed:

(a) What decision ought you to make?

(b) What, if any, would be the benefits to you?

(c) What, if any, would be the disadvantages to you?

(d) What, if any, would be the benefits to the others involved?

(e) What, if any, would be the disadvantages to the others?

(f) If you were the disadvantaged person, would it be right to act on the decision? Why or why not?

(g) Here is a similar case _____.
Would you make the same decision in this case? Why or why not?

(h) Would you want everyone to make the same decision in this case? Why or why not?

Evaluation of responses should be based on the following criteria. (1) Students can identify the consequences to themselves and others. (2) Students have fairly clear ideas of what is in their own best interest. (3) Students are able to put themselves in the shoes of the other person and consider that person's needs, interests, and feelings. (4) Students are able to judge the universal consequences of their decisions. (5) Students are able to consider other similar cases and state why their decision applies or does not apply in the new cases. (6) Students are willing, where appropriate, to put aside prudential concerns and make decisions that do not harm others. (7) In group decision-making sessions, students are willing to seek advice and consider the views of others in the group.

Here is an example that incorporates many of the questions posed above.[1]

> In the town of Actum there is an downtown area that contains many heritage houses. The town council is approached by a developer who wants to build a much-needed shopping centre that will revitalize the downtown area. If the shopping centre is built, the business community will be delighted. But the people who live in the heritage houses do not wish to move.

1. If the shopping centre is built, what problem would this cause?

(a) There would be too many shops.

(b) People would lose their homes.

(c) There would be too many people in the downtown area.

2. If the shopping centre is built, who will be most disadvantaged?

(a) The people who live in the heritage houses.

(b) The developer.

(c) The shoppers.

3. If the shopping centre were built, how would you feel if you were one of the people who lived in the heritage houses?

(a) Happy because you would get a new house.

(b) Unhappy because you did not want to move.

(c) Happy because you would have more stores to shop in.

(d) Unhappy because you like the furniture in your house.

4. What is the best way to make the decision?

(a) Let everyone in the town decide.

(b) Let the developer decide.

(c) Let the business people decide.

You could then pose other questions about alternative solutions to this problem, and about the best solution, and ask students whether their decision would be different if the facts of the case were different. For example:

5. Suppose the heritage houses were the only examples left in Canada of this type of house. Would this make a difference to your decision?

You can use this sort of item as the basis for a performance or authentic assessment. Listen to a group of students and keep a record of their deliberations as they try to resolve the problem. Place particular emphasis on how well they define the problem, generate alternatives and consequences for proposed actions, and argue for a particular solution. In the intermediate grades, students could write a letter to the editor of their local newspaper stating how they would resolve the issue. Evaluate the letter using the criteria outlined above.

ACTIVITY 21-D

This test is for you.[2] It is designed to assess how well you would lead a class discussion on a value issue. For each example, decide which is the best question to ask.

1. TEACHER: Students shouldn't take school paper home for their personal use.

STUDENT: Well, our parents pay for it, so why shouldn't we?

What should you (as teacher) say?

(a) Let's take a vote. Who agrees with that and who doesn't?

(b) How many of you take paper home for your personal use?

(c) What would happen if the principal caught you?

(d) Your parents also help pay for the video machines.

Should you take them home for your personal use?

2. TEACHER: Should you help other people even if it inconveniences you? Suppose a person in a wheelchair needs help getting the chair into a building and you are in a rush to get to a movie. Should you help?
STUDENT: No, the person in the wheelchair shouldn't go places where it is difficult for wheelchairs.

What should you (as teacher) say?

(a) Would you think it was right if nobody helped you if you were in a wheelchair?

(b) Should there be laws to make all buildings wheelchair accessible?

(c) Would *you* help? (*to another student*)

3. TEACHER: Don't walk on the running track. It's against the school rules.
STUDENT: But what harm does it do if I walk on the track?

What should you (as teacher) say?

(a) I'm telling you it's against the rules.

(b) But what would happen if everyone did that?

(c) Are you saying it's not against school rules?

(d) How would you feel if you were me?

4. TEACHER: Should we allow more refugees into Canada?
STUDENT: They would take jobs away from Canadians.

What should you (as teacher) say?

(a) Have you any evidence for saying that?

(b) Does it matter if they take jobs away from Canadians?

(c) Do you all agree that they take jobs away from Canadians?

(d) Do you have any other reasons?

5. TEACHER: Is it fair that Derek chose Alex for the team, and not Ian, even though Ian is the better player?
STUDENT. Yes, because Alex is Derek's brother and Alex would be upset if he wasn't chosen.

What would you (as teacher) say?

(a) Do you think Ian is the better player?

(b) Ian, do you think it's fair?

(c) Alex, do you think it's fair?

(d) Suppose Derek was in charge of surgery at a hospital and chose his brother to perform an operation, even though another doctor was a much better surgeon. Would this be right?

Wherever judgments are made, attitudes will be brought into play. As teachers, we may wish to find out what attitudes students have toward something, and we might want to change students' attitudes. The following types of attitude measures should not be used to *evaluate* students. They should be used to (1) find out what individuals think, so that what is taught takes into account students' attitudes, and (2) discover whether attitudes change over time. Attitude measures are administered in a pre-test/post-test format. They should be anonymous, so that students will be more likely to divulge their true feelings than write what they think the teacher wants them to write.

Here are some examples of ways in which student attitudes can be determined.

1. On meeting a uniformed member of the police force, I feel:

2. Members of the police force are friendly.

Strongly Agree	Agree	Don't Know	Disagree	Strongly Disagree
☐	☐	☐	☐	☐

3. Members of the police force are:

Bad	_____	Good	_____
Hardworking	_____	Lazy	_____
Stupid	_____	Clever	_____
Brave	_____	Cowardly	_____

4. Circle the words that tell what you feel about the police force:

interesting	worthwhile	necessary
important	exciting	dull

5. If you were to study the police force, what topics would interest you? Put a 1 against your first choice, 2 against your second, and so on.

Police Dog Handling and Training	_____
Police Cars	_____
How the Police Are Trained	_____
A Typical Day in the Life of a Police Officer	_____
Crimefighting	_____

6. When I see a member of the police force I think _____

_____.

ACTIVITY 21-E

Create an instrument to determine students' attitudes toward one of the following: the study of Canadian history or geography; gun laws in Canada; recycling; violence on television.

One other evaluation technique is to observe students' behaviours. Here we infer students' motivations, feelings, and attitudes from their speech and behaviour and note them down, either as anecdotal records or on a checklist. However, we must remember that what is in students' minds cannot be accurately identified by observing their actions. For example, it may be a mistake to infer that students are staying after class to work on a project because they have positive attitudes toward their work. They may be staying late to impress the teacher; or because they're afraid of getting a poor grade; or because they have nothing better to do; or because they are "latchkey" children who do not wish to be at home on their own before a parent returns.

OTHER ACTIVITIES

1. How would you ascertain the attitudes of Grade 6 students toward the Canadian government's immigration policy?

2. How would you evaluate the ability of Grade 1 students to make decisions?

3. How would you determine if Grade 3 students can put themselves into another person's role?

NOTES

1. Adapted from C. Bognar and W. Cassidy, *Social Studies in British Columbia: Technical Report of the 1989 Social Studies Assessment* (Victoria, B.C.: Assessment, Examinations and Reporting Branch of the Ministry of Education, 1991).

2. Adapted from the work of the Association for Values Education and Research, University of British Columbia.

PART 4

Unit Planning

C H A P T E R 22 Writing a unit plan

RATIONALE & SCOPE

In this last chapter, we synthesize all the material covered in previous chapters into a unit plan. To begin the task of unit planning:

1. Choose a grade level/class. Answer the following questions.

(a) What does the curriculum guide suggest that students at this grade level or in this class should learn?

(b) Do you think this would be relevant, interesting, significant, and worthwhile?

(c) Would it be within the students' capabilities?

(d) If the curriculum guide allows you to choose your own topic, is there a skill/sensitivity/concept/problem/generalization that seems especially relevant to you and/or your students—for example, a current event? If there is, can you give positive answers to questions (b) and (c) above?

2. Having chosen the topic, write down some good reasons for teaching it. You may think of other reasons as your planning becomes more specific. This is to be expected, as unit planning is not linear but interactive. Here is an example for a Grade 2 unit on the community.

EXAMPLE

Topic: The Community.   *Grade 2*.

Rationale. The curriculum guide suggests this be studied in Grade 2. Given that students interact constantly with the community, it is a significant topic. The community provides opportunities for students to learn about the interactions of people and people's interactions with the environment. This knowledge can then be built upon in later grades when students learn about other communities in the world. Students can begin to realize that a community is a microcosm of the wider world and that the concept of interdependence applies in all contexts. A community study can provide the concrete experiences that young students require. Further, a variety of skills can be developed—simple mapping, graphing, interviewing, and so on. All these skills are significant in the further pursuit of Social Studies goals and in everyday life. Resource materials are easily found in the community.

3. How can the chosen topic be broken down into subtopics?

◖EXAMPLE

Topic:

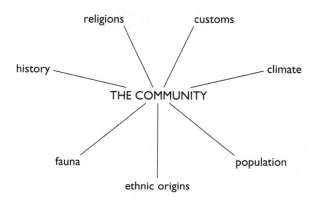

religions   customs

history ————   —— climate

THE COMMUNITY

fauna   population

ethnic origins

4. It may be impossible to study all these subtopics, so a decision has to be made about which one(s) will be included in your unit. Rather than trying to cover everything, thereby creating a kind of "trivial pursuits" unit, choose a focus— e.g., a study of change in the community; a particular community problem; how the concept of interdependence relates to the community; how the behaviours of community members are influenced by customs, rules, laws, and so on.

When you have identified a focus, then a rationale has to be provided for it. Of course, if you have chosen a particular focus at the outset, then you will have already provided a rationale and your next task is to present a rationale for the instrumental content you are using to exemplify your focus. For example, if you decide to tackle "multiculturalism" or "pollution," you have to decide what content is suitable for your particular grade level. If you were to select "change" as your focus, your rationale might look like the following:

◖EXAMPLE

Topic: Change.   *Grade 2*.

Rationale. Change is constant, and students should begin to consider how and why change occurs and what influence they can have on the process of change in particular contexts. Students experience change in themselves (in growth, in learning, in how they behave) and in their community (new buildings, more pollution, etc.). Both contexts are suitable vehicles for this age group to begin to comprehend the concept of change.

Now choose the content that will exemplify your focus.

EXAMPLE

Topic: Change in the Community.   *Grade 2*.

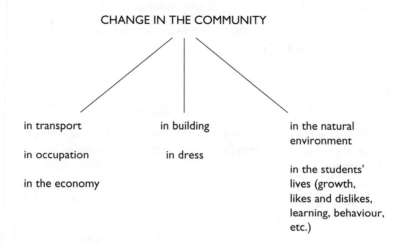

CHANGE IN THE COMMUNITY

in transport   in building   in the natural environment

in occupation   in dress

in the economy   in the students' lives (growth, likes and dislikes, learning, behaviour, etc.)

Your choices will also be determined by time constraints and by the availability of resources. They may also be influenced by what is being studied in other subject areas. You may decide to integrate what you intend to do in Social Studies with other subject areas. Because there are no scientific formulae for designing units, you have to use your judgment.

5. What follows is an example of a unit plan in which the focus is on *interdependence* and the ways in which "rules" often define the roles we play and the ways in which we relate to others. By "rules" we mean the customary behaviours that are culturally observed but not enforced (such as shaking hands when meeting someone); rules that are enforced by authorities (e.g., school rules, community regulations, and laws); and rules that relate to subject areas (such as grammatical rules, mathematical rules, and so on).

   Related to the concept of rules is "responsibility." People in interdependent relationships are responsible for upholding the rules that pertain to their roles. For instance, we as teachers are not legally bound to comfort students who are upset, but it is a customary rule that we do so.

EXAMPLE

Topic: Community Interdependence and Rules.   *Grade 2*.

Interdependence is a key concept in Social Studies and can be explored by studying the interactions between the student and the community. By studying interdependence, students can see how their actions affect others and how the actions of others affect them. This knowledge will help them realize the interdependent and interconnected nature of the world and how they can help (or hinder) progress toward a better world. Insofar as communities are rule-governed, the influence of rules on community interdependence will be explored. This understanding will lead to greater student insight into how people interact and will eventually help students evaluate the customs, regulations, and laws that impinge on their lives.

Having settled on the topic of "Community Interdependence and Rules," we then have to choose the content and provide reasons for our choices.

EXAMPLE

Topic: Community Interdependence and Rules. *Grade 2*.

Because the school is a major focus and the teacher an important person in the students' lives, one example of interdependence will be a study of the interactions between the student, the teacher, and the wider community. Schools are rule-governed institutions, so the effects of rules on student/school interactions can be explored. The knowledge gained can be extended by studying the police force—e.g., how police officers relate to the wider community and their role in enforcing the law.

6. Now that it is clear what students are to study, some objectives should come to mind. List the objectives even if they are somewhat vague at this stage.

EXAMPLE

(a) Students will be able to describe the jobs of teachers and police officers.

(b) Students will be able to state why these jobs are important to the community.

(c) Students will be able to give examples of interdependence.

(d) Students will be able to state how different kinds of rules affect community life and how rules relate to interdependence.

7. These broad objectives need to be analyzed so that specific ideas about what to teach and how to teach are noted.

EXAMPLE

Police Force: what laws they uphold; how they attempt to prevent crime; what jobs they do—traffic control, investigating crimes, attending court to give evidence, etc.

Activities. Have a police officer come to the school to answer student questions. Draw police officers performing specific tasks. Make a mural showing the tasks the police perform. Set up a vocabulary list of words related to the police. Produce a chart showing how the police help students. Role-play what would happen if there were no police. Collect pictures of police. Produce a graph showing amount of time spent by police on various tasks per day. Create a map showing routes patrolled by police. List the rules affecting students that are enforced by police.

8. When choices have been made, objectives can be stated in more specific terms. If the objective is to learn about the tasks police officers perform, the objective can be stated thus: "The student will correctly name tasks performed by police officers." The next section is designed to help you write clear objectives.

WRITING CLEAR OBJECTIVES

Suppose your topic is the history of the local community. You might write the objective as "Students will know about the history of the community," but this is too vague to be useful. If the objective is unclear, then so too will be your evaluation of student learning. Thus, teachers need to specify objectives as clearly as possible.

ACTIVITY 22-A

From the objectives below, identify the ones that are clearly stated.

(a) The student will really understand the history of the Riel Rebellion.

(b) The student will write a three-page essay on the life of Jacques Cartier.

(c) The student will correctly write a definition of the term "gillnetter."

(d) The student will interpret a map.

(e) The student, when given a map, will be able to measure accurately the distance between two points.

(f) When given the name of a country, the student will identify the capital city of that country.

(g) The student will know capital cities.

Clear objectives use verbs such as list, identify, draw, explain, define, model, measure, and solve. They derive from the broad aims of the unit and are statements of value judgments about what students should learn.

ACTIVITY 22-B

Your objective is:

(a) Students will know about New Brunswick. Make up three specific objectives that would relate to "knowing about New Brunswick."

(b) Students will understand the economic impact of the St. Lawrence Seaway on the provinces of Quebec and Ontario. State three specific objectives that would help realize this objective.

Having identified knowledge objectives, the next task is to determine the skills necessary to attain the knowledge objectives. For example, if the student is to use an atlas to find the distance between Montreal and Paris, she or he must locate the appropriate map (use the index and reference system to find Montreal and Paris) and use the map scale and a suitable measuring instrument to ascertain the distance between the two cities.

ACTIVITY 22-C

For each of the following objectives, identify the skills and abilities that the student would be practising/learning.

OBJECTIVE: Using floor plans and pictures of a Roman villa, the student will write a description of the villa.

OBJECTIVE: Using library resources, the student will draw five forms of transport used by gold seekers to travel from the coast of British Columbia to the Cariboo in the 1860s.

OBJECTIVE: Students, in groups, will tour the local supermarket and, as a group, arrive at a list of jobs done in the supermarket.

Social Studies is not merely concerned with objectives concerning "knowing that" and "knowing how"; it is also concerned with dispositions, sensitivities, and appreciations. These are often labelled "affective" objectives. Basically, "affective" objectives state how we want students to be disposed toward something, or what we want students to value. In the above objectives, we may wish students to *appreciate* the hardships suffered by gold miners. In studies of cultures or ethnic groups, we will want students to *respect* cultural differences. In decision-making, we will wish students to be *willing* to consider points of view that differ from their own. In studies of disadvantaged people, we would like students to feel *empathy*. It is often difficult to write these objectives in specific terms. For example, we could specify that the demonstration of a positive attitude toward disadvantaged people would consist of giving money to a charitable organization, but this is only one aspect of what we might consider "a positive attitude." In the case of appreciating the hardships of miners, we might interpret a student's statement "I'm glad I'm not him" as an indication that the student has some appreciation. When stating "affective" objectives, you should have some idea of what would constitute successful performance, even through your criteria are "subjective."

SEQUENCE

9. Having now obtained a broad perspective on the scope of the unit, it is time to put it into a logical sequence.

(a) What kind of prior knowledge will students need to have? Do specific concepts and skills have to be taught before the unit is actually taught?

(b) Would it be best to start with something students are familiar with, or with something they are not familiar with?

(c) Could another topic in a different subject area act as a springboard for this unit?

(d) What would be a logical sequence once a starting point has been ascertained?

(e) How can the unit be organized so that the major findings are synthesized?

(f) Can the unit be sequenced so that the content or skills covered relate to other subject areas?

EXAMPLE

(a) Start with a stimulating question within the familiar context of the school. Show how the roles of students, teachers, principal, secretary, custodian, and so on are interdependent.

(b) Examine how rules impinge on school life and how they relate to interdependence. Integrate the material with other curriculum areas, such as rules followed in playing games in physical education.

(c) Study the police force and how members of the force relate to school and community life.

(d) Synthesize the above so that generalizations concerning interdependence and rules are formulated.

10. We are now in a position to chart the subtopics and activities in sequence. At this stage, we are not planning specific lessons; rather, we are attempting to get a broad overview of the unit. First, we need an opener.

OPENERS

Presumably, you want your students to be interested in the topic. Stating, "Today, class, we're going to study X; open your textbooks at page Y" may not motivate students. Below are some ideas that are designed to spark student interest.

ACTIVITY 22-D

Study the photographs below.

(a) In what country (countries) were these photographs taken?

(b) What led you to this conclusion? What clues did you use?

(c) On the basis of your experience with the six photographs above, predict how well you will do in identifying photos of the above country X from a number of photos that may or may not be of country X.

(d) Which of these photos are of country X? Answers are in the ANSWERS section.

Why were you successful/unsuccessful in identifying these photos?

The above procedure is an adaptation of the *discrepant data technique*. First, you identify a stereotype that you think people hold. In this case, the stereotype was that you can easily identify photos of Canadian scenes. Second, you reinforce this stereotype by showing pictures that fit the stereotype. Third, you introduce discrepant data that do not fit the stereotype, so that, fourth, you have to re-examine the stereotype and formulate a new generalization.

Suppose children have stereotypic views about the continent of Africa—for example, only black people live there; all the people are hunters or farmers, and so on. Show pictures of people who live in Africa that fit the students' stereotypes and ask them, "Who are these people?" and "Where do they live?" Then, having ascertained that all the pictures are of people who live in Africa, say, "I'm going to show you some more pictures and I want you to tell me where *these* people live." Display pictures of people who live in Africa that do not fit the stereotype. If students incorrectly identify the pictures (and in my experience they will), then state that all the pictures were of people who live in Africa. The new information will have to be reinforced during your unit, as some students may not believe you.

Another opener is to show students an object or picture of something unknown to them. Students have to guess what the object is by asking questions that demand a *yes* or *no* answer only; i.e., the question "What is it?" is not allowed, but the question "Is it an X?" is.

ACTIVITY 22-E

Using the above technique, try to ascertain from your instructor what the picture below depicts. (The answer appears in the ANSWERS section.)

All these ideas are meant to puzzle students. The next idea can be a real puzzler if you use it when introducing a unit on culture in the intermediate grades.

ACTIVITY 22-F

Read the following passage and answer the question, "Who are the Nacirema?" (The answer appears in the ANSWERS section.)

THE NACIREMA[1]

The Nacirema inhabit a large area of the North American continent. Because of their belief that the human body is ugly and that its natural tendency is towards illness, everyone tries to avoid disease and ugliness by various ceremonies performed in a shrine. Every house has one or more of these shrines and people are judged to be wealthy if they have a lot of shrines in their homes.

The ceremonies performed in the shrine are private and secret. The most important thing in the shrine is a box, or chest, built into the wall. In this chest are kept many charms and magical liquids without which no native believes he could live. Most of these charms and magical liquids are obtained from medicine people who are rewarded for these by large gifts. However, the medicine people only decide what ingredients should go into the liquid or charm by writing these down in a secret language that only medicine people and herbalists understand; it is the herbalist who, for another large gift, provides the actual charm.

Even after the charm has had its effect, it is not thrown away, but is placed in the charm box in the shrine. The charm box is therefore filled to overflowing, often with useless junk. The natives therefore must believe old charms still protect them.

Beneath the charm box is a small basin. Every day each member of the family enters the shrine, bows his or her head before the charm box, mixes different sorts of holy water in the basin, and performs a washing ceremony.

There is also a mouth ceremony, when a bundle of small sticks is put in the mouth along with certain magical powders and the bundle moved in a very specific way. Despite this magic to protect the teeth, once or twice a year the natives visit a holy mouth person. He or she, with a number of probes, prods, and sharp, pointed tools, puts the native through a painful ceremony. The native's teeth are prodded and decay is removed. Magic materials are put into holes and sometimes whole teeth are pulled out in a torturous way. The whole thing is done because the natives believe that they will lose their friends unless they have these ceremonies performed.

EPISODES

11. We are now in a position to plan the individual episodes of the unit. We need to know:

(a) The subtopic and/or questions.

(b) The information that students will use.

(c) The activities students will perform

(d) The way(s) in which students will present their information.

(e) Any opportunities for integration with other subject areas.

(f) The following examples consist of "bites" of content that have some structural unity. It might be possible to teach a particular episode in one lesson of 30–45 minutes or a particular episode might entail several lessons.

EXAMPLE: Opener

Topic School.

Question What would happen if you didn't have to attend school? Would these consequences be desirable or undesirable?

Information Student hypotheses. Teacher's list of consequences.

Activities Discussion. Each student draws a picture of one consequence (for him/herself, family, teachers, retailers, recreational facilities, etc.) and states why it would be desirable or undesirable.

Presentation Class mural showing consequences and decisions about their desirability.

EXAMPLE: Episode I

Topic Interdependence in the School.

Question How are people in the school dependent upon one another?

Information Roles of various school personnel.

Activities Interviewing. Listening to people in the school telling what they do. List of tasks performed by school personnel.

Presentation Diagram showing how students, teachers, etc., interact within the school community.

Integration Stories about schools.
(Some of the questions posed and activities presented in Chapter 12 could be used here).

EXAMPLE: Episode II

Topic Role of Rules in the School.

Question How do rules affect school interactions?

Information Pictures of school activities. Teacher and student contributions.

Activities List of activities carried out in school (extension of Episode I). Discuss rules behind each activity; categorize rules as customs, school rules, legal rules, and subject-matter rules (e.g., spelling, grammatical rules).

Presentation Role-play of following/not following a particular custom, school rule, or legal rule. Inclusion of rules that exist in the interactions diagrammed in Episode I.

Integration In all other subject areas.

EXAMPLE: Episode III

Topic Rules.

Question What makes a good rule?

Information List of rules. Criteria for good rules (see Activity 20-G).

Activities Discussion of each rule. Students draw a picture of the consequences if a good rule is not followed. Relating rules to the diagram generated in Episode I. What would be the effect on interdependent relationships if rules were not followed?

Presentation Each student takes a particular interaction (student–teacher: student–principal, etc.) and writes a sentence about a rule that affects the interaction and why it is a good (or bad) rule.

Integration Discussion of what constitutes good rules for safety purposes in PE and science, and for learning in general in other subject areas. Stories of rule-following (or not following) behaviour.

EXAMPLE: Episode IV

Topic School Rules and Laws.

Question Who enforces school rules and who enforces laws?

Information Series of vignettes (e.g., Alice runs in the school corridor, which is against the school rules. Can the police arrest her?). Student- and teacher-generated list of rules and laws that directly affect students in school.

Activities Discussion. Role-play of vignettes (e.g., police officer attempting to arrest Alice, and Alice's reactions).

Presentation Class list of rules showing who enforces each one.
(Activities proposed in the law-related education section of Chapter 20 could be carried out in this episode).

EXAMPLE: Episode V

Topic Tasks of Police Officers.

Question What do police officers do?

Information Field trip to police station.

Activities Listen to presentations made by members of the police force. Interview police officers. Observe or take photos of the activities they perform.

Presentation A "radio" program in which students play the role of a police officer and are interviewed by other students.

EXAMPLE: Episode VI

Topic: The Relationship of the Police to the Community.

Question How do the police relate to the Community?

Information Visit by police to class.

Activities Listen to presentation; ask questions. Discuss what would happen if there were no police in the community.

Presentation Webbing diagram showing police–community interactions.

EXAMPLE: Synthesis

Topic Interdependence and Rules.

Question   How do students, the school, and the police relate to the community, and what effects do rules have on these interactions?

Information   All information gathered during the unit.

Activities   Drawing a phenomenon in the community and a picture of a student, teacher, and police officer. Where there is an interaction, coloured string is used to show the links. For each link (if feasible), the rule or rules that affect the interaction are identified—e.g., students by law have to attend school; students follow certain rules in their interactions with teachers; students and teachers customarily behave in certain ways in their interactions. Students discuss what would happen if rules were not followed, or new rules were created, or one of the components in an interdependent relationship was weakened or disappeared.

Presentation   Students write a short paragraph to demonstrate their understanding.

Now that an outline has been formulated, more questions may be generated. To answer them, more activities will be needed, and thus more objectives will need to be stated.

Throughout, you will need to ascertain whether or not students have realized the objectives. So, it will be necessary to determine procedures for evaluating students' learning (see Chapters 15 and 21). Even though this section comes at the end of the unit plan, this does not mean that evaluation should occur only at the end of the unit. You should be constantly monitoring student performance so that you can diagnose any student problems and modify your instruction where necessary. The ideas presented here could be implemented at any appropriate time during the unit.

EXAMPLE: Evaluation

Objective   The student will list and describe tasks performed by police officers.

Evaluation   Have the student draw a picture that correctly identifies a task performed by a police officer. If asked, can the student give an accurate description of the task? If given a number of pictures of various tasks, can the student correctly identify which ones are carried out by police officers?

Objective   The student will be able to give an example of "interdependence."

Evaluation   Give the student a sheet of paper with the name of a particular community phenomenon written in the middle, and have the student draw all the other phenomena that are linked to it. Interview the student to ascertain how well the student can explain the webbing diagram.

Unit planning is a complex activity because there are so many factors to take into account and so many opportunities that could be pursued. For example, in the unit outlined in this chapter, students could study a variety of other community interactions: they could inquire into the relationships between the physical and social environment and the rules that govern each; they could inquire more deeply into the school as a social institution; they could look at images of the police as portrayed on TV; they could study the rules and conventions followed by people in different cultures; they could discuss the sorts of rules necessary for the smooth functioning of a multicultural society, etc.

For various reasons, most plans have to be modified in the actual implementation (e.g., a movie is unavailable on the day it is needed; students have to be taught X before the unit can continue; and, most frequently, students find something to be very interesting and you decide to spend time on this rather than what was originally intended).

This chapter has presented one way of unit planning—but not the only way. Students can also be involved in planning. For example, after a visit to the police station, students could pose their own questions, carry out their own research, and make a presentation. They might choose to write a poem about the police, or to find out how many police shows there are on TV. Students could read laws that affect their lives and rewrite them in language that a Grade 2 student could understand. Any of these activities could be encouraged even though you hadn't planned for them.

Other ways of proceeding are to use Egan's story-telling approach (see Chapter 6) or a social issues (decision-making) approach (see Chapters 18, 19, and 20); or you could let students take what interests them and design their own unit. You should also look at textbooks and kits, such as the McGraw-Hill Ryerson *Social and Environmental Studies* program and the Douglas and McIntyre *Explorations* program.

Finally, the unit needs to be evaluated. Below is a list of suggested questions.

1. Was the topic worth teaching?

2. Did students realize the objectives?

3. Did students find it interesting?

4. Could students cope with the unit? Was it within their capabilities?

5. Were the resource materials used appropriate?

6. Was I interested in teaching the unit?

7. Were the objectives congruent with the teaching/learning and evaluation procedures?

8. Was the sequence logical?

9. If I taught the unit again, what, if anything, would I change?

NOTES

1. Adapted from H. Miner, "Body ritual among the Nacirema," *American Anthropologist* 58:3 (June 1956), 503–7. Not for further reproduction.

ANSWERS TO ACTIVITIES

ACTIVITY 1-B

All the vignettes could be considered Social Studies *if* the objectives for engaging students in the activities are Social Studies ones.

ACTIVITY 2-B

1. Citizenship Transmission.
2. Reflective Inquiry, although it could be Critical Reflection.
3. Citizenship Transmission.
4. Critical Reflection.
5. Social Science.
6. Citizenship Transmission.
7. Citizenship Transmission.
8. Reflective Inquiry, although it could be Critical Reflection.
9. Critical Reflection.

ACTIVITY 5-B

1. Lee Mong Kow family, Victoria, British Columbia.
2. Arctic hares, family Leporidae.
3. Hutterite family, Alberta.
4. Quatsino Indians at a potlatch.
5. Group of East Indians at North Pacific Lumber Co. in Barnet, British Columbia.
6. A.G. Johnson, proprietor of Poplar Creek store, British Columbia.

ACTIVITY 5-F

The concept is "immigrant."

ACTIVITY 5-G

The concept is "tradition." If you look at the last sentence, it sounds odd to say that watching television news every night is not a "custom" (which would be a sensible choice to fill all the other blanks). This practice seems to have many of the attributes of "custom" in that it is regularly practised over some extended period of time, it is an act of persons who, in most cases, can either do or refrain from doing it, it is usually done with full awareness of what one is doing, and one may believe that one ought to do it. However, unlike some other customs where there there are sanctions applied if they are not followed, refraining from watching television news is not a punishable offence.

"Tradition" has the same sorts of characteristics as "custom." However, a tradition may be more robust than certain customs; it may be handed down orally and deliberately from generation to generation (whereas a custom may endure for only one generation and not be formally taught); it may be based on very strong beliefs, which if contradicted may seriously undermine group cohesiveness and may lead to extreme sanctions (whereas not all customs have these characteristics); and it sounds a bit odd to say, "X is my individual tradition which no one else practises," whereas it is normal to say, "X is my custom even though no one else practises it." Yet words change in meaning over time, and one often hears people say that they are starting a tradition just for themselves (which would be incorrect usage if a necessary attribute of the word was that a tradition had to be passed down from generation to generation), and we may find that the words "tradition" and "custom" become almost interchangeable in ordinary language.

ACTIVITY 5-H

Examples of "authority" are numbers 1, 2, 5, 6, and possibly 7 (depending on whether or not the principal really has authority to do this). Notice that in the other cases there is the exercise of power without the requisite authority.

CHAPTER 5. OTHER ACTIVITIES (3)

The teacher has implemented Taba's concept development procedure well. She/he has ensured that students have (1) correctly classified items, (2) decided whether items could be classified in more than one category, and (3) created categories useful for study of the topic.

ACTIVITY 7-D

As I find many problems in using Sanders's and Bloom's taxonomies, the answers provided are, in some cases, debatable.

Type of Question	Level of Question (highest is indicated)
1. Empirical	Memory
2. Empirical	Memory
3. Empirical	Synthesis
4. Empirical	Translation
5. Conceptual	Memory

Type of Question	Level of Question (highest is indicated)
6. Conceptual	Analysis
7. Value	Evaluation
8. Value	Evaluation
9. Value	Evaluation
10. Empirical/logical If you accept the two premises, then logically you must accept the con- clusion.	Analysis

ACTIVITY 8-B

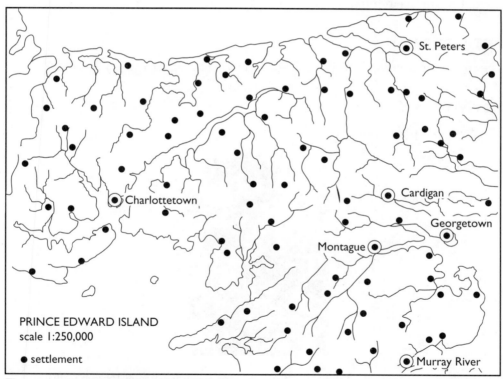

PRINCE EDWARD ISLAND
scale 1:250,000

● settlement

St. Peters
Cardigan
Georgetown
Montague
Charlottetown
Murray River

The map depicts part of Prince Edward Island.

ACTIVITY 8-D

Life in China (a)
Internment of the Japanese (a)

ACTIVITY 8-E

1. (a)

2. (b)

3. (a)

ACTIVITY 8-F

The inference statements are (c), (d), (f), and (h). All are plausible.

ACTIVITY 8-H

If inquiry is defined as the testing of hypotheses, then 4, 7, and possibly 10 would qualify as inquiry. In 10, students make a series of hypotheses and receive immediate feedback on each one. There is no real testing of hypotheses. Thus, *I* would not define this as inquiry.

ACTIVITY 8-I

The following assumptions would be made: (b), (c), (e), (f), (g), (h), (i), and (j).

ACTIVITY 10-A

The complete photograph looks like this.

The second photograph shows the dragon dance in Vancouver, British Columbia.

ACTIVITY 11-F

In 1818, the British government helped army personnel settle in Canada. Settlers received free transportation and some food for the first year, and privates were given forty hectares (a hundred acres) of free land. According to Andrew Haydon,

Pioneer Sketches in the District of Bathurst (Toronto: Ryerson, 1925, p. 64), the head of each family was entitled to receive: 1 axe, 1 broadaxe, 1 mattock, 1 pickaxe, 1 spade, 1 shovel, 1 hoe, 1 scythe, 1 drawknife, 1 hammer, 1 handsaw, 2 scythe stones, 12 panes of glass, 0.5 kg (1 lb.) of putty, 5.4 kg (12 lb.) of wrought iron nails in three sizes, 1 camp kettle, 1 bed tick, and 1 blanket.

ACTIVITY 12-A

The teacher has forgotten to obtain permission from parents or legal guardians for their child to go on the field trip. This is a legal requirement and thus is obligatory before any field trip is undertaken.

CHAPTER 13. OTHER ACTIVITIES (2)

The scale is incorrect. The room would be 5 km long. Further, the chair is bigger than the bed. The scale should read 1 cm : ___, not 1 cm = ___. If south is at the top of the room, then east and west are incorrect; if the east and west are correct, then north and south are reversed. The perspective is confused—the bed, chair, and pictures are not drawn from the pilot's eye-view.

ACTIVITY 14-A

Every sentence, bar the last one, is a generalization. Each one is presumed to be universally true.

ACTIVITY 14-F

The following generalizations are assumed:
1. All recent immigrants are good workers.
2. Boys don't cry.
3. Immigrants create cultural and economic change.
4. Working-class girls have problems in school.
5. It rains all the time in the summer in Vancouver.
6. People from India wear turbans.
7. Girls aren't good at baseball.

ACTIVITY 15-B

1. Far too many correct answers are possible.
2. Stems (a), (b), and (c) are possible answers; (d) does not grammatically follow from the question. Also, (c) is a value statement and can be "right" or "wrong" only on the basis of a value principle or standard.
3. Far too broad. What would count as a good answer?

4. Some explorers may have to contend with all these factors, whereas others did not. The entire statement is neither true nor false.

5. Confusing. Doesn't state which native peoples are being discussed. If (f) was the correct answer, this would include (e) and would be illogical.

6. A crib? A house? May? 1860? What would count as a correct answer?

7. Bad matching—far too obvious.

ACTIVITY 17-B

1. Value conclusion: Students should work in cooperative groups.

2. Value conclusion: Students at age 9 should learn conventional map symbols.

3. Value conclusion: Students should understand the Canadian Charter of Rights and Freedoms.

CHAPTER 17. OTHER ACTIVITIES

1. People should be treated with respect.

2. Child abuse is morally wrong.

3. Students who wear glasses should not be given special consideration in school classrooms. Or: Only handicapped people should receive special consideration in classrooms.

4. Children should not be allowed to do things that are harmful to them.

CHAPTER 19. OTHER ACTIVITIES

The teacher has not implemented the decision-making procedure in an appropriate way. She/he has (1) allowed the problem to be wrongly defined; (2) limited the number of alternatives to be considered; (3) invented new information; (4) held a vote when this is inappropriate (to decide whether or not an empirical claim concerning the teasers is true); and (5) imposed his/her own decision on the class and cut off any further discussion.

ACTIVITY 20-D

1. Overgeneralization. Just because one recent immigrant is hardworking does not mean that all recent immigrants will be.

2. False cause (*post hoc ergo propter hoc*). There are other reasons for the high unemployment.

3. Appeal to tradition. Just because immigrants came from Europe in the past, it does not follow that they should today.

4. Appeal to authority. Are business people experts on whether the secretary of state should give money to ethnic groups?

5. "Black or white" (either this or that). This form of argument presents an over-simplication: Canada's economy could crumble (if it was going to crumble) for a variety of reasons.

6. Slippery slope (in which it is argued that you must not accept as desirable the first event in a supposed chain of events that will lead eventually to something undersirable). In this case, you could agree to allowing native peoples to govern themselves without agreeing to the rest.

ACTIVITY 22-D

Photographs 1–6 were all taken in Canada.

1. Quebec City, Quebec
2. Igloolik, Northwest Territories
3. Canadian Pacific locomotive (somewhere in Canada)
4. Vancouver, British Columbia
5. Toronto, Ontario
6. Ottawa, Ontario
7. Denver, Colorado
8. Borneo
9. Richmond, British Columbia
10. Quebec City, Quebec
11. Dr. Sun Yat-Sen Garden, Vancouver, British Columbia
12. Cloverdale, British Columbia

ACTIVITY 22-E

Map of the world as known to Europeans, 1398.

ACTIVITY 22-F

Nacirema = American.

A SELECTED BIBLIOGRAPHY

GENERAL ELEMENTARY SOCIAL STUDIES METHODS TEXTS

Banks, J. *Teaching Strategies for the Social Studies*, 4th ed. New York: Longman, 1990.

Chapin, J., and R. Messick. *Elementary Social Studies: A Practical Guide.* New York: Longman, 1989.

Ellis, A. *Teaching and Learning Elementary Social Studies*, 4th ed. Boston: Allyn and Bacon, 1991.

Evans, J., and M. Brueckner. *Elementary Social Studies for Today and Tomorrow.* Boston: Allyn and Bacon, 1990.

Fraenkel, J. *Helping Students Think and Value: Strategies for Teaching the Social Studies*, 2nd ed. Englewood Cliffs, N.J.: Prentice-Hall, 1980.

Hennings, D., G. Hennings, and S. Banich. *Today's Elementary Social Studies,* 2nd ed. New York: Harper and Row, 1989.

Hunkins, F. *Social Studies in the Elementary School.* Columbus, Ohio: Merrill, 1982.

Jarolimek, J. *Social Studies in Elementary Education*, 7th ed. New York: Macmillan, 1986.

Kaltsounis, T. *Teaching Social Studies in the Elementary School: The Basics for Citizenship.* Englewood Cliffs, N.J.: Prentice-Hall, 1987.

Kirman, J. *Elementary Social Studies.* Scarborough, Ont.: Prentice-Hall, 1991.

Martorella, P. *Elementary Social Studies: Developing Reflective, Competent and Concerned Citizens.* Boston: Little, Brown, 1985.

Maxim, G. *Social Studies and the Elementary School Child*, 3rd ed. Columbus, Ohio: Merrill, 1987.

Michaelis, J. *Social Studies for Children*, 9th ed. Englewood Cliffs, N.J.: Prentice-Hall, 1988.

Michaelis, J., and H. Rushdoony. *Elementary Social Studies Handbook.* San Diego, Calif: Harcourt Brace Jovanovich, 1987.

Naylor, D., and R. Dien. *Elementary and Middle School Social Studies.* New York: Random House, 1987.

Nelson, M., *Children and Social Studies*, 2nd. ed. Fort Worth, Tex.: Harcourt Brace Jovanovich, 1990.

Parsons, J., G. Milburn, and M. Van Manen, eds. *A Canadian Social Studies.* Edmonton, Alta.: Faculty of Education Publication Services, University of Alberta, 1983.

Preston, R., and W. Herman. *Teaching Social Studies in the Elementary School,* 5th ed. New York: Holt, Rinehart and Winston, 1981.

Savage, T., and P. Armstrong. *Effective Teaching in Elementary Social Studies.* New York: Macmillan, 1987.

Seefeldt, C. *Social Studies for the Preschool-Primary Child*, 2nd ed. Columbus, Ohio: Merrill, 1984.

Servey, R. *Elementary Social Studies: A Skills Emphasis.* Boston: Allyn and Bacon, 1981.

Sunal, C. *Early Childhood Social Studies.* Columbus, Ohio: Merrill, 1990.

Sunal, C., and M. Haas. *Social Studies and the Elementary/Middle School Student.* Fort Worth, Tex.: Harcourt Brace Jovanovich, 1993.

Van Cleaf, D. *Action in Elementary Social Studies.* Englewood Cliffs, N.J.: Prentice-Hall, 1991.

Walsh, H. *Introducing the Young Child to the Social World.* New York: Macmillan, 1980.

Welton, D., and J. Mallan. *Children and Their World,* 3rd ed. Boston: Houghton Mifflin, 1988.

PART 1: THE NATURE & PURPOSES OF SOCIAL STUDIES

Barth, J. "Social Studies: There is a history, there is a body, but is it worth saving?" *Social Education* 57:2 (1993), 56–57.

Brophy, J., and J. Alleman. "Elementary Social Studies should be driven by major social education goals." *Social Education* 57:1 (1993), 27–32.

Chamberlin, C. "Citizenship as the goal of Social Studies: Passive knower or active doer?" *Canadian Social Studies* 26:1 (1991), 23–26.

Egan, K. "Herodotus, Thucydides and modern students." *The History and Social Science Teacher* 17:4 (1982), 9–15.

Egan, K. "What children know best." *Social Education* 43:2 (1979), 130–39.

Epstein, T., and R. Evans, eds. "Reactions to *Charting a Course: Social Studies for the 21st Century.*" *Social Education* 54:7 (1990), 427-46.

Hartoonian, M. "A guide for redefining Social Studies." *Social Education* 57:2 (1993), 59–60.

Myers, J. "The trouble with history." *The History and Social Science Teacher* 25:2 (1990), 68–70.

National Council for the Social Studies. Report of the National Council for the Social Studies Task Force on Scope and Sequence. *Social Education* 53:6 (1989), 376–87.

Nelson, J. "New criticism and Social Education." *Social Education* 49:5 (1985), 368–405.

Scope and Sequence: Alternatives for Social Studies. Special issue of *Social Education* 50:7 (1986).

Scope and Sequence in the Social Studies. Special issue of *Social Education* 48:4 (1984).

Sheehan, N. "The future of Social Studies: An historian's perspective." *The History and Social Science Teacher* 22:3 (1987), 143–48.

Social Sciences in the Social Studies. Special issue of *The Social Studies* 73:5 (1982).

Tomkins, G. "The Social Studies in Canada." In J. Parsons, G. Milburn, and M. Van Manen, eds. *A Canadian Social Studies.* Edmonton, Alta.: Publication Services, Faculty of Education, University of Alberta, 1983.

Tooke, M. "A view from Canada." *Social Education* 52:6 (1988), 414-20.

VanSickle, R. "The personal relevance of the Social Studies." *Social Education* 54:1 (1990), 23–27/59.

PART: 2 EMPIRICAL & CONCEPTUAL CLAIMS & QUESTIONS

Concept Teaching & Learning

Bolton, N. *Concept Formation.* Toronto: Pergamon Press, 1977.

Dueck, K. "Teaching concepts: From theory to practice." *The History and Social Science Teacher* 14:2 (1979), 103-12.

Gray, D. "Teaching concepts in Social Studies." In J. Parsons, G. Milburn, and M. Van Manen, eds. *A Canadian Social Studies.* Edmonton, Alta.: Faculty of Education Publication Services, University of Alberta, 1983.

Kleg, M., and M. Mahlios. "Delineating concept meanings: The case of terrorism." *Social Education* 54:6 (1990), 389–92.

Langford, P. *Concept Development in the Primary School.* London: Croom Helm, 1987.

Wilson, J. *Thinking with Concepts.* Cambridge: The University Press, 1969.

Exposition, Narrative & the Teaching of History

Clarke, G., and J. Smyth. "Stories in elementary history and the Social Studies." *Canadian Social Studies* 27:2 (1993), 76–78.

Hickey, M. "And then what happened, Grandpa?: Oral history projects in the elementary classroom." *Social Education* 55:4 (1991), 216–17.

History and the Social Studies. Special issue of *Social Studies and the Young Learner* 2:2 (1989).

Saxe, D. "Resolving students' confusion about indefinite time expressions." *The Social Studies* 83:5 (1992), 188–92.

Sears, A., and G. Bidlake, "A senior citizens' tea: A connecting point for oral history in the elementary school Social Studies." *The Social Studies* 82:4 (1991), 133–35.

Smith, J., and D. Dobson. "Teaching with historical novels: A four step approach." *Social Studies and the Young Learner* 5:3 (1993), 19–22.

Zarnowski, M. "The question-and-answer book: A format for young historians." *Social Studies and the Young Learner* 4:2 (1991), 5–7.

Questions, Critical Thinking & Inquiry

Baron, J., and R. Sternberg, eds. *Teaching Thinking Skills: Theory and Practice*. New York: W.H. Freeman, 1987.

Beyer, B. "Critical Thinking revisited." *Social Education* 49:4 (1985), 268–310.

Beyer, B. "Improving the teaching of thinking skills in Social Studies." *The History and Social Science Teacher* 19:4 (1984), 229–37.

Beyer, B. *Inquiry in the Social Studies Classroom*. Columbus, Ohio: Merrill, 1971.

Beyer, B. *Teaching Thinking in Social Studies*. Ohio: Merrill, 1979.

Boyd, B. *Thinking about Inquiry*. Toronto: McGraw-Hill Ryerson, 1971.

Critical Thinking. Special issue of *The History and Social Science Teacher* 21:3 (1986).

Dhand, H. "The source method to teach Social Studies." *Canadian Social Studies* 26:4 (1992), 165–69.

Ennis, R. "Critical thinking and the curriculum." *National Forum* 65:1 (1985), 28–31.

Evans, R. "Group investigation." *Canadian Social Studies* 26:2 (1991), 65–67.

Hickey, M. "Reading and Social Studies: The critical connection." *Social Education* 54:3 (1990), 175–79.

Hunkins, F. *Involving Students in Questioning*. Boston: Allyn and Bacon, 1976.

Parker, W., J. McDaniel, and S. Valencia. "Helping students think about public issues: Instruction versus prompting." *Social Education* 55:1 (1991), 41–44/67.

Paul, R., J. Binker, and M.Charbonneau. *Critical Thinking Handbook: K–3 Guide for Remodelling Lesson Plans*. Also available for Grades 4–6. Rohnert Park, Calif.: Center for Critical Thinking and Moral Critique, Sonoma State University (no date).

Ryan, F., and A. Ellis. *Instructional Implications of Inquiry*. Englewood Cliffs, N.J.: Prentice-Hall, 1974.

Wright, I., and C. LaBar. *Critical Thinking and Social Studies*. Toronto: Grolier, 1987.

Group Inquiry/Cooperative Learning

Dueck, K. "Preparing students for group work in elementary Social Studies." *The History and Social Science Teacher* 18:2 (1982), 65–73.

Johnson, D., R. Johnson, and E. Holubec. *Structuring Cooperative Learning: Lesson Plans for Teachers*. Edina, Minn.: Interaction Book Company, 1987.

Johnson, D., R. Johnson, E. Holubec, and P. Roy. *Circles of Learning: Cooperation in the Classroom*. Alexandria, Va.: Association for Supervision and Curriculum Development, 1984.

Kagan, S. *Cooperative Learning: Resources for Teachers*. Riverside, Calif.: University of Calif., 1988.

Manning, M., and R. Lucking. "The what, why, and how of cooperative learning." *The Social Studies* 82:3 (1991), 120–24.

Morton, T. "Growing cooperation." *Canadian Social Studies* 26:2 (1991), 74–77.

Morton, T. "Pyramids and buffalo jumps: An exercise combining inquiry with cooperative learning." *The History and Social Science Teacher* 25:4 (1990), 202–9.

Myers, J., L. Cox, and R. Evans. "Getting started strategies and cooperative learning." *Canadian Social Studies* 26:2 (1991), 68–71.

Myers, J., and C. Lemon. "The jigsaw strategy: Co-operative learning in Social Studies." *The History and Social Science Teacher* 24:1 (1988), 18–22.

Schniedewind, N., and E. Davidson. *Cooperative Learning: Cooperative Lives*. Dubuque, Iowa: Wm. C. Brown, 1987.

Stahl, R., and R. VanSickle, eds. *Cooperative Learning in the Social Studies Classroom*. New York: National Council for the Social Studies, 1992.

Steinbrink, J., and R. Jones. "Team learning in Social Studies." *Social Studies and the Young Learner* 2:3 (1990), 3–5.

Windrim, R. "Co-operative learning as an agent of inquiry." *The History and Social Science Teacher* 25:4 (1990), 193–96.

Working Together: Learning Together. Department of Cooperation and Cooperative Development (Education Unit), Saskatchewan, 1983.

Using Instructional Resources

Computers and Social Studies. Special issue of *The Social Studies* 78:1 (1987).

Computers in Social Studies. Special issue of *Social Education* 51:1 (1987).

Crowley, T. "Understanding Canada's aboriginal people: A regional guide." *Canadian Social Studies* 27:2 (1993), 71–74.

Gibson, S. "Putting the focus on current affairs." *Canadian Social Studies* 26:4 (1992), 161–63.

Kirman, J. "Using newspapers to study media bias." *Social Education* 56:1 (1992), 47–51.

Levesque, J. "Using computers to motivate learners." *Social Studies and the Young Learner* 2:1 (1989), 9–12.

McCoy, J. "Databases in the Social Studies: Not why but how." *Social Studies and the Young Learner* 3:2 (1990), 13–15.

Martorella, P. "Harnessing new technologies to the Social Studies curriculum." *Social Education* 55:1 (1991), 55–57.

Patton, W. *Improving the Use of Social Studies Textbooks.* Washington, D.C.: National Council for the Social Studies, 1980.

Riecken, T., and M. Miller. "Introduce children to problem-solving and decision-making by using children's literature." *The Social Studies* 81:2 (1990), 59–64.

Ruef, S. "A study of the effects of computer-assisted instruction in the social studies." *The Social Studies* 81:2 (1990), 73–76.

The Textbook as Teaching Tool. Special issue of *Social Education* 44:2 (1980).

Wooster, J. "Getting the most from textbooks: Making instruction motivating." *Social Studies and the Young Learner* 2:1 (1989), 13–15.

Maps, Mapping & the Teaching of Geography

Allen, R., and J. Hoge. "Literature study for geographic literacy." *Social Studies and the Young Learner* 2:4 (1990), 3–5.

Blyth, J. *Place and Time with Children Five to Nine.* London: Croom Helm, 1984.

Carey, H. *How to Use Maps and Globes.* New York: Franklin Watts, 1983.

Carswell, R. "Atlas skills for learning rather than learning atlas skills." *The History and Social Science Teacher* 22:1 (1986), 19–23.

Cochrane, K., ed. "China: A case study in using geography to understand culture." Pull-out feature, *Social Studies and the Young Learner* 4:3 (1992).

de Leeuw, G., and N. Waters. "Computerized atlases: The potential of computers in Social Studies." *The History and Social Science Teacher* 22:1 (1986), 6–14.

Kirman, J. "Elementary age children and remote sensing: Research from the Omega Project." *Canadian Social Studies* 26:1 (1991), 17–19.

Maier, J. "Relating here to there: Globes and world maps as advanced organizers." *Social Studies and the Young Learner* 5:3 (1993), 9–11.

Milburn, D. "Children in time and space." In J. Parsons, G. Milburn, and M. Van Manen, eds. *A Canadian Social Studies.* Edmonton, Alta.: Faculty of Education Publication Services, University of Alberta, 1983.

Milburn, D. "Mapping and young children." In R. Choquette, J. Wolforth, and M. Villemure, eds. *Canadian Geographical Education.* Ottawa: Canadian Association of Geographers, University of Ottawa Press, 1980.

Mills, D., ed. *Geographical Work in the Primary and Middle Schools*. Sheffield, England: The Geographical Association, 1988.

Muessig, R. "Building map skills to advance geographic understanding." *Social Education* 49:1 (1985), 28–47.

Natoli, S., ed. *Strengthening Geography in the Social Studies*. New York: National Council for the Social Studies, 1988.

Osmers, K. "Remote sensing and the environment." *Canadian Social Studies* 26:1 (1991), 14–16.

Sunal, C. "Mapping for the young child." *The Social Studies* 78:4 (1987), 178–82.

Wentworth, D., J. Couchman, J. MacBean, and A. Stecher. *Mapping Small Places*. Toronto: Holt, Rinehart and Winston, 1976.

Simulation Games

Basaraborvich, Y., J. Coglon, and D. Mertz. "My school game: A grade one game." *Canadian Social Studies* 26:4 (1992), 170–71.

Boocock, S., and E. Schild. *Simulation Games in Learning*. Beverly Hills, Calif.: Sage, 1968.

Haas, M. "The role of Social Studies games in the elementary classroom." *Social Studies and the Young Learner* 3:2 (1990), 9–12.

Livingstone, S., and C. Stoll. *Simulation Games: An Introduction for the Social Studies Teacher*. New York: Free Press, 1973.

MacArthur, B., J. Magdalinski, and R. Smilar. "The long haul: A grade five game." *Canadian Social Studies* 26:3 (1992), 123–25.

Muir, S. "Simulation games for elementary Social Studies." *Social Education* 44:1 (1980), 35–39.

Tansey, P., and D. Unwin. *Simulation and Gaming in Education*. New York: Methuen, 1969.

Turner, T. "Simulation games are for younger learners too." *The Social Studies* 73:3 (1982), 130–34.

PART 3: VALUE CLAIMS & QUESTIONS

Values Education

Beck, C., N. Meloy, and J. Bradley-Cameron. *Reflecting on Values*. Toronto: Ontario Institute for Studies in Education, 1980.

Chester, M., and R. Fox. *Role-Playing Methods in the Classroom*. Chicago: SRA, 1966.

Dinkmeyer, D. *Developing Understanding of Self and Others*. Circle Pines, Minn.: American Guidance Service, 1970.

Edwards, C. *Promoting Social and Moral Development in Young Children: Creative Approaches for the Classroom*. New York: Teachers College Press, 1986.

Fraenkel, J. *How to Teach about Values*. Englewood Cliffs, N.J.: Prentice-Hall, 1977.

Hickey, M. "Folk literature as a vehicle for values education." *Social Studies and the Young Learner* 2:3 (1990), 6–8.

Kurfman, D., ed. *Developing Decision-Making Skills*. Washington, D.C.: National Council for the Social Studies, 1977.

LaBar, C., and I. Wright. "Critical thinking and moral reasoning." In I. Wright and C. LaBar, eds. *Critical Thinking and Social Studies*. Toronto: Grolier, 1987.

Lamme, L., S. Krogh, and K. Yachmetz. *Literature-Based Moral Education: Children's Books and Activities for Teaching Values, Responsibility, and Good Judgment in the Elementary School*. Phoenix, Ariz.: Oryx Press, 1992.

Lipman, M., A. Sharp, and F. Oscanyan. *Ethical Inquiry: Instructional Manual to Accompany Lisa*. New Jersey: Institute for the Advancement of Philosophy for Children, Montclair State University, 1977.

Lockward, A. "Character education: The ten percent solution." *Social Education* 55:4 (1991) 246–48.

Shaftel, F., and G. Shaftel. *Role-Playing for Social Values*, 2nd ed. Englewood Cliffs, N.J.: Prentice-Hall, 1982.

Walsh, H. *Introducing the Young Child to the Social World.* New York: Macmillan, 1980.

Wright, I. "Teaching values in the Social Studies." In J. Parsons, G. Milburn, and M. Van Manen, eds. *A Canadian Social Studies.* Edmonton, Alta.: Faculty of Education, Publication Services, University of Alberta, 1983.

Citizenship Education

Botting, D., K. Botting, K. Osborne, J. Seymour, and R. Swyston. *Politics and You.* Scarborough, Ont.: Nelson, 1986.

Canadian Education Association. *Canada and Citizenship Education.* Toronto: Canadian Education Association, 1988.

Chamberlin, C. "Knowledge + commitment = action." In J. Parsons, G. Milburn, and M. Van Manen, eds., *A Canadian Social Studies.* Edmonton, Alta.: Faculty of Education, University of Alberta, 1983.

Civitas: A Framework for Civic Education. New York: National Council for the Social Studies, 1992.

Dueck, K. "Social action in elementary Social Studies." *The History and Social Science Teacher* 15:4 (1980), 245–51.

Dynneson, T. "What's hot and what's not in effective citizenship instruction." *The Social Studies* 83:5 (1992), 197–200.

Hepburn, M., ed. *Democratic Education in Schools and Classrooms.* Washington, D.C.: National Council for the Social Studies, 1983.

Holmes, E. "Democracy in the elementary school classes." *Social Education* 55:3 (1991), 176–78.

Lewis, B. "Cleanup crusade: Citizenship in action." *Social Education* 54:4 (1990), 238–40.

Meyer, J. "Democratic values and their development." *The Social Studies* 81:5 (1990), 197–201.

Osborne, K. *Teaching for Democratic Citizenship.* Our Schools, Our Selves Education Foundation: Toronto, 1991.

Osborne, K., and J. Seymour. "Political education in upper elementary schools." *International Journal of Social Education* 3:2 (1988), 63–77.

Parker, W., and J. Jarolimek. *Citizenship and the Critical Role of the Social Studies.* Washington, D.C.: National Council for the Social Studies, 1984.

Participatory Citizenship. Special issue of *Social Education* 53:6 (1989).

Pereira, C., J. Dolenga, and C. Rolinzinski. "Teaching citizenship through community service." Pull-out feature, *Social Studies and the Young Learner* 3:2 (1990).

Raus, R., and R. Remy. *Citizenship Decision-Making.* Reading, Mass.: Addison-Wesley, 1978.

Shaver, J., ed. *Building Rationales for Citizenship Education.* Washington, D.C.: National Council for the Social Studies, 1977.

Teaching for Citizenship. Special issue of *Social Education* 45:7 (1981).

Wright, I. "Citizenship education and decision-making." *International Journal of Social Education* 3:2 (1988), 55–62.

Multicultural Education

Appraising Multiculturalism. Special issue of *The History and Social Science Teacher* 17:1 (1981).

Appreciating Diversity. Special issue of *Social Studies and the Young Learner* 1:4 (1989).

Beck, C. "Presenting a multicultural inquiry lesson based on a pictorial format." *Social Studies and the Young Learner* 5:3 (1993), 12–14.

Bransone, M., and J. Torney-Purta, eds. *International Human Rights, Society, and Its Schools.* Washington, D.C.: National Council for the Social Studies, 1982.

Connors, B. "A multicultural curriculum as action for social justice." In S. Shapson and V. D'Oyley, eds., *Bilingual and Multicultural Education: Canadian Perspectives.* Avon, England: Multilingual Matters, 1984.

Enhancing the Multicultural Climate of the School. Special issue of *The History and Social Science Teacher* 19:2 (1983).

Lesourd, S. "A review of methodologies for cross-cultural education." *The Social Studies* 83:1 (1992), 30–35.

Stereotypes and Racism. Special edition of *Social Studies and the Young Learner* 5:2 (1992).

Wright, I., and C. LaBar. "Multiculturalism and morality." In S. Shapson and V. D'Oyley, eds. *Bilingual and Multicultural Education: Canadian Perspectives.* Avon, England: Multilingual Matters, 1984.

Wright, I., and C. LaBar. "Multiculturalism in the teaching of Social Studies." In V. D'Oyley and S. Shapson, eds., *Innovative Multicultural Teaching.* Toronto: Kagan and Woo, 1990.

Global Education & Peace Education

Angell, A., and P. Avery. "Examining global issues in the elementary classroom." *The Social Studies* 83:3 (1992), 113–17.

Blackburn, A. "Teaching about the global environment." *Social Education* 49:3 (1985), 198–219.

Fisher, S., and D. Hicks. *World Studies 8–13. A Teacher's Handbook.* Edinburgh: Oliver and Boyd, 1985.

Fountain, S. *Learning Together: Global Education Age 4–7.* World Wildlife Fund, U.K. (1990). Available from Educational Awareness, P.O. Box 572, Stn. A., Scarborough, Ont. M1K 5C4.

Global Education. Special issue of *Social Education* 50:6 (1986).

Global Education. Special issue of *The History and Social Science Teacher* 22:2 (1986–1987).

Hicks, D. *Exploring Alternative Futures: A Teacher's Interim Guide.* London: Global Futures Project, Institute of Education, University of London, 1991.

Hicks, D. *World Studies 8–13.* Harlow, Essex: Oliver and Boyd, 1985.

Hicks, D., and Steiner, M. *Making Global Connections.* Harlow, Essex: Oliver and Boyd, 1989.

Johnson, J., and J. Benegar. "Global issues in the elementary school." *Social Education* 47:2 (1983) 131–37.

Lacks, C. "Sharing a world of difference: International education in the early years." *Social Studies and the Young Learner* 4:3 (1992), 6–8.

Peace Education. Special issue of *The History and Social Science Teacher* 20:3, 4 (1985).

Pike, G., and D. Selby. *Global Teacher: Global Learner.* Toronto: Hodder Stoughton, 1988.

Schniedewind, N., and E. Davidson. *Open Minds to Equality: A Sourcebook of Learning Activities to Promote Race, Sex, Class, and Age Equity.* Englewood Cliffs, N.J.: Prentice-Hall, 1983.

Teaching about International Development. Special issue of *Social Education* 53:4 (1989).

Teaching about the United Nations. Special edition of *Social Education* 53:5 (1989).

Teaching about World Hunger. Special issue of *The Social Studies* 74:4 (1983).

Vocke, D. "Those varying perspectives on global education." *The Social Studies* 79:1 (1988), 18–20.

Walter, V. *War and Peace: Literature for Children and Young Adults.* Phoenix, Ariz.: Oryx Press, 1993.

Werner, W. "Conceptions of Peace Education." *History and Social Science Teacher* 20:3/4 (1985), 29–32.

Human Rights & Law-Related Education

Alberta Human Rights Commission. *Human Rights: Respecting Our Differences.* Edmonton, Alta.: 1978.

Anderson, C. "Promoting responsible citizenship through elementary law-related education." *Social Education* 44:5 (1980), 383–86.

Baldwin, P., and D. Baldwin. "The portrayal of women in classroom textbooks." *Canadian Social Studies* 26:3 (1992), 110–14.

Center for Sex Equity. *Guide to Nonsexist Teaching Activities.* Phoenix, Ariz.: Oryx Press, 1983.

Edmonds, B., and W. Fernekes, eds. "The convention on the rights of the child: A challenge for Social Studies education." *Social Education* 56:4 (1992), 203–35.

Fountain, S. *Gender Issues: The Gender File*. York, England: The Centre for Global Education, University of York, 1991.

Hickey, M. "Mock trials for children." *Social Education* 54:1 (1990), 43–44.

Hickey, M. "... and justice for all: Teaching kids about the law." *The Social Studies* 81:2 (1990), 77–79.

Law in a Free Society: Multimedia Instructional Materials. Calabas, Calif.: Law in a Free Society, 1977.

Phi Delta Kappa. *A Guide for Improving Public School Practices in Human Rights*. Bloomington, Ind.: Phi Delta Kappa, 1975.

Rights and Freedoms: Universal Declaration of Human Rights. New York: United Nations, 1983.

The Rights of Children Series (The Storybook Children. The Children Who Learned to Smile. The Girl with No Name. The Child Who Cried at Night. The Boy with Two Eyes. The Boy and His Robot. The Children and the Silly Kings. A Town without Children. The Giant Child. Annie, the Invisible Girl). Rexdale, Ont.: John Wiley and Sons, 1978.

Teaching Law. Special issue of *The History and Social Science Teacher* 24:2 (1989).

Totten, S. "Teaching about international human rights."*Social Education* 49:6 (1985), 444–538.

United Nations. *The ABC of Teaching Human Rights*. New York: United Nations Human Rights Center, United Nations, 1989.

Women, Gender and the Social Studies. Special issue of *Social Education* 51:3 (1987).

Evaluation

Student Assessment in Social Studies. Special section in *Social Education* 56:2 (1992), 89–111.

PHOTO ACKNOWLEDGMENTS

British Columbia Archives and Records Service, page 44/HP6603. Used with permission.

Canadian Museum of Contemporary Photography, page 112/62-5573T. T. Grant. Used with permission.

Canadian Pacific, page 274. Used with permission.

City of Vancouver Archives, page 110/William Bros. AIR P.108, c. 1966; page 111/ W.H. Roozebaum. CVA 23-12c, 1973. Used with permission.

Fitzhenry and Whiteside Limited (*Growth of a Nation,* "Canadian History Study Print Program," by Daniel R. Birch et al.), page 191. Used with permission.

National Capital Commission, page 275/01-05-986. Denis Drever, 1990. Used with permission.

National Film Board Photothèque, page 44/75-2267K. George Hunter; page 44/75-1339KC. Kryn Taconis; page 69/75-3237K. Terry Pearse; page 69/75-3224KC. Terry Pearse; page 112/62-5573. T. Grant (Canadian Museum of Contemporary Photography); page 273/75-3205KC. Terry Pearse. Used with permission.

Native Indian Teacher Education Program, Leadership seminar, 1989–90. Faculty of Education, University of British Columbia. page 111. Used with permission.

Metropolitan Toronto Convention and Visitors Association, page 274. Used with permission.

A. Morrison, page 110; page 277. Used with permission.

R. Rustad, page 276. Used with permission.

Royal Canadian Mounted Police, page 250/93-3 (E9). Used with permission.

Tourisme Québec, page 273/TQ 29-20-64. Used with permission.

University Endowment Lands Fire Department (Vancouver, B.C.), pages 192–193/Photos by J. Ostermeier. Used with permission of Chief W.J. Ferguson.

Vancouver Public Library, page 44/14082; page 44/7641; page 44/199. Used with permission.

All other photographs by the author.

INDEX

To the owner of this book

We hope that you have enjoyed *Elementary Social Studies,* and we would like to know as much about your experiences as you would care to offer. Only through your comments and those of others can we learn how to make this a better text for future readers.

School _____   Your instructor's name _____

Course _____   Was the text required? _____   Recommended? _____

1. What did you like the most about *Elementary Social Studies?*

_____

_____

_____

2. How useful was this text for your course?

_____

_____

_____

3. Do you have any recommendations for ways to improve the next edition of this text?

_____

_____

_____

4. In the space below or in a separate letter, please write any other comments you have about the book. (For example, please feel free to comment on reading level, writing style, terminology, design features, and learning aids.)

_____

_____

_____

_____

Optional

Your name _____   Date _____

May Nelson Canada quote you, either in promotion for *Elementary Social Studies* or in future publishing ventures?

Yes _____   No _____

Thanks!

- FOLD HERE -

MAIL ➤ POSTE

Canada Post Corporation / Société canadienne des postes

Postage paid	**Port payé**
if mailed in Canada	si posté au Canada
Business	**Réponse**
Reply	**d'affaires**

0107077099 01

Nelson

0107077099-M1K5G4-BR01

Nelson Canada
College Editorial Department
1120 Birchmount Rd.
Scarborough, ON M1K 9Z9